praise for rebel

"Donald Spoto examines [Dean] with perception and ... originality. ... [Rebel] has the ring of truth."
—*Washington Post Book World*

"[Spoto] does bring a new clarity to the fog that has enveloped the Dean mystique."
—*Seattle Post-Intelligencer*

"Packed with details."
—*Indianapolis Star*

"[Spoto's] passion gives wings to his writing. ... [He] shines the light of truth through the stained-glass window figure that others would make of the man who is every teenager for every generation."
—*Beacon Journal*

"In the first complete, fully documented biography of this enigmatic hero, Spoto offers a startlingly revelatory look at the short, greatly misunderstood life of an icon frozen in time."
—*Herald-Republic*

rebel

THE LIFE AND LEGEND OF JAMES DEAN

DONALD SPOTO

HarperPaperbacks
A Division of HarperCollins*Publishers*

HarperPaperbacks
A Division of HarperCollinsPublishers
10 East 53rd Street, New York, N.Y. 10022-5299

ISBN 0-06-109400-5

HarperCollins®, 🔥®, and HarperPaperbacks™ are trademarks of HarperCollinsPublishers, Inc.

Cover photo © 1955 Motion Picture and Television Archive

A hardcover edition of this book was published in 1996 by HarperCollinsPublishers.

First HarperPaperbacks printing: May 1997

Printed in the United States of America

Visit HarperPaperbacks on the World Wide Web at
http://www.harpercollins.com/paperbacks

❖ 10 9 8 7 6 5 4 3 2 1

for Fred McCashland—
like James Dean, a son of Indiana:
with love and gratitude
for four decades of friendship

And as I gazed with dazzled eyes,
    A gleaming smile lit up his lips
    As his bright soul from its eclipse
Went flashing into Paradise.
Then tardy Fame came through the door
And found a picture—nothing more.

JAMES WHITCOMB RILEY, "FAME" (1877)

acknowledgments

During the course of my research and writing, I have been the grateful recipient of many kinds of assistance.

For important interviews, the following people generously and courteously offered reminiscences that contributed to a fuller representation of James Dean's life:

Corey Allen, Eric Bentley, Dick Clayton, Mart Crowley, Jonathan Gilmore, Julie Harris, Elia Kazan, Kenneth Kendall, Jud Kinberg, Jack Larson, Ernest Lehman, Arthur Loew, Jr., Beverly Long, Vivian Matalon, Andrew McCullough, Faye Nuell Mayo, William Orr, Leonard Rosenman, James Sheldon, Elizabeth Sheridan, Steffi Sidney, Ray Stark, Stewart Stern, Christine White and James Whitmore.

Marcus Winslow, Jr.—James Dean's cousin—welcomed me to his home and graciously shared memories.

In libraries and archives across the country, crucial material turned up with the astute assistance of:

Ned Comstock, in the Cinema and Television Library at the University of Southern California;

Lavedah Craw and Gene Peterson, at the Fairmount (Indiana) Historical Museum;

June Felton and Barbara A. Love, at the Marion (Indiana) Public Library;

Sam Gill, Stacey Behlmer and the entire staff at the Academy of Motion Picture Arts and Sciences, Beverly Hills;

Lenny Prussack, Heidi Goodpaster and Luke Williams at the James Dean Gallery in Fairmount;

Margaret Hedrick, librarian at the New School for Social Research, New York;

and the staffs at the Billy Rose Theatre Collection, Lincoln Center Public Library, New York; at the Museum of Television & Radio, New York; and at University Research Library at the University of California at Los Angeles.

Invaluable help was provided by Robert R. Rees, an archivist, writer and James Dean enthusiast, who provided me with copies of a number of Dean's television appearances that would otherwise have been unavailable for viewing.

For various other kind and concrete gestures of help, I am indebted to Matt Battaglia, Gail McCashland, Patrick Miller, Nelson Price and Joshua Samuel Smith.

My publishers and editors, as usual, have never failed to provide their professional wisdom and friendly counsel, as well as their unfailing encouragement. At HarperCollins Publishers, New York, I rejoice in the friendship of Gladys Justin Carr, Vice President and Associate Publisher, who has guided me with her unfailingly acute and perceptive judgments, her great kindness and the leaven of her good humor throughout the production of *Rebel*, our fourth book together. In her offices, Cynthia Barrett, Deirdre O'Brien and Elissa Altman offer a warm welcome and constant cheerful assistance that make the writer's life so much easier.

Also at HarperCollins, Jack McKeown, Vice President and Publisher of the Trade Group, was a most enthusiastic supporter of this book from the start. To him and to his colleagues—among them, Diane Reverand, Steven Sorrentino, Jessica Jonap, Joseph Montebello, Kim Lewis and Sue Llewellyn— my heartfelt appreciation.

I am fortunate, too, in the friendship of my many foreign publishers, and if I mention only Richard Johnson, at HarperCollins, London; and Renaud Bombard and Sophie Thiebault, at Presses de la Cité, Paris, that is because I have come to know them personally and to be as enriched by the warmth of their friendship as by their professional support and wise advice.

It is impossible to imagine where I would be without my literary representatives. In the acknowledgments of each book, I have the task of trying to articulate with some sort of fresh diction my loving gratitude for my agent, Elaine Markson, a devoted confidante for almost twenty years. Everyone who knows Elaine will nod knowingly at these words: she is the soul of prudence, erudition, attentive affection and unfailing loyalty. She is also, I can testify, a marvelous traveling companion and the most splendid cook—what more can any client seek? I am among the many blessed people who love her dearly and cannot imagine life without her.

Part of Elaine's brilliant judgment is reflected in her choice of colleagues: in the offices of Elaine

Markson Literary Agency, New York, I am grateful for the vigilance, friendship and daily help of Geri Thoma, Sally Wofford Girand, Pari Berk and Sara DeNobrega. I cannot imagine that any writer has ever benefited from so scrupulous and faithful a team of representatives.

Just so, in London, my interests are looked after by Abner Stein, Octavia Wiseman and their colleagues. No visit to London is complete without their delightful company, not to say their superb and attentive work on my behalf.

In Paris, my agent Mary Kling, at La Nouvelle Agence, has for years enabled me to work with the finest French publishers; her friendship and superb judgment have never failed me, and I am glad for her collaboration and that of her staff.

I cannot think how bleak and impoverished my days would be without the constant devotion of my friends, many of whom are named above; the others know, too, how precious they are to me.

Among them is my superb research and personal assistant, Greg Dietrich. He read and outlined books, tracked down obscure texts, historical documents and archival sources, made careful studies of major themes in American culture and literature and generally made himself an indispensable colleague. Working together daily could be a strain on any friendship, but this is a glorious exception. Greg is not only a gifted and perceptive researcher whose keen intelligence, quick humor, pointed observations and timely questions enrich my work at every stage; he is also the best companion a writer could have. Whatever the weather, his daily arrival at our offices brings sunshine.

On the dedication page of this book is the name of a faithful friend for almost thirty-seven years. I first met Fred McCashland when we were college students, and he has never failed to be my staunch and dear ally. We have laughed together, and we have shared gray as well as glad times. Fred is also a brilliant educator, much admired and rightly honored with impressive awards in his native Indiana. And so—*dignum et justum est*—I offer this book to Fred McCashland with gratitude and devotion. James Dean, too, would have valued his friendship.

D.S.
1 November 1995
The Feast of All the Saints

rebel

THE LIFE AND LEGEND OF JAMES DEAN

chapter one

Saint: a dead sinner,
revised and edited.
AMBROSE BIERCE

From thirty-four states and eleven foreign countries, they came to the small Indiana town of Fairmount—from as near as Indianapolis and as far as Australia. It was September 30, 1995.

"This trip has been fifteen years in the making," said thirty-three-year-old Brian McKay, who traveled from Perth, "and now I know it's worth it." Outside the church, he mingled with Frank Minerva, twenty-six, who had seen *Rebel Without a Cause* at the age of twelve. "I've been addicted to Jimmy ever since then," he said. "I went into debt coming from Brooklyn, New York, for this day. Jimmy was unique. Cool." Nearby were the Etheridge sisters, Michele and Diane, who had driven fourteen hours to be present. They were chatting with Erika Pearson, who had flown in from San Francisco, where she had taken time off from her job at the Wells Fargo Bank.

"You could see he was special," said Frederick Storms of Brewster, New Jersey. "I started a scrapbook in 1955. I still have it, plus a collection of T-shirts, magazines, tapes and so forth. The legend still lives, forty years later."

"Jimmy died when I was ten and my brother and his friend were thirteen," said New Yorker Joanne Milazzo. "We thought he was great, so we decided to hold a séance in the basement of our house to contact him. Over the table was a pipe from which a lot of metal hangers were suspended. We agreed that when Jimmy was in our sphere, he'd signal his presence by rattling the hangers. It happened! I felt the thrilling shock of it all, and my big brother and his friends scrambled upstairs to safety. My mom still lives in that house, and I always think of James Dean when I see those hangers."

A woman named Patricia Rich said that her son, a great James Dean fan, had died in 1989 at the age of thirty-one. "He copied [Dean's] walk and his gestures. I still have an album which he created containing all the old pictures and stories—anything to do with James Dean. It has the greatest sentimental value to me."

A middle-aged man had traveled from Vancouver, Canada, playing tapes of James Dean's movies all the way—not the music, but the complete dialogue, which he knew by heart. He said that his wife, who did not accompany him, thought he was crazy. As he stood outside the church, the glow on his face and the radiance in his eyes showed the joy of the true believer.

A secretary from Lyons, France, stood shyly to one side, trying to negotiate a few English sentences with a man from Burma, who had rearranged a season's work schedule to be here in Fairmount. Just about everyone seemed to sport a likeness of his hero—on shirts or neckties, scarves or pendants. A few dozen bold people showed off their Dean tattoos.

The week-long James Dean Festival had been a glorious success. Songs by crooner Tommy Sands and tunes by the Crickets brought the music of the 1950s back to Fairmount. James Dean's three feature films, made in 1954 and 1955, had been screened. In Fairmount and nearby Gas City, there were exhibits of vintage automobiles from the 1950s. And there was the internationally famous James Dean Look-Alike Contest, although no one seemed to know what the winner received.

On September 30, 1955, Dean had died at age twenty-four in an auto accident on a lonely stretch of California road. Now, exactly forty years later, a service to mark the anniversary would conclude the week's memorial activities. By eleven o'clock on this sunny, warm September day, hundreds of cars and trucks had already arrived. The small, red brick Back Creek Friends Church, flanked by a vast cornfield and the village cemetery on one side and a lovely white farmhouse on the other, could accommodate only ninety fortunate worshippers; the rest gathered beneath large shade trees and along the roadway, where they heard the ceremony over loudspeakers. Some of the devout who managed to squeeze into the church were young and healthy; others limped, leaned on canes or had to be brought in wheelchairs.

Just after noon, a lady withdrew from her satchel a book of music, switched on an electronic organ and began a medley from "Popular Classics." Everyone fell silent, listening to the familiar tunes "Goin' Home," "Aura Lee" and "Amazing Grace." As the organist played, a small basket of silk flowers on the organ suddenly tumbled to the floor and was repositioned by a guest. "To my beloved Jimmy," said the message on the card. "You will always be my Giant." It was signed "Still lovin' you from Maryland."

At last, promptly at one o'clock, a dozen guest speakers took their places beneath a fresco of the Good Shepherd. The figure in the painting looked like a buffed and brilliantly trained college football player who had suddenly stumbled into a field of disenchanted sheep.

Of the speakers, only three had known James Dean personally. But the others were just as effective in moving the congregation to grief, pride and gratitude. Teenage girls, young women in their twenties and white-haired grandmothers wept openly for the boy they had lost, the lover they always longed for, the son they never had. Young and middle-aged men looked somehow gray and solemn, as if suddenly bereaved, robbed of a close friend or brother.

"Of all places on the planet you could choose to be today, you've picked the right spot," said Tom Berghuis, the master of ceremonies. He wore a tie with a large image of James Dean, and he gazed over the congregation, many of whom wore shirts or sweaters bearing the legend "James Dean Forever" on the front and "Disciples of James Dean" on the back. Others wore replicas of the famous red windbreaker Dean had worn in *Rebel Without a Cause*. People clutched their devotional books—homemade albums or published volumes of the star's photos.

"You are about to hear, from people who personally knew Jimmy Dean, how that gift affected their lives," continued Berghuis. Then, to polite applause, Bob Pulley walked to the podium. He recalled the fast car rides, the games of ice hockey and pleasant times at Fairmount High School with his classmate James Dean a half-century earlier. "You couldn't ask for anything better than the way it was," he said. "Fans come to me and the wife all the time, and I say I'm always happy to talk to anybody about Jimmy." A wave of contentment rippled through the church.

Next at the podium was Frank Mazzola, who had just arrived from Los Angeles. He had played one of the gang members in *Rebel Without a Cause*. "When I met Jimmy, something changed," he said, and then told a story about "racing with him in a Porsche along Mulholland Drive."

Mazzola was followed by a man from Japan named Kazoo. "East is East and West is West," he said, "but *East of Eden* is *East of Eden*." That brought the first really big round of applause from the audience. "This film changed my life when I was a high-school student. Of course I had parents and a younger brother and our family loves each other, but this film made me awake to the love of a family *in my mind*!" He gave special emphasis to those last three words, and with that curious announcement, the tears could again be seen gliding down the cheeks of a few worshippers. Kazoo resumed his place after promising that "like General MacArthur, I shall return—I shall return—I shall return to Fairmount!" A bigger round of applause.

Then a fifty-year-old woman rose to testify. She had lived in Fairmount all her life and had clear memories of the 1950s. "It was a very, very conservative time in a very conservative place, and like most young people I had a lot of conflict with my parents. And then one day in 1955 I went to a movie, *Rebel Without a Cause*. I was ten years old, and for the first time in my life, I fell in love. James Dean was the embodiment of every romantic, idyllic feeling that my body, heart and mind possessed. And then I remember when he died. I remember lying in bed, praying and crying and asking God to take my life and to bring Jimmy back. Soon after I started a James Dean Fan Club. I know I could've been Mrs. James Dean." Louder applause followed this confession, as many girls and women, now weeping copiously, fumbled for handkerchiefs. More speakers came forth, struggled to find the right words in praise of their revered hero, and sat down to more clapping.

A little lady in a wheelchair, who had been positioned up front, smiled occasionally, looked around the room and, if this or that speaker went on too long, dropped off to sleep for a few moments. When she was Jimmy's high-school teacher, back in the 1940s, her name was Adeline Brookshire; now she was known as Mrs. Nall. She was eighty-nine, and she uttered not a word that afternoon, but she seemed to know who and where she was. Over the last fifty years, she had spoken about James Dean every chance she got. Now, trotted out for the thousandth time as one of the original eyewitnesses, she was perhaps a little tired or even confused.

Lew Bracker, who had been James Dean's insurance agent in California, rose to say that the afternoon made him think of the movie *Close Encounters of the Third Kind*, "because, just like in that picture, some power has compelled us to go to the mountain—and in this case, Jimmy is the mountain." With that, as if on cue, a gentle breeze drifted in through the church windows and toppled a few photos of the mountain. "We were two young guys in that fabulous L.A. scene at the time," continued Bracker. "One day, Jimmy said to me, 'You know, we have to get married,' and I said, 'To each other?'" No one laughed, but Bracker went on as if someone had. "Oh, Jimmy didn't want to joke about it! He had made a scenario—he wanted a family! Jimmy and I were as close as two straight guys could ever be." At this news, most men in the congregation nodded gravely: what a wonderful thing to hear, and what a relief! Two women then bent over to pick up the fallen photos of Jimmy and replaced them on the dais and organ console. The congregation gazed lovingly at these sacred mementos of an actor in costume—images of James Dean, an icon role-playing in shots from a movie.

At the end of the speeches, a man who called himself Nicky Bazooka rose to thank everyone for coming to the service. From cap to boots, he was dressed completely in black leather, except for a fuchsia neckerchief.

By three o'clock the service was over, but not the pilgrimage. James Dean, it had been said, was not just an actor: he was a great creative genius. James Dean was not merely a young man in search of himself: he was a deeply religious person. James

Dean was not just a charmingly awkward fellow: he was a man who had a clear and definite path ahead of him. James Dean was not merely a man who made an impression in three movies forty years ago: he was a hero of our time. There was more to say: he was affable, devoted, clean, sober, intelligent, gifted, unselfish, prayerful, loving, brave, kind. He was a wistful wanderer, a vulnerable, shy artist. He was good. He was cool. He was great. He was a saint. He was everything that everyone wanted him to be— he was even everything everyone there wanted to be. Here present were all the faithful, to testify to the beloved's greatness. Some of them, on crutches or leaning on friends for help, had come long distances to weep and pray at the graveside. There were whispers and tears all day.

A long procession then formed, and everyone headed for James Dean's final resting place in nearby Park Cemetery, where they took photographs of one another standing over the grave or embracing the headstone, which bore the red imprint of many lipstick kisses. Some people dabbed at their eyes. Others smoked nervously. Most people went up to touch the little old lady in the wheelchair who had been Jimmy's teacher. A few recognized fans from previous years and embraced tightly. It was a kind of homecoming. They had come to honor their best beloved, and they had not been disappointed. Their faith had been deepened, their hope confirmed, their love sealed for another year. There were thousands—tens of thousands in America, hundreds of thousands around the world—who shared their beliefs.

Later that afternoon, there was a brief ceremony as a

new bust of James Dean was installed, the work of
artist Kenneth Kendall, who had devoted much of his
life and talent to celebrating James Dean. A previous
bust by Kendall had been stolen, but that would never
happen again. "The neck [of the new bust] is designed
in a way that it can't be sawed off," said Marcus
Winslow, Jr., Jimmy's cousin.

Throughout the evening, the pilgrimage wound its
way to the James Dean Gallery, where one could see
original letters and notes that James Dean had scrib-
bled, high-school book reports, an address book he had
written, a laundry receipt he had touched, sketches he
had made, paintings of him done by others—as well as
mementos, replicas of his clothes and devotional articles in his honor, of every sort, on sale for the faithful.
Nearby, the Fairmount Historical Museum contained
even more relics in abundance—schoolbooks, trophies
and check stubs once owned by James Dean.

The town where he had lived for only nine years
had certainly been enriched by those who came to
offer homage—not only on this special anniversary,
but all through the year. Here in the heartland of
America, you could gaze at the holy objects in abundance; you could go away with artifacts that were like
sacraments of the beloved's presence. Everywhere
were articles bearing the image of James Dean—
he was on postcards and posters, on shirts and
sweaters, on pocket combs and pens, on coffee mugs,
refrigerator magnets and key chains.

Life could be very full indeed.

chapter two

> Let a man turn to his own
> childhood—no further—if he
> will renew his sense of
> remoteness, and of the
> mystery of change.
>
> ALICE MEYNELL

Early in the hot afternoon of July 26, 1930, the Reverend Zeno Doan, a Methodist minister in Marion, Indiana, was hastily summoned to his parlor to perform an unscheduled marriage. Before him were Winton Dean, a quiet, slim, handsome man with blond hair and blue eyes, and Mildred Wilson, a plump, dark-haired girl with a shy, wistful appearance and a rueful smile. The groom was twenty-two, the bride nineteen, and by all accounts they had had no plans to marry that summer, if at all; indeed, they had just obtained a marriage license that very morning. The haste was occasioned by the fact that Mildred had learned, in mid-July, that she was two months pregnant. Her father, as the rural Indiana folk would have put it, was ready to load up the shotgun if Winton failed to do the honorable thing.

After residing several months with some of Winton's relatives in Fairmount, eleven miles south of Marion, the newlyweds returned to Marion and rented a room at the Seven Gables, a boardinghouse as gloomily Gothic as its name. At 430 East Fourth Street, the Gables, a few steps from the railroad tracks, shook ominously as the long freight trains rumbled by several times each day and night. Although the landlady's sons whitewashed the house every spring and the house had survived the seasonal rush of Indiana tornadoes, the paint was always chipped and peeling inside and out, the shutters slammed in the autumn rainstorms, and a damp, cold wind moaned through the house when winter came to Grant County.

On February 8, 1931, at this inauspicious address, Mildred Wilson Dean bore a healthy, eight-pound boy after a brief and uncomplicated labor, and with only a midwife attending. The infant was named James Byron Dean, in honor of two loyal and discreet friends, James Emmick and Byron Feist, who, like Winton, worked in the dental laboratory at Marion's Veterans Administration Medical Center. When copies of the Deans' marriage certificate were altered years later, bearing the more respectable date of 1929, Emmick and Feist kept the secret.

James Dean's great-grandfather, Calvin Dean—unlike most serious Indiana Christian folks of his day—might not have been much upset about his grandson's conduct had he lived to see Jimmy mature. According to one friend, Cal was "an earthy, flamboyant and colorful man with considerable histrionic ability, a fund of risqué stories and a flair for show-manship," qualities that made him and his son Purl much in demand as auction agents, if not dinner guests. When he died in Fairmount at age seventy-four in 1918, Cal was cited by the local press as "one of the best-known and most successful auctioneers in the West, and one of the most widely known men in Indiana." Although he was perhaps not so widely known or discussed as a band of robbers who terror-ized farm folk that year, Calvin Dean was eulogized at a funeral that drew hundreds.

Cal's other son, Charles Dean, chose the quieter life of a farmer, working a few hundred acres in a stretch of rich land called Jonesboro, snug against the some-what vague borders of Fairmount. In 1900, at the age of twenty-one, Charles married a sturdy sixteen-year-old girl named Emma Woollen. The Dean and Woollen families had, by that time, lived in Grant County for more than sixty years and were friendly. It was not much of an exaggeration to say that most of the two thousand people in Fairmount and Jonesboro knew a good deal about their neighbors.

As it happened, there was not much to know in the case of the Deans: Charles and Emma worked the farm and faithfully attended the Fairmount Methodist Church, and she was a staunch supporter of the Back Creek Woman's Christian Temperance Union. A glass of elderberry wine—and then only if Charles or one of their children suffered from influenza—was the strongest liquor brought into Emma's house. Church suppers, quilting bees, county fairs, Bible study groups: the Dean family's country life right through the 1920s seemed to bear little resemblance to the swiftly changing urban sprawls of Fort Wayne and Indianapolis.

"We're not rich, but we're not poor, either," said Emma Dean after more than a half-century of marriage to Charles. His sober diligence generated enough cash to build a modest but comfortable farmhouse for them and their children, Charlie, Winton and Ortense. "So long as I live," Emma added, "I'll always have a porch to sit on, a rocking chair to rock in, and a clock that strikes." She and her husband were, by all accounts, uncomplicated, simple and devoted to work and family. In 1961, Charles and Emma Dean, at eighty-one and seventy-five, died within two months of each other; much earlier, they had turned the house in Jonesboro over to their daughter Ortense and her husband Marcus Winslow, who expanded the place and raised their two children there. A century after the foundation was laid, visitors can still find an unpretentious, tidy place where modernization has not spoiled the original, cozy simplicity.

Charles and Emma Dean's son Winton, who was born January 17, 1908, in Fairmount, was a dexterous tinkerer but not much interested in agrarian life. He was trained as a dental technician by the government after landing a job at the Veterans Administration in Marion, where his job was molding false teeth, bridges and crowns. After work, during the first warm spring days of 1930, he and a few co-workers liked to ride or stroll near the banks of the Mississinewa River or in a shady park. His slender form and taciturn manner, his blond hair and deep blue eyes appealed to the young ladies who drifted out of offices and factories, some of them imitating movie glamour queens, fanning themselves and sprinkling their handkerchiefs with lavender water. For themselves and for young men they knew (or hoped to know), the girls often stopped to buy bottles of ginger ale or sarsaparilla as they headed for a park bench: only a very few brave souls would have dared defy Prohibition and obtain beer or spirits. One April day, Winton met Mildred Wilson as she sat alone in a pleasant grove.

Marion, with a population of about eleven thousand in 1930, had known a boom time at the turn of the century, when oil and gas companies sprang up and attracted platoons of workers. Even when the wells ran dry, auto and glass factories prospered, and there were always jobs for girls eager to escape country life for Marion, which by comparison passed for an exciting place. The Great Depression shut down many companies, but the Indiana General Assembly prepared a Commission on Unemployment Relief that specified the creation of some jobs for single women. Mildred Wilson was one of the refugees who sought work in Marion, and by the time she met Winton, she had a clerical job.

Born in Marion on September 15, 1910, Mildred Marie Wilson had been raised in nearby Gas City, whose name was a dubious (not to say unimaginative) tribute to its original industry. There, Mildred's father, John, worked variously as a box maker, a barber and a farmhand; his wife, the former Minnie May Slaughter, raised two sons and three daughters. In the spring of 1927, just before Mildred completed high-school, her mother fell ill with cancer, and in January 1929, at age forty-six, Minnie died. Mildred, who adored her, was almost hysterical with grief, and for several weeks she did little but sit forlornly at home, wrapped in her mother's shawl, her eyes brimmed with tears. And then, that summer, another terrible thing happened to Mildred. John Wilson began to court a widow named Cordelia Smithson, and at Christmas he told his children that he would soon remarry. With that, Mildred made her decision. In March 1930, she packed a cardboard suitcase and left for Marion. The following month, she wandered into a park and sat under a chestnut tree, Winton Dean strolled by, and in May she was pregnant.

Everything happened so quickly that Winton and Mildred had little time really to know each other. It is easy to understand Mildred's loneliness and her ready response to male attention, as well as the evident reasons for her attraction to Winton: he was handsome, protective and employed. Had she not been pregnant, however, she might not have married him, nor would he have asked her, for apart from the obvious initial chemistry they seem to have had nothing in common. She wanted to learn, she liked music, she had a gift for mimicry and a quick sense of humor, she lost all track of time when reading novels, and she longed to travel abroad—in other words, Mildred Wilson Dean wanted a better life.

Winton, on the other hand, was satisfied with a regular income and required little else. He was a man utterly without intellectual curiosity, much less esthetic pretensions, and he saw no need to travel outside Grant County for anything. But it was Indiana, 1930, and the scenario of an unmarried woman who could point out the father of her illegitimate child appealed to neither of them; worse, it would have caused sheer hell among their families.

Initially, Winton saw in Mildred an irresistible, almost exotic, gypsylike quality. Sometimes he called her his "little bohemian," especially when she went to the movies or, whenever she had saved small change, boarded a bus for Indianapolis and saw a variety show, a dance recital or a play at the Indianapolis Civic Theater, the nation's oldest continuously operating theatrical institution. At home, she often tried to entertain Winton by reciting generous portions of poetry, particularly the works of Indiana's own James Whitcomb Riley, but the words fell on apathetic ears. And so with her cultural interests and her absorption with the chores of motherhood, Mildred Wilson Dean tried to leaven for herself the demands of what can only be called an indifferent marriage.

As for Winton, he was neither a warm nor a demonstrative man, and this may have derived from the fact that he had contracted a marriage he had not really desired. To his credit, it must be said that he was a dutiful husband and father, if also a remote and humorless one. Whatever anxieties and resentments he may have felt on finding himself suddenly burdened with fresh responsibilities, Winton Dean did not—at first—try to escape the obligations he had not foreseen during that passionate springtide of 1930.

Just about the time Winton and Mildred marked Jimmy's first birthday, they abandoned the Seven Gables; between 1932 and 1936, they lived in a quartet of apartments and rented houses in Jonesboro, Fairmount and Marion. Each time they moved, no matter how clean the new rooms, Mildred insisted on painting the walls fresh, bright new colors. None of them could be called lavish homes, but as the Great Depression wore on, displacing and bankrupting millions of families, Mildred was grateful for Winton's weekly paycheck from the Veterans Administration, which also provided the family with medical care. With almost half the workforce idle, the Deans could count their blessings.

But with a baby at home, her cultural forays out of town ceased, and she had to invent her own entertainment. This Mildred did with considerable success, to the constant delight of her attentive audience of one. She read to Jimmy, sang and played music on a wind-up gramophone and distracted him from the miseries of childhood illnesses by acting out nursery rhymes and tall tales from American folklore.

The familiarity with frontier humor and legend was a critical part of Jimmy's early education. The unrestraint, the sense of gaiety and passionate individuality, the impetus toward sophisticated urban values—these were the characteristics of tall tales, and in the telling by Mildred they evoked from the young listener a sense of colorful drama.

Usually diffident and demure with peers, Mildred was expansive and unrestrained with her son, who quickly caught her imaginative spirit. When she told him about the mythic Paul Bunyan, the giant lumberjack who symbolized the vitality of the American frontier, Jimmy jumped right into the story, improvising the roles of Babe the Blue Ox and Johnny Inkslinger. Neighbors were sometimes alarmed, sometimes delighted to see mother and son on the stage of their front porch, fighting imaginary enemies, negotiating invisible rapids or winter storms and impersonating everything from Indians to raccoons.

In a more pacific tone, Jimmy retold after just one hearing the true story of John Chapman, the missionary nurseryman of the frontier who collected apple seeds from cider presses and planted trees from Pennsylvania through Ohio and beyond. This colorful and eccentric character died near Fort Wayne in 1845 and, as the legendary and beloved "Johnny Appleseed," had become something of a local patron saint. He sprang to life when Jimmy Dean asked his mother for apple seeds and tried to raise a grove in his back yard, transmuting all this action into an amusing little playlet for the benefit of neighborhood children. Alas, the Deans moved again before Jimmy's husbandry could flourish.

But the new house had a front porch, too, and for weeks after mother and son saw the Disney cartoon *The Three Little Pigs*, four-year-old Jimmy mimicked all the characters, dancing and singing, then huffing and puffing to blow the house down. After Mildred read him the stories, he also pretended to be Mike Fink, the rowdy Mississippi keelboatman; Captain Stormalong, whose ship was driven by a hurricane between the Americas and who magically dug the Panama Canal; and Davy Crockett, the backwoods Tennessee marksman. At his fifth birthday party, in February 1936, Jimmy prepared his own rendition of Goldilocks and the Three Bears, which he apparently enacted with such impressive conviction that two of the invited playmates ran to their mothers in fright.

Mildred applauded her little Barrymore. Winton, on the other hand, held the common view that acting was something done by people who were a bit queer. He preferred to see Jimmy in more rough-and-tumble activities, and for that same birthday had bought him a child's baseball, bat and catcher's mitt. On the first warm Saturdays of spring, father and son were seen tossing a ball back and forth—an enterprise at which the boy failed miserably, incurring the stony resentment of his father. When Mildred insisted that Jimmy was not clumsy but simply could not see much farther than the end of his nose, Winton whisked the boy off to the Medical Center. Mother was right: the child was severely nearsighted and had to be fitted for eyeglasses. By June, he was catching and tossing the ball vigorously and even asking Winton for a basketball.

Still, nothing Jimmy did pleased his father. The boy seemed destined to be resented simply for being. "I never understood him," he said years later of his father.

> I never understood what he was after, what sort of person he'd been, because he never tried to get on my side of the fence, or to try and see things the way I saw them when I was little. I was always with Mom and we were very close.

As for Winton, he noticed that Jimmy required a lot of diversion: "He had a large anxiety to do many different things. He had to try everything, and he soon outgrew most of the toys we bought him. He always seemed to be getting ahead of himself."

Images of an idyllic childhood have been served up by chroniclers of James Dean since long before his death. But in addition to the domestic tensions and the very different attitudes of Winton and Mildred toward their son, which would cause deep and unarticulated conflict, there were also frightening facts of public life. Even a quick review of rural Indiana history indicates that it was nothing like the mythic "heartland of America," which, if that phrase implies utopian innocence and an epidemic of neighborly sweetness, never existed anywhere except in Hollywood fantasies and bad fiction.

In February 1931, for example—the month James Dean was born—his hometown of Marion ranked eighth among Indiana towns for violent crime. Everywhere people spoke of the notorious Brady Gang, a band of cutthroats led by twenty-one-year-old Alfred Brady. With four companions, he cut a path of violence from Indiana to Maine, and before they were brought down in 1937 he and his gang could count two hundred armed robberies, a dozen murders and countless assaults.

The Brady Gang were folks acting in a long and established Indiana Hoosier tradition going back to the 1870s and 1880s, the era of the infamous Peanut Gang of Perkinsville. These twelve- and thirteen-year-old boys ("peanuts," in the contemporary diction) were psychopathic juvenile delinquents who began by annoying girls at cotillions and, when that got them some local celebrity, swiftly moved on to stealing and murder. "Oh, they were just a bunch of wild boys who had some bad luck," said the people of Perkinsville, attempting to protect their community's reputation when the national press took notice. Not nearly as much bad luck, one might reply, as their unfortunate victims.

Nor were acts of lunacy invented only in late twentieth-century urban America. In 1893, six members of the Wratten family were butchered in their Indiana home by their neighbor James "Bud" Stone, who had intended to kill his own family but, in a mad stupor, wandered into the wrong house. In 1908, a beloved Indiana farm lady named Belle Gunness had the doubtful distinction of becoming one of the country's first serial killers. She slew her two children and her husband and went along in an uninterrupted vocation of carnage by killing two more husbands and a dozen more neighbors until she made the mistake of discussing her history over cocoa one afternoon with a friendly parson.

Perhaps the best-known Indiana criminal was John Dillinger, who was twenty-seven when Jimmy was born. A native of Indianapolis, he left school at sixteen and moved with his family to Mooresville, where he seemed destined for the rustic life of a farm boy. But Dillinger preferred more exciting prospects, and after a series of petty burglaries he rose to auto theft in 1923. Someone with good intentions suggested he join the Navy, which he did—and soon deserted. Back in Mooresville, Dillinger lost no time returning to his real talent. He held up a grocer, and this landed him a nine-year prison term, during which he reinforced his connections to the criminal underworld. Paroled in 1933, when Jimmy was two, Dillinger achieved the remarkable record of a dozen major bank robberies in eight months—most of them in Indiana but some in Ohio and Michigan. At the height of the Depression, Dillinger made an easy fortune and inspired literally thousands of copycat crooks: among the best-known were Ma Barker, Bonnie and Clyde, and Pretty Boy Floyd. They were all major newsmakers in the 1930s, and from that time forward there was always a big audience for movie versions of their stories.

Caught and imprisoned, Dillinger escaped, and locksmiths and gunsmiths made small fortunes from frightened citizens in every city and hamlet of Indiana. More arrests were followed by more escapes, and at the time when Jimmy was hearing tall tales from Mildred, the newspapers and radio blared frightening news. The Indiana American Legion offered to arm its thirty thousand members to patrol Indiana highways in search of the fugitive Dillinger and his growing band of unmerry men; by this time, the dapper, nattily dressed outlaw had the loyalty of George "Baby Face" Nelson (dismissed from the service of Al Capone, who considered Nelson too bloodthirsty).

Fear gripped all Indiana. Governor Paul McNutt increased the state budget for police and firearms, and newspapers from Gary to Fort Wayne to Indianapolis begged the United States attorney general to resolve a dreadful public menace. A $10,000 reward was offered for Dillinger's capture, but he eluded the FBI and local authorities until 1934, when, with the compliance of a brothel madam named Anna Sage (later known as "the Lady in Red"), he emerged from a Chicago movie theater and was shot dead at age thirty-one. His body was returned to Indianapolis for burial.

In some ways even more shocking were the routines of the Ku Klux Klan, whose major stronghold in the

North had always been in Indiana. Black men whom the Klan suspected of anything more than uncivil language were routinely dragged out to a convenient tree and lynched. For the most part, police looked the other way, and the Klan flourished well into the 1930s, when the fierce outcries of Indiana's Roman Catholics (a despised minority like the "coloreds") threatened to boycott every Klan-connected merchant in the state. James Dean was born not into a safe and folksy "heartland" but into a society ravaged by crime, a county in the grip of poverty and fear, and a family riddled with remorse and resentments.

During the summer of 1936, just before he was to be enrolled in kindergarten class, Jimmy suddenly displayed a variety of physical maladies much more alarming than myopia. No longer rambunctious and extroverted, he became listless and easily fatigued, and he had a chronic low-grade fever. His face was pale, then a rash appeared on his arms, torso and legs. Days later, things worsened: he was vomiting a fetid, inky fluid and passing tarry stools. Mildred, who had seen her mother endure similar symptoms, was beside herself: she was convinced that the boy, who remained eerily calm, was dying of cancer.

Two days of tests at the Veterans Administration Medical Center revealed a less malignant condition: it was severe anemia, which, if left untreated much longer, could become life-threatening. Blood transfusions and vitamin therapy comprised the only treatment at the time, and physicians, unaware of the cause, could offer no guarantee the anemia would not return. The family diet was not meager, nor did the child seem to have been exposed to any poisons. In any case, the acute phase of the illness passed by the end of July.

But in fact Jimmy had been exposed to poisons. Sixty years later, it is possible to suggest the etiology of what seems to have been a disease known as erythema infectiosum—commonly called fifth disease not because it usually afflicted children at the age of five or six (which it did), but because in the standard early-twentieth-century literature of pediatric medicine, erythema infectiosum was the fifth entry on the list.

This condition seems to have occurred because of Mildred's habit of painting the rooms of each new home. At the time, ordinary house paints contained alarming quantities of lead: from infancy at the Seven Gables, with its exterior peeling and its interior chips, to the seasonal paints applied to each new residence, Jimmy inhaled considerable amounts of potentially lethal chemicals—not always dangerous for healthy adults, but invariably so for children, who are often tempted to munch paint chips like cookies.

Released from the hospital, the boy and his mother went to stay at the Winslow farm in Jonesboro, where Winton's sister Ortense installed them in a cheerful little cottage, and joined Mildred in pampering Jimmy back to health. In addition to the ministrations of his mother and aunt, there was a lively cousin, ten-year-old Joan. It was, to summarize the atmosphere, a pleasant place to recuperate.

At the same time, Winton—for reasons that remain unclear but may suggest a temporary rift in the marriage—remained at a rented apartment on South Adams Street in Marion. "I thought so much of Mildred," Ortense said fifty years later. "We had such a good time together." As for Jimmy: "He wasn't afraid of anybody or anything. He was a pretty boy, fair-skinned, rosy cheeks, and his mother dressed him cute."

Ortense Dean Winslow, seven years older than her brother Winton, was born April 1, 1901, in Fairmount. A quiet, pretty girl with alert eyes and a gentle disposition, she was a devout Quaker, became organist at the Back Creek Friends Church and worked in and around Fairmount as a secretary and bookkeeper. At age twenty-three, in June 1924, she married Marcus Winslow and moved with him to the Winslow farm in Jonesboro, close to the Friends Church. While Marcus supervised the farm (two hundred acres of oats, corn, hay and livestock), Ortense transformed the house into a home; their daughter Joan was born there in 1926. By the time Mildred and Jimmy came to the farm, Ortense was quite respected as a charter member of the local Woman's Christian Temperance Union and of something called the Fairmount Bonnet Club. Her husband, Marcus, a slight but strong man, was born December 15, 1900, in Fairmount; he was a life-long farmer.

Into this picturesque rural scene, Winton came one day in early September with astonishing news. The government had posted a call for dental technicians at the Veterans Administration Hospital in the western sector of Los Angeles, and he was considering accepting the offer of a transfer. This need not be permanent, he added: those who were unhappy could eventually return to their original posts. Why should he not travel out to Southern California for a few weeks or months, scout the possibility of a new life for the family, and then return to bring them back with him?

There was at this time a rift in the Dean marriage, and Winton may have reasoned he could go west for more than a few months—perhaps remain permanently, without wife and son. But his wife received the news joyously and started to make plans at once. For Mildred, Los Angeles spelled a taste of freedom, the first chance in her life to cross the borders of Indiana. Los Angeles meant Hollywood, the movies, a touch of glamour, an ascendancy above the dreary dullness she had known in her twenty-six years. However much she liked the Winslows, she was a guest. Life in sunny California also meant a hospitable climate for her recovering boy. Early that autumn, Charles and Emma Dean accompanied Winton, Mildred and Jimmy to the railway station. Everyone promised an early reunion.

The Deans settled into their new California life quickly. While Winton drove early each weekday to the hospital in Westwood, Mildred made a home for them in their small, rented California Craftsman-style bungalow at 1422 Twenty-third Street, Santa Monica. There were two small bedrooms and a parlor, a lush front lawn with a palm tree, and a rear garden; to Mildred's delight, the house was also just two miles from the Pacific Ocean. On weekends, holidays and often after Jimmy's days in first grade at the Brentwood School (on Gretna Green, just off San Vicente Boulevard), mother and son took the streetcar to the Santa Monica pier or to the grassy promenade above the highway.

At the same time, Mildred did not forsake the private tutelage she had begun earlier. In addition to a little cardboard theater with puppet figures to poke onstage into impromptu skits, Mildred put into effect more refined projects. "When I was five, my mother had me playing the violin," Jimmy recalled later, "and then soon I was tap-dancing." Apart from a few over-enthusiastic Dean fans decades later, no one made great claims about the results of these childhood lessons, at which Mildred was invariably present. There was, however, one ambiguous side effect. Of her goodwill and devotion to her son there is no doubt, but her constant presence in his life after school denied him time with playmates his own age. In providing what she thought were the best diversions, games and instruction, Mildred short-circuited some critical forms of normal socializing. Very few classmates or teachers recall anything at all about the boy during his time at the school to which he transferred after one term in Brentwood—McKinley Elementary on Santa Monica Boulevard, just around the corner from his home. From 1938 to 1940, Jimmy passed through grades one, two and three at McKinley.

Mildred's benevolent but somewhat overbearing management of her son's life was perhaps at least partly undertaken to distract her from a marriage that had very much cooled. Winton, in any case, became even more remote a figure in Jimmy's life, and occasional attempts at exerting paternal authority were doomed. "You'd try," Winton later said of this time, "to order him to do or not to do something and he'd just sit there with his little face all screwed up and closed. It didn't take you very long to realize that you weren't going to get anywhere with him. Spanking didn't help. Scolding didn't. And you couldn't bribe him." Eventually, Winton seems to have abandoned all these tactics.

The distance separating father and son widened in the autumn of 1939 when Mildred fell ill with what seemed to be a stomach virus. Then, as the mild Southern California winter wore on, with its misty fogs and temperate dampness, she began to lose weight rapidly, and vague abdominal pains were complicated by intermittent nausea. She agreed to see a doctor only in early April, after almost two weeks of anorexia: once brisk and buxom, Mildred then lost an alarming thirty pounds in less than a month. The diagnosis of advanced ovarian cancer was confirmed at Eastertide.

In June, Mildred was admitted to a hospital. "I tried to get it across to him," said Winton of his awkward conversations with Jimmy, "to prepare him in some way, but he just couldn't seem to take it in. I told him straight out one evening: 'Your mother's never coming home again.' All he did was stare at me!" Many strong adults, one might have replied—not to mention a sheltered child almost inordinately bound to his mother— would react similarly to such devastating news. "Jim and I," Winton commented awkwardly, "well, we've never had that closeness. It's nobody's fault, really. Just circumstances."

The circumstances swiftly became morbid. Emma Dean arrived from Fairmount to find her daughter-in-law virtually unrecognizable, and by early July the doctors said death could occur any day. The disease had swiftly taken its toll, Emma wrote to the family back home, adding that Mildred's only concern was that "she didn't want to die and leave Jimmy until she could get him raised."

On the afternoon of July 12, Winton was at work while his mother and son visited his wife. Now it was no longer Mildred who read to Jimmy, but he who sat reading a magazine article to her, his voice falling to a whisper as he watched his mother drift in and out of consciousness. "I just knew she was asleep before I got through the story," he recalled. "Then she woke up and said, 'I'm listening, Jimmy. I only had my eyes closed.'" The next day, she was permitted to go home, and there, just before three on the afternoon of July 14, 1940, the struggle ended: Mildred Wilson Dean was dead at age twenty-nine. When Emma and Winton told nine-year-old Jimmy the news, he sat blankly, his tearless gaze fixed and distant.

But his mother's death was not the only announcement. Winton had been making plans for the boy's future, and Emma had written to and received replies from Ortense and Marcus Winslow. And so, along with the shattering loss of maternal love, the boy was to be shipped back, with his grandmother and with his mother's coffin, to Indiana. Mildred was to be buried in Marion, and Jimmy would return to Fairmount, there to be raised by his aunt and uncle.

It is difficult to comprehend Winton Dean's remarkably cold and calculated action. For decades, family partisans maintained that his wife's illness had depleted his finances, and that he had neither the time nor the money to devote to the care of a child. Jimmy's best interest, according to this scenario, was back in Fairmount, far from the unhappiness of 1939 and 1940. But this defense does not take into account the fact that the cost of Mildred's medical care was completely provided by the federal government, for which Winton worked.

More to the point, it is hard to understand why Winton neither accompanied his wife's body back to

Indiana nor supervised her memorial service. His nine-year-old son had just endured a terrible loss, but all Winton could see was the burden of raising the boy. Why did he not at least go to Indiana with Jimmy, there to discuss the matter, in his presence, with the Winslows? Could he have been so callous? So it seems, and the reason for his conduct lies in the fact that Jimmy was, from conception, an unwanted child. Winton resented the boy's very existence, the marriage into which the child had forced him, and the freedom the marriage had aborted. If Winton had indeed wanted to come to California alone, now, at least, he could remain there unfettered by obligations at last.

Winton could easily have obtained leave from his job for the journey to Indiana, and if he was actually cash poor (which he was not), his parents or in-laws would gladly have volunteered to cover the expense of his trip—as they covered the return trips of Emma, Jimmy and the remains of Mildred. Winton chose, however, to pack off the child with the casket, blithely burying a ten-year chapter of his life along with his wife's body. "It seemed to me worse than dying itself," said James Dean of this dreadful experience, from which he never recovered.

The train journey was grim aboard the Challenger as it made its way from California to Indiana. Emma, who tried to speak of the familiar things to which her grandson would presently return, could not restrain Jimmy from jumping out at every stop and racing to the baggage compartment: he was afraid that someone might have removed his mother's coffin. Before they arrived in Indiana, Jimmy asked a conductor for a memento of the train and was given a cup and saucer with the monogram of the Challenger. These he kept for years.

Six days after she died, Mildred Marie Wilson Dean was safely interred in Grant Memorial Park Cemetery in Marion, her hometown. Only her parents, her in-laws and her dazed child stood at the graveside. For months after, Jimmy traveled each week from the farm in Jonesboro to Marion, where the Winslows sought him out as he hugged the gravestone—crying, as they gently drew him away, "Oh, Mother, why did you have to leave me?"

chapter three

> Youth is the period of
> assumed personalities and
> disguises. It is the time of
> the sincerely insincere.
>   V. S. PRITCHETT

Of course he was upset when he came
back," said his aunt Ortense.
"Everyone felt sorry for him, and we bent over backwards to make him happy."

Indeed, it is no exaggeration to say that the Winslows, in an excess of zeal to comfort and encourage an essentially orphaned boy, indulged Jimmy to the point of pampering him. When, that first day in July 1940, Jimmy said he liked their bedroom furniture, they moved it into his room. This set an unwise precedent, for any of the boy's preferences or caprices were instantly provided whenever possible. He was invited to help with farm chores, but only if he really wanted to, and he was never pressed into servitude. Ortense and Marcus Winslow were slow to scold and slower still to withhold privileges if Jimmy exhibited bad conduct; in any case, correction never took the form of corporal punishment. The result, to no one's surprise, was that the boy was too much indulged—spoiled, in fact. Patience with his moods became excessive tolerance of pranks and peccadilloes, and misdemeanors, too, often went unchecked.

Their lenience was understandable, and equally so his testing of it. The boy's wariness, doubtless springing from a fear that at any moment the Winslows, too, might send him away, led to a somewhat impervious aloofness. "He shut it all inside him," said his cousin Joan. "The only person he could ever have talked with was lying there in the coffin." Reticence was taken for unhappiness, which afflicted him often enough; but life did have to proceed. "Understandably, in light of what had happened, he had a very needy childhood from this point," according to his intimate friend and confidante, the actress Elizabeth "Dizzy" Sheridan, who spent time at the farm with Jimmy a dozen years later. "His uncle and aunt were really lovely people, and they adored him. But his mother's death and the sudden separation from his father made him very, very lonely."

That summer, the Winslows, the grandparents Dean and a few neighbors familiarized Jimmy with the surrounding territory, which had first been settled in 1830 by Marcus's ancestor, Joseph Winslow. (Greater Fairmount, as it might be called, included the Winslow farm in Jonesboro, five minutes by car from Fairmount.) The area could count white residents for just over a century, and everywhere were relics of the prior Native American culture—well-worn paths, former camp grounds and even shards of artifacts no one could trace to European-Caucasian traditions.

Good water and some of the richest farmland in America primed the area for planting corn, barley, oats and wheat—staples of Marcus Winslow's farm—and natural gas was for years abundant. By 1900, the area included fifty-three hundred residents, a number cut in half when the gas wells failed a few years later. Booth Tarkington's popular *Penrod* novels of rural Indiana life had celebrated an era before World War I, when, as he wrote, "the stable was empty but not yet rebuilt into a garage." Nineteen-forty was a midpoint in time: the Winslows had both a stable and a garage.

Of this summertime, and whenever he was not in school, Jimmy mostly remembered the kindness of the Winslows—and an introduction to farm chores, for which he was entirely unsuited by experience and temperament and which he dispatched with the fluctuating intensity typical of a schoolboy.

My uncle's place was a real farm, and I worked like crazy—as long as someone was watching me. Forty acres of oats made a huge stage, and when the audience left, I took a nap and nothing got plowed or harrowed. Then I met a friend who lived over in Marion, and he taught me how to wrestle and kill cats and other things boys do behind barns.

Notwithstanding the complete acceptance of Jimmy into the Winslow home, the activities, interests and atmosphere were completely opposite to what Jimmy had known with his mother. Instead of books and music, there were cows to be herded and barns to sweep; replacing tall tales were lists of spring planting chores; puppets and drawings were superseded by harvesting tasks and manure raking. None of these was his alone, and the more exacting tasks were left to farmhands. The fact is, as Jimmy admitted years later to close friends, "I was never a farmer. I always wanted out of there, but I never ran away, because I never wanted to hurt anyone." And where, one might have asked, could he go but to an orphanage? Beginning in September, the Winslows noticed that Jimmy kept very much to the farm after school hours, preferring the protective company of his aunt and uncle.

In early 1942 came the news that Winton, now freed of domestic responsibility, had been drafted into the Army Medical Corps; from that time, Jimmy began to call the Winslows "Mom and Dad." The following year, Ortense gave birth to her second child, Marcus, Jr., but Jimmy was not denied attention. "Jimmy was such an unusual child," said Ortense. "He kind of demanded it."

Often left to amuse himself while Ortense took care of baby Markie, Jimmy liked to sit with a family photo album or sketch with crayons. The art became more and more proficient, and extant artwork from his seventh and eighth grades reveals a sure hand in his drawings of cars and trucks, of the cotton gin and the reaper, of carefully rendered cross-sections of plants, roots and human organs in his high-school biology workbook.

At school, every child seemed familiar to every other—and he was the loner, the new boy, the isolate. Ortense noted the same facile dissatisfaction, the "anxiety to do many different things" that Winton observed.

"Once he learned or mastered something," according to Ortense, "Jimmy had to go on to something new. He was like that when Marcus got a new piece of farm machinery. He had to know all about it—then he dropped it." Joan agreed: "Jimmy was never one to sit still. He always had to be the best in everything."

At school, recalled one of his teachers, a lady with the splendidly rustic name India Nose, "He was sometimes moody and often unexplainably stubborn. He could be forgetful, too, as if he were in a daze. Sudden noises would startle him, and questions in class seemed to interrupt some faraway thoughts." One day she had her explanation when Jimmy burst into tears before the entire class and, when Miss Nose asked the reason, he sobbed, "I miss my mother."

While World War II raged abroad, there was considerable tension on the home front, when the Federal Bureau of Investigation announced in 1941 that the Hoosier state led the nation in reported car thefts and burglaries; worse, Indiana ranked third in the total number of murders. So much for the safety and security of simple midwestern country life.

There was more to come. During the summer of 1943, a vicious murder, reported all over the country, occurred in downtown Indianapolis. At the Claypool Hotel, an army corporal named Maoma Little Ridings was found slashed to death. That was followed, for a year beginning in early 1944, by a series of appalling sex murders in Fort Wayne. Neither the Indianapolis nor the Fort Wayne killer was caught, and the people of Indiana were, according to a survey, frightened, ashamed, angry and confused. While farm wives clucked about the good old days and their husbands called for stricter anticrime laws, it seemed the charming days of *Penrod* were (if they ever existed outside Tarkington's imagination) vanishing into oblivion.

Precisely at these times, as if inspired by the news of the day, Jimmy found a cache of books and almanacs that provided stories like those his mother had told him: soon, as his confidence with the family grew, he entertained them with skits like those he had improvised with Mildred. For the Winslows and sometimes a gathering of their friends, he brought to life the violent criminals of previous generations—for starters, the Wild Bunch, those notorious outlaws who rustled horses and cattle at the end of the nineteenth century. There, right before the family in the parlor, Jimmy seemed to disappear, replaced by the Bunch's amiable leader, Butch Cassidy, and his sidekick, Elzy Lay. Jimmy acted out the train robbery, the shootings, the sentencing, the escapes, the pardons. He also brought to life the daring thefts committed by America's fastest gunslinger, Harry Longabaugh, who rechristened himself "the Sundance Kid." These and other legends could be heard on the radio, too: from 1930, *The Lone Ranger* and *Death Valley Days* were staples of boyhood life in America and inspired costumes and skits for a generation of boys.

But more often than any role, Jimmy loved to play Billy the Kid, of whom he had first learned in school in California, and who now became a kind of demigod for him. Billy, too, had lost a parent; and Billy, Jimmy insisted naively, was innocent of almost every vicious crime attributed to him. Billy was "just a kid," as Jimmy said in his act—and really not so lawless as legend indicated. Adapted for young readers, *Riders of the*

Purple Sage and other books by Zane Grey (from neighboring Ohio) were entertaining enough, but the unvarnished truth about Billy the Kid appealed more to Jimmy Dean.

William H. Bonney, Jr. (most likely, Billy's true name) was born in 1860 in New York and migrated as a child to Kansas with his parents. His father died, and eventually Billy fell into a career of robbery, wandering across the Southwest and into Mexico. By the age of eighteen, he had been charged with a dozen killings and was sentenced to hang for two. He then escaped from jail, was tracked down and was finally shot dead at the age of twenty-one on July 14, 1881 (the date of Mildred's death, as her son pointed out). Jimmy's little playlet about Billy the Kid impressed the family, their friends and his own: Jimmy was alternately menacing and funny, violent and touching—especially in the surprisingly effective conclusion, when Billy was shot and lay dying in tears, calling for his dead father. This scene, above all others, gained Jimmy some brief popularity at school.

As for his other earlier cultural pursuits: "The violin was buried with my mother," he told columnist Hedda Hopper years later, and the tap shoes were replaced with heavy boots for farm work and sensible Buster Browns for school. He wore brogans while riding ponies and, later, the motor scooters and motorbikes for which he developed such a passion.

The first bike was a birthday gift from the Winslows; it helped gratify his need for attention, which extended beyond parlor skits and the dramatic exploitation of his own moods. After the Winslows gave him, on his sixteenth birthday, his first motorbike—a one-and-a-half-

horsepower Czech-made machine that raced to fifty
miles an hour—they may have had some regrets, for at
once noise and speed announced Jimmy Dean all over
the county. The elder Deans always knew when he was
a mile from their front door; schoolmates had to leap
out of his way as he zoomed toward Fairmount High;
and the Winslows feared for Jimmy's life. "They called
him One-Speed Dean," said Marvin Carter, whose
motorcycle shop in Fairmount was virtually the boy's
second home. "With his noise and speed, he had everyone in a riot."

"If he'd fallen only once," Marcus said years later,
"things might have been different [at the end]. Trouble
is, he never got hurt and he never found anything he
couldn't do well almost the first time he tried it. Just
one fall off that first bike and maybe he'd have been
afraid of speed. But he was without fear." According to
his childhood friend Robert Middleton, "Jimmy didn't
like anything to defeat him. The bigger the challenge,
the better he liked it. He liked to do everything and he
tried to do everything well." As he did for the rest of
his short life, during which he owned, successively, an
English motorcycle, a Harley, a Norton, an Indian 500,
an Italian Lancia and a British Triumph—each of which
he pushed beyond speed limits.

But machines were never such a passion as playacting, which extended beyond his homespun performances; as it happened, Jimmy became something of a
notorious mimic. "If Grandpa Dean sat with his legs
crossed, Jimmy crossed his," according to Ortense. "If
Grandpa stretched his legs out, Jimmy did, too. It was
more than just mocking Grandpa's gestures. Jimmy
seemed able to be another person. . . . His gift for

make-believe had us helpless with laughter one moment and gripped the next moment by a sudden change of mood."

As he quickly learned, this was still another way of gaining attention, often from others to himself. The Winslows soon sensed that their nephew had what Ortense called "a real talent for making you share his emotions. If he came home and was sad about something or someone had hurt him, it made you want to just go out and get whoever had made him unhappy. On the other hand, if he was in a good mood, you had to feel happy with him." This ability to manipulate others' emotions became, in time, a more and more powerful weapon in his arsenal of attention-getting devices.

So began James Dean's lifelong struggle to establish a sense of himself as someone to reckon with. Thereafter, fighting constantly to win approval and affirmation, he sought to excel at sport, to take risks and chances, and sometimes simply to make noise as methods to win admiration. In acting, he assumed the identity of another—it was his moment to escape himself, to wrap Jimmy Dean in another's personality—and simultaneously to astonish, to shock, to control the emotions and reactions of others before they controlled him. He was, in other words, the essence of a singular type of budding actor.

"I felt a need to prove myself," he said of this time. And to do so at school, he turned to sports. Just as he had to excel in playacting, so he had to gain respect in school games, and beginning in eighth grade, in 1944, he was a hellion on the ball field and basketball court, and a fiercely determined racer on the track. In this regard, he partook of the legendary "Hoosier fever" for racing and basketball and developed a certain reputation for ornery prankishness.

To outdo the competition, he risked his health; to attract admiration, he performed astounding leaps, catches, crashes into opponents—and often enough the results were almost disastrous and at least expensive. "He broke fifteen pair of glasses doing athletics," Marcus Winslow said with some exasperation. "He broke them as fast as I could get them." There were more dramatic gambles, too, as when he attempted a trapeze act in the barn and fell, knocking out two front teeth. Fortunately, Winton was expected on a return trip, and so Jimmy's father fashioned a bridge. This, too, the boy turned into a shock tactic: unprepared visitors stared in horror when Jim Dean calmly took out two false teeth and dropped them into a glass or pretended he had just coughed them out. "You either wanted to skin him or love him, one or the other," according to Marcus Winslow.

There were other ways to satisfy his need to be the center of attention. "He liked to perform at home, as his grandmother Emma Dean told me," recalled Adeline Brookshire, the teacher who most influenced Jimmy at Fairmount High.* "He loved to get up on a table or chair and be heard, give readings or perform. And so the first things he did in public were little recitations and parts in tableaux for the WCTU"—the Woman's Christian Temperance Union. But there was a problem: Jimmy refused to attend rehearsals with a group. As church and WCTU tutor Helen Kirkpatrick recalled, "He just did things his own way. He was— well, a little different."

---

*Farmount High was later replaced by Madison–Grant High School.

Ortense Winslow was a devout adherent to the principles of the WCTU, which had been founded in 1883 by Frances Willard. A lobbyist, expert in pressure politics and leader of the Prohibition Party, Willard used her superb oratorical skills toward her goal of abolishing the sale and consumption of liquor. Thus her followers, after her death in 1898, continued the tradition of sponsoring dramatic speaking competitions about the evils of drink. When one such contest was announced for Fairmount in 1945, Ortense urged Jimmy to put his talent at the service of God's cause. A thundering recitation of a little morality monologue called "Bars" would be just the thing for her friends and his reputation. The title, Jimmy first learned, was a stern double meaning: frequenting liquor bars led to a life behind the iron type.

He needed some coaching, and so he sought the assistance of Adeline Brookshire (formerly Mrs. Nall, to which name she reverted after divorcing Brookshire, her second husband), who taught Jimmy Spanish, speech and drama during his high-school years. In the first he very nearly failed, because languages did not interest him; in the others, he excelled. "Jimmy was very aggressive about getting what he wanted," according to Ortense. "He had a bright mind—but didn't always apply himself. He used to say, 'I'd rather not get good grades than be called a sissy.'" That was a real risk, since he did not make friends easily and was, according to classmates and teachers, usually alone. "He was a little different from most boys," according to basketball coach Paul Weaver. "He was usually alone, and when the team arrived, usually kids came together. But Jimmy would usually arrive alone."

Longing for acceptance, he had a simultaneous fear of rejection that kept him at a distance from everyone: no offer of friendship was readily accepted. "He seemed to feel uncomfortable with everyone," according to Weaver, who—like others at Fairmount High— could never remember the shy Dean with a girlfriend, or even a date.

Only Adeline Brookshire took the time to see the proficiency behind the eccentricity. Born in Marion in 1906, Adeline Brookshire was a sprightly, perceptive and (so the townsfolk thought) slightly offbeat little bird of a woman who resembled nothing so much as Mrs. Pampinelli, that colorful eccentric from the pages of *The Torchbearers*, playwright George Kelly's sharp satire of amateur theatricals. Bitten in her twenties by the acting bug, she had never been able to shake the virus and, after failing to take the Chicago circuit by storm, settled down to the more realistic life of a drama teacher at Fairmount High in 1940.

"He could be moody and unpredictable, to keep people off their guard—and rude, to attract attention," Adeline Brookshire remembered of their early meetings in 1945. "One day, to shock everybody, he offered me a cigarette right in the middle of class. I almost popped him one for that. And if he didn't win a competition in something—oh, he could pout and rant like I don't know what. But I also recognized a natural talent. The boy had a gift—he knew it and I knew it." The growth of that talent, however, was impeded by Jimmy's inability to take correction: "Frankly, he couldn't take criticism," she added. "Marcus [Winslow] came to school and told me, 'Don't let it bother you. He's very critical—he's that way at home.' He was kind of hard for me to get along with. I didn't have time to sit down and talk everything over about his every part in every play."

"Jim knew how to play people," Brookshire admitted years later. "He could work me around his little finger." Before or after James Dean, she never met a more seductive student: young James Dean used the pity of others for his own ends, and his remote manner to turn vulnerability into a powerful asset. "He was often nothing more than a kid, showing off for the hometown folks. In a way, that's about all he ever was."

And so teacher and student set to work on "Bars," for which they agreed that a chair with rungs would be a neat prop, although the rules of the contest forbade props. With the chair, Jimmy could sit, then turn the chair around and use the top as a bar, and then finally kneel behind it and grasp the vertical rungs like a man imprisoned. "Bars! Bars! Iron bars!" he shrieked during his private rehearsals, his voice echoing along the third floor corridor outside Room 21.

> No matter which way I look I see them always before me! Long, menacing, iron bars that mock and sneer at me, even in my sleep. At times I think I hear them shout, "You killed a man! You killed a man!" Then I shout back at them, "I didn't! I didn't! I tell you, I didn't!" But did I? My God above, did I—I who as a boy could not bear to inflict pain on anyone?

Frances Willard and company would have swooned for joy. One classmate did not, however, and could not

resist poking fun at a run-through. Jimmy challenged
the boy to a fistfight, which led to a temporary suspen-
sion from school.

The judges of the oratory contest applied a more
devastating sanction: adhering religiously to the no-
prop regulation, they took the chair away from the
performer when he stepped up for his speech. Without
it, he stood, wordless and stubborn, perhaps hoping
the jury would return the chair to him so the evening
could move along. But he was gently pulled offstage,
the next speaker took his place, and that was that.
Instead of apologizing to Adeline Brookshire, he threw
a temper tantrum, accused her of sabotaging his prize
and would not look at her for weeks. "He did the
dumbest things," she said with a sigh. And of that
unfortunate evening Ortense reasoned, "I was sure
then of what I had known all along: you couldn't make
Jimmy Dean do things he didn't want to do." So
passed the most public moment of his freshman year
in high-school.

Adeline Brookshire had a male counterpart, and
James Dean another surrogate father, in a young minister who came to Fairmount in 1946, just after military service. The Reverend James A. De Weerd, then
thirty, had studied in California and at Cambridge
(England), won several medals for bravery as an
Army chaplain, and returned to civilian life as pastor
of the Fairmount Wesleyan Methodist Church. Stocky,
single, slightly baroque in manner and speech and
almost frighteningly gifted when he mounted the pul-
pit, De Weerd preached in the old tradition of extreme
emotionalism; he could, it was said, wring tears from
a teenage boy and strike fear into a hardened atheist.

Outside churchly duties, he was a kind of all-around mentor to the boys at Fairmount High, introducing them to the art museum in Indianapolis, putting recordings of Tchaikovsky on the gramophone, encouraging them to write poetry and showing them eight-millimeter films of exotic lands, dancers and bullfighters. And so (it was perhaps inevitable), after De Weerd's death at age fifty-six in 1972, some imaginative journalists decided that an unmarried country parson just had to have been a sex offender, and for years stories circulated about De Weerd and Dean. Their relationship was carnal, ran the stories. Jimmy was so hungry for the loving affirmation of an older man that he succumbed to the irresistible charms of the seductive minister. Hence, the story concludes, James Dean was introduced to the gay life in early adolescence.

This account provides tangy spice for the otherwise unexceptional history of James Dean's high-school years: the problem, however, is that there is not a single shred of evidence for such a relationship. De Weerd was indeed, by all accounts, an eccentric—even flamboyant—character, and his preference for the exclusive company of country boys suggests perhaps at least some kind of veiled erotic component in his attitude toward them. But there is nothing in his character to suggest abusive conduct; in fact, his life in Fairmount proceeded without a hint of scandal, and he was subsequently a college president and the author of several highly regarded religious tracts. Moreover, it would have been difficult for him to risk anything like homosexual activities with teenagers and not be exposed in so intimate a community as Fairmount, a place not known as a hotbed of sexual

libertinism. Most significant of all, not one young person—
then or later—ever accused James De Weerd of inappropriate conduct. The truth of the matter was that De
Weerd was, for a brief time, another temporary father
figure to James Dean, and in this regard he had a brief,
benevolent influence. Jimmy took his unhappy memories
of his mother's death to De Weerd, who told him no, that
tragedy was not his fault. "Jimmy was usually happiest
stretched out on my library floor," De Weerd said after
Dean's death. "He loved good music playing softly in the
background." And that, during 1947 and 1948, was that.
A lonely boy sought out a single, older man who supplemented spiritual comfort with an introduction to art
books and music.

Continuing his obsession with excellence, Jimmy
Dean continued to work hard at sports—sometimes
with a fierce temper if he did not win or disagreed
with a referee's decision. Any threat to his success he
took as almost a threat to his life, not to say his honor,
and teammates who got in his way were deeply
resented. "He was not always as thoughtful and considerate as he might have been," according to coach
Weaver. "I felt sometimes that he had an inferiority
complex that he was covering up. In any case, he
wasn't too coachable and couldn't take criticism in
front of others."

At home, he used free time to play hand (or bongo)
drums, which the Winslows did not much appreciate;
and to sketch in pencils and pastels, which they did.
For friends' and relatives' birthdays, he frequently presented a landscape or floral drawing, much to the
amazement of the recipients, most of whom saw him as
a skittish, unsociable lad who made no effort to make

himself agreeable. Winton Dean got no such present when he showed up for a visit, discharged from the service and squiring—to everyone's surprise—his new wife, a nervous little woman named Ethel Case. She and her stepson eyed each other warily, and during that week Jimmy made himself very scarce around the Winslow farm. He was torn between a consuming desire for love and approval and a deeply rooted bitterness and suspicion that everyone would, sooner or later, let him down, and so to hell with the world.

In his sophomore year of high-school (1946–47), Jimmy's acting career began, although hardly auspiciously: his first two roles were in creaky melodramas chosen by Adeline Brookshire. The first was *The Monkey's Paw*, a damp little supernatural thriller about wishes and a curse, by W. W. Jacobs and Louis N. Parker. In this three-scene melodrama, a favorite of school and amateur groups, Jimmy played Herbert White, a London factory laborer who lives with his parents. "My work doesn't go with alcohol," says Herbert, and Jimmy shaded the line with just the right callow moralism. "I've got to keep a cool head, a steady eye and a still hand." And then, ominously: "The fly-wheel might gobble me up"—which is of course exactly his fate. In the audience, Grandma Dean and Aunt Ortense applauded the character's sentiments of virtuous temperance; and moments later, they wept, when Herbert White, sober as a WCTU chairlady, was killed in a machine—mercifully, offstage.

His second appearance at Fairmount High was in something just as unfortunate: a short romance titled *Mooncalf Mugford*, by Brainerd Duffield and Helen and Nolan Leary. Jimmy played the title character, a demented old man who draws his wife into the world of his dreams and delusions, eventually excluding them both from anything like normal life. Those who attended the play that winter remembered only one unusually affecting moment—at the conclusion, when Jimmy took the arm of the girl playing his wife and led her to the shore, pointing out the starry sky and the sound of gentle waves on the beach. What world, his gestures said, could be more real, more beautiful than this? It was only a teenage actor's momentary glance— a gaze of ineffable longing on the face of a man disconnected from a troubled world—but the spectators were silent, and some students were haunted for days by the spirit of the play. In those few final moments, Jimmy Dean evoked and established something that would be part of his later trademark—an amalgam of tenderness and confusion that never failed to touch audiences. That night, Adeline Brookshire decided she had a talent on her hands.

In October 1947, he had another chance onstage, this time a minor role that required him again to play a man much older than himself. Cornelia Otis Skinner and Emily Kimbrough's memoirs, *Our Hearts Were Young and Gay*, had been successfully dramatized by Jean Kerr the previous year; it was a screwball comedy chronicling the misadventures of two nineteen-year-old college girls who leave Muncie, Indiana, and travel, unchaperoned, to Paris. Attempting a façade of sophisticated savoir faire as they are pursued by two Harvard boys, the untried girls are caught up in the usual comic mayhem. Jimmy held the stage as actor Otis Skinner, the father of one, and in the role he fearlessly sliced through the ham with the conviction of a once-grand thespian: "You'll be lucky if this old tub gets out of the harbor!" he bellowed ominously. "I know what this reminds me of! The tomb scene! 'Shall we stay in this palace of dim night? . . .

"'Alack, what blood is this which stains the stony entrance of this sepulchre? . . .

"'Lady, come away from this nest of death, contagion and unnatural sleep.'"

The scene, students and teachers remembered, was amusing but not foolishly overwrought. He would like, Jimmy told his teacher privately after the final performance, to play Shakespeare—the real thing, not a parody. Reverend De Weerd, he added, had told him that Jimmy would be the perfect romantic hero—Romeo, perhaps, or Ferdinand. Well, there would be time for that later, said Adeline. No need to rush. She did not say what he might have guessed: that he may have been the only student capable of scenes from Shakespeare.

Eager to learn every aspect of the actor's craft, Jimmy had concocted his own makeup for Otis Skinner, from the pancake base to the eyeliner and the talcum-powdered hair, and during his first moments onstage no one recognized him. But that was nothing compared to his appearance as mustached, spiteful villain in a Fairmount Halloween revue that fall of 1948. He made sure he stole the show by appearing a few minutes after the final curtain in the auditorium—as Frankenstein's monster, for which he had devised a face so grotesque that some students and teachers, unsmiling, drew back.

Coach Weaver was among the staff, and Bob Pulley one of the students, who could not recall Jimmy with a high-school girlfriend. "The girls liked him," said Barbara Garner, summing up the general recollection, "but I guess he wasn't interested." In fact no matter his skill on the basketball court and playing field, regardless of the loud applause he earned onstage and the quiet awe inspired by exploits on his motorbike, Jimmy Dean was, throughout high-school, a loner.

In the spring of 1948, a new principal at Fairmount High asked students to write a short autobiography, and James Dean turned in "My Case Study."

I, James Byron Dean, was born February 8, 1931, Marion, Indiana. My parents, Winton Dean and Mildred Dean, formerly Mildred Wilson and myself existed in the state of Indiana until I was six years of age. Dad's work with the government caused a change so Dad, a dental mechanic, was transferred to California. There we lived until the fourth year. Mom became ill and passed out of my life at the age of nine. I never knew the reason for mom's death, in fact it still preys on my mind.

I had always lived such a talented life. I studied violin, played in concerts, tap-danced on theatre stages but most of all I like art, to mold and create things with my hands. I came back to Indiana to live with my uncle. I lost the dancing and violin but not the art. I think my life will be devoted to art and dramatics. And there are so many different fields of art it would be hard to foul up, and if I did there are so many different things to do—farm, sports, science, geology, coaching, teaching, music. I got it and I know if I better myself then there will be no match. A fellow must have confidence.

When living in California my young eyes experienced many things . . . My hobby, or what I do in my spare time, is motorcycle. I know a lot about them mechanically and I love to ride. I have been in a few races and I have done well. I own a small cycle myself. When I'm not doing that I'm usually engaged in athletics, the heartbeat of every American boy. As one strives to make a goal in life in a game there should be a goal in this crazy world for each of us. I hope I know what mine is—anyway, I'm after it.

The tone of his little autobiography was appropriately serious, but Jimmy was quite casual about his studies, as his report card for February 1948 revealed (D+ in English, C- in American history, in geometry and in safety driving, and A- in art). Even as he told the new principal that he hoped for a goal "in this crazy world," he seemed to find something truthful only when he was not himself—only when he was rehearsing a part with Mrs. Brookshire. The characters might be downright silly, but the more outrageous they were, the greater the challenge to him, and the farther the distance from himself.

No doubt about it, James Dean loved the applause he heard at the end of a play, just as he had since his childhood pageants with his mother, presented for neighboring children. The desire for approval and respect was an incentive to excel in sports, too, and by senior year, 1948–49, he was hailed in the yearbook as a "brilliant guard in basketball—one of the main cogs in the Quaker line-up this season. Jim was rated one of the most outstanding guards in the county." But none of this gave him any lasting satisfaction: congratulations faded, praise was never enough, and he always longed for yet more and more endorsement.

For years it was alleged that, on his eighteenth birthday (February 8, 1949), James Byron Dean registered with his local Selective Service System, or draft board, claiming that he was a homosexual and thus assuring that he would be exempt from military duty. But neither his board papers nor his draft card confirm this rumor, and in the absence of those documents it can only be presumed that James Dean would certainly not have claimed, in the conservative atmosphere of Fairmount, Indiana, what gay men in New York or Los Angeles only very rarely admitted on official documents at the time. To do so would have been effectively to ruin one's chances of a career.

Such a step, for which there is absolutely no evidence, would have meant instant social ostracism at home and at school—such records were, after all, available for public scrutiny—and, far worse, there would at once follow a permanent public record of "undesirable character." (There were no secrets in Fairmount, especially when the issue related to sex.) Thus Dean would have been ineligible for any respectable occupation. Ex-convicts, at that time, were in fact hired more readily than the few courageous, avowed homosexuals.

Just as J. Edgar Hoover and Joseph McCarthy were sharpening their weapons, claiming that "perverts" were poisoning the life of America, fear was struck into the hearts of boys all over the country. The merest hint or whisper, fantasy or wonder about attraction to the same sex was enough to drive many men and women to thoughts of suicide (and often, alas, to more than thoughts), and others to expensive, protracted psychotherapy in hopeless attempts to alter something fundamental in their natures. James Dean, who precisely at that time was considering a life in the theater, knew very well that (hurrah for the triumph of image-making) homosexuality or bisexuality was "unknown" among theater folk (not to say any other profession) in America. It would take years before anything was known about the complicated private lives (so different from the perception created by the studio) of Rock Hudson, Tyrone Power, Marlene Dietrich, Cary Grant, Montgomery Clift or Greta Garbo, to name only a few among thousands whose lives were sexually unconventional.

During his last year at Fairmount High, from the autumn of 1948 through the spring of 1949, most of Jimmy's time was devoted to the playing field and the rehearsal room. His accomplishments in speech class and with the Thespians led Adeline Brookshire and James De Weerd, his second "Mom and Dad" beside Ortense and Marcus, to encourage him when he mentioned a career as an actor. Even in debate tournaments, a sense of drama infused the project. On February 13, 1949, for example, Jimmy was heard on the *Voice of Youth* program, broadcast at the Marion Public Library—addressing, of all things, America's postwar economic boom. Remarkably, he made the speech, patched together from news stories and given final form by two teachers and the principal, sound as thrilling as a report from the floor of the basketball court.

He would have accepted the substantial role of Martin Vanderhof in Kaufman and Hart's *You Can't Take It With You*, Fairmount's spring play, but at the same time he was preparing for a state and national competition in an important oratory contest. And so Jimmy took on the smaller character role of Boris Kolenkhov, the eccentric Russian ballet master—"hairy, loud and very, very Russian," as the authors indicated. Besides, said Adeline, no other student could manage the accent and the touch of madness in the role. Heavily bearded (again, with his own makeup), Jimmy tore through his scenes, rhapsodizing over women and Russia and leaping into the dance and wrestling episodes with appropriately farcical panache. By now, no one was surprised when he got the loudest applause. "Life is chasing around inside of me, like a squirrel!" he said as Boris. In just these words, he spoke of himself to his drama teacher, with a wink and a smile.

Yet the touch of comic madness Adeline saw as essential to that role was in fact obvious to her every day in a far darker and more terrifying way as she worked with Jimmy on a dramatic presentation of "A Madman's Manuscript" from Charles Dickens's *Pickwick Papers*. This he planned to recite at the state finals of the National Forensic League—and, if he won there, at the nationwide competition later that month. A text written in the Gothic-horror style of Edgar Allan Poe's short story "The Tell-Tale Heart," the Dickens selection is a monologue told by a lunatic: he drives his poor wife to madness and death, attempts to kill her brother, and is hunted down and committed to an asylum—from which he recounts this frightening tale of derangement and murder.

From the start, Jimmy's serious preparations got him in trouble, for one of his classmates was only too willing to be critic and judge.

Jimmy began brilliantly, and at once the students snapped to attention as he shouted madly:

> Yes! A madman! How that word would have struck to my heart, many years ago! How it would have roused the terror that used to come upon me sometimes, sending the blood hissing and tingling through my veins, till the cold dew of fear stood in large drops upon my skin, and my knees knocked together with fright!

His entire appearance altered before their eyes. His voice dropped to a whisper, and some of the students were visibly shaken as he continued, his voice hard as steel, his teeth clenched, jaw set and eyes glazed with insane purpose:

> It's a grand thing to be mad, to be peeped at like a wild lion through the iron bars, to gnash one's teeth and howl through the long, still night, to the merry ring of a heavy chain—and to roll and whine among the straw . . .

He leaped to a corner of the classroom and crouched with feral menace, his voice edged with fear and loathing:

> Large, dusky forms with sly and jeering faces crouch in the corner of my room and bend over my bed at night, tempting me to madness. They tell me in low whispers that the floor of the old house in which my grandfather died was stained with his own blood, shed by his own hand in raging madness . . .

As he continued, his tone and mood were as mercurial as a madman's, his color changing from pale to livid as he threatened to kill his lovely wife—an oppressive act of intimidation that drove her over the brink to lunacy and confinement. "And all this was food for my secret mirth, and I laughed behind the white handkerchief which I held up to my face." A few girls in the class began to shiver and weep, and boys shifted uneasily at their desks—right through to the violent ending, with the shrieks of the madman in his cell. The performance—it could hardly be called a "speech"—had lasted almost fourteen minutes. During the entire time, the classroom was frozen at attention; at the finale, when Jimmy bowed his head and moved to take his seat, there was no applause for almost a minute. The atmosphere in Room 21 was thick with shock.

And then, at his final open rehearsal a few days later, a junior student named David Fox decided, perhaps from either jealousy or simple perversity, to sabotage the act. As Jimmy shifted into high gear, Fox—who was sitting in a front seat, turned around to gaze at his classmates, smirked, choked back a mocking laugh and drew the attention of classmates away from the star and toward himself and his rude critique. *What is this stupid stuff?* his manner asked.

Five minutes into the monologue, as if he had become the madman himself, Jimmy broke character, tore after Fox, caught him at the bottom of a stairwell and began to throttle him—much like the character he had just enacted. It took the principal and two teachers to break up the fight, and a half-hour for school activity to return to normal. Jimmy was suspended from classes for two days. (In the traditional "Class Will," in which graduating seniors make a bequest to juniors, he bequeathed his "short temper to David Fox.")

When he returned, he had the text of "A Madman's Manuscript" memorized to perfection. Still, Adeline warned, it was two minutes too long: the rules were strict about a twelve-minute limit. "But every part of it is necessary," he replied when she repeated the criticism to him. "He was a temperamental artist," Adeline said years later, "and I didn't press the issue." It would have done her no good in any case, for Jimmy was a stubborn student. He had to do the piece as he felt it, he insisted—just as he refused to wear the customary coat, white shirt and tie expected of entrants. "I've got to go crazy in this speech! How the heck can I go crazy in a shirt and tie?" Adeline had to concede that, but the timing bothered her.

On April 8, Adeline and Jimmy drove to Peru, Indiana, about an hour northeast of Fairmount, for the

regional contest. "The effect was chilling," according to
Adeline, and the first-round judge, Frieda Bedwell of
Terre Haute, agreed: "I was deeply moved. I was espe-
cially impressed with the eerie expression in his eyes.
They actually looked glassy and mad at times." The
judges were lenient about the time, although they cau-
tioned Adeline about the finals. But the outcome in
Peru brought Jimmy—and he brought Fairmount
High—a touch of glory. He won first place in Dramatic
Declamation in the Indiana State Finals.

And so, on Wednesday morning, April 27, teacher
and student boarded the train for Chicago and changed
there for the Zephyr, which took them to the National
Finals in Longmont, Colorado (less than two hours
north of Denver). There Jimmy had to go up against one
hundred contestants from twenty-four states in the contest held at the local high-school on Saturday, April 30.

In the first round that morning, Jimmy was warned
by a judge less lenient than Mrs. Bedwell and the
Indiana locals. "If I were to judge you with an equally
good speaker, time would have to be an element in my
decision," Jimmy was told. "It might be splitting a hair,
but I would have to use that against you." But the boy
who was a star in Fairmount was too confident in
Longmont. Insisting on the integrity of the Dickens
text, he refused to cut the speech during the final round
that afternoon. Jimmy placed sixth and so was ineligible for the last round.

Adeline was, of course, sorely disappointed for her
star pupil. But her distress turned to anxiety when she
could not locate him. He was not in his assigned room,
not in the cafeteria, not with the resigned group of
losers drowning their sorrows at a soda fountain.

Finally she found him huddled high in the gymnasium bleachers, and she could not coax a word out of him for hours. When at last she got him to speak, he muttered coldly that his loss was entirely her fault: she did not back him before the judges, he complained; the timing was part of the art, and some of the critical points she had offered him during rehearsals had thrown him off the mark. He lost his primacy, he insisted, because of her. With that, Adeline, too, was speechless.

The moment was not unlike Paul Weaver's recollection that Jimmy was uncoachable on the basketball team, obstinate and unwilling to take correction. Perhaps he saw teachers as parent figures, and their advice as reproof; perhaps, on the other hand, in a perverse way he wanted their disapproval, wanted to proclaim himself against them—to do things entirely his own way. He would do the rejecting first, even if this meant harm to himself or his destiny. This kind of conduct formed a disappointing pattern in relationships to come.

What might have been a great triumph was, therefore, aborted by sheer self-will and infantile arrogance—and more was the pity, since the eyewitness testimony of the Longmont contest indicates that his dramatic reading was superb. "The odd thing," said Adeline, "was that offstage Jimmy could be just as crazy as onstage, very changeable from one minute to the next, just like—well, I'd say just like an adjustable lunatic."

Throughout the school year, the Fairmount seniors had gathered every few weeks for "Penny Suppers," at which they shared—for only one cent a serving—

sumptuous pot-luck buffet meals donated by their families. By virtue of adolescent appetites, the suppers realized their goal: the money to finance a three-day trip to Washington, D.C., during which Jimmy constantly entertained them with sharp impersonations of teachers they knew and tourists they met. One evening, after a peaceful boat ride along the Potomac, Jimmy and two classmates got hold of a case of beer. Back at the hotel, there were the inevitable results of youthful imbibing that night—pranks aimed at innocent boys, kisses stolen from unwary girls and the highjinks typical of eighteen-year-olds in 1949. Because Jimmy was the leader of the outlaws, his antics were censurable by faculty monitors, who wisely chose not to spoil the journey by imposing any sentence harsher than an early curfew the next night.

Fairmount High's commencement exercises were held at the Bethel Tabernacle of the Wesleyan-Methodist camp grounds on Monday, May 16. Of forty-nine graduates in the class of '49, Jimmy ranked twentieth from the top. "Good, but handicapped by a lack of application," noted the principal, Roland DuBois, on Dean's record. But this referred only to academic achievement, at which Jimmy never attained anything like excellence. Instead, he took enormous pride in his achievements as a basketball player, which he managed despite his full adult height of just five feet, eight inches, which he reached that year.

Basketball hero or no, his height—or lack of it, as he believed—was a source of discomfiture for the rest of his life, and he often used the word "runty" to describe himself; he rarely weighed in at more than 140 pounds, and his tendency to slouch and lope never made him seem robust—much less self-confident. That quality was reserved for his inchoate acting talent—for which he could, in 1949, be considered first-rate only in comparison with other high-school actors. Still, Adeline Brookshire was right to see that there could be good uses for the obstinacy, the moodiness, the unpredictability, the sense of marginality and rejection she discerned in young James Dean.

At home, the Winslows were pleased with whatever he did well and never complained about his mediocre reports. Although they were not particularly analytical or concerned about Jimmy's mercurial moods and lack of self-discipline, Ortense and Marcus were distressed by his lack of trust in them. Of Jimmy's last year in Indiana, his uncle recalled, "He pulled into himself and didn't share with us anymore. Then suddenly he left us."

chapter four

There is a period near the
beginning of every man's
life when he has little to
cling to except his unman-
ageable dream, little to
support him except good
health, and nowhere to go
but all over the place.
                    E. B. WHITE

The departure was really no surprise
to anyone; Jimmy had planned it for
several months that spring, and on June 14 he boarded
the train for California. There he intended to study acting, a goal he kept to himself: he told the Winslows
only that he wanted to visit his father and consider
attending college in Los Angeles.

His family expected only that eventually he would
get a good job and settle down. After all, in 1949 the
country was booming. The American standard of living
had risen dramatically after World War II (and did so
nowhere else in the world), and a new materialism was

taking root. Americans were now more prosperous
than at any time in history: they owned more things,
drove more automobiles, had more leisure time.
Luxuries were turning into necessities, privileges into
expectations.

Consumer goods were produced in astonishing
volume; the first portable radios were on the market;
almost ten percent of American homes had little
seven- or ten-inch black-and-white television sets
(often with magnifying "bubbles" positioned in front
of them to enlarge the image); and automatic washing
machines prophesied the liberation of the American
housewife. The first strip malls, shopping centers and
fast-food drive-ins appeared. Banks had drive-up
windows and post offices drive-up letter boxes. More
dubiously, there were at least three drive-up windows
at Los Angeles funeral parlors: visitors could avoid
the awkwardness of in-person condolences by
remaining in their cars and simply glancing for a
moment at the remains of the deceased, conveniently
visible behind a glass window, rather like a dozing
bank teller. Then the driver-visitor shifted gears and
drove away, perhaps to one of the McDonald ham-
burger eateries, the first of which opened in Southern
California in 1940: in 1948, the brothers McDonald
converted it to a self-service restaurant and were
beginning to franchise their name to other fast-food
entrepreneurs.

In the nation's cities and towns, the Consumer Price
Index was stable; the minimum wage rose to seventy-
five cents an hour; and the Housing Act authorized
construction of almost a million homes, some of them
built according to the mass construction techniques

introduced by Levitt and Sons, the company that developed low-cost suburban housing developments for veterans. In Levittown, Long Island (the first of several
communities of that name), thousands of dwellings
were identical, built according to a rigidly uniform
plan; it was very often difficult to distinguish one from
another—a visual emblem, it later seemed, of the social
and cognitive uniformity so sadly misperceived as
unity in postwar America. It was much the same way
in Southern California, where the San Fernando Valley
(the area of Los Angeles County separated from
Hollywood and the West Side by the Santa Monica
Mountains) blossomed like the desert; between the end
of 1947 and early 1950, hundreds of thousands of new
homes and apartments dotted former ranches and fruit
groves. From all over the country and south of the border, people flocked to the good life in the Golden State.
The population of Los Angeles County, which had
been 2.7 million in 1940, was 4.2 million at the end of
1949.

But that year, Hollywood folks were under the
worst cloud of suspicion in the history of the business.
The House Committee on Un-American Activities
(HUAC) was on the rampage, tearing up the lives of
filmmakers, writers, actors and professors in a search
to root out the specter of Communism among "dangerous" artists and intellectuals. If traitorous Americans
were not exposed (so ran the conventional wisdom),
then Russians would creep into the house while you
were asleep, and suddenly the United States would be
under the control of the Soviets. They were probably
already embarking on a plan to atomize the minds of
innocent Americans: according to a very active (but

misguided) citizens' group, the numbing of America was to be achieved when Communists got their way and put fluoride in the nation's water supply.

The paranoia that gripped postwar America had several causes. China fell to a Communist regime in 1948; Moscow announced the detonation of an atomic bomb in 1949; Communist troops were preparing for the war (beginning in 1950) against American-supported armies in Korea; and there were, alas, some authentic cases of treason and espionage (mostly of atomic secrets) on the home front.

The triumph over fascism in Europe and the hitherto unimaginable display of power demonstrated by America's atomic bombs at the end of World War II bestowed, in their wake, an unspoken presumption that there was something like a divine mandate to protect everything "pure" about American values and American success. In June 1949, peace and prosperity were proofs of that. A certain moral smugness often occurs in such circumstances, the odd but unspoken hunch that God is an American. Hence the coagulation of pride and paranoia.

In October 1947, the HUAC, which had developed unchecked from a 1938 congressional committee to investigate suspicious activities among American intellectuals, swung into action like medieval crusaders. Nineteen prominent men in Hollywood were ordered to testify about their involvement in Communist activities. The first group (who came to be known as "the Hollywood Ten") at first refused to testify and at once lost their jobs, were sentenced to prison and were fined for contempt of Congress.* Studio executives initially condemned the witch-hunt, but when threatened with the loss of financial backing from East Coast banks, they became friends of the HUAC. The deepest loyalties of moguls are always to the cashier.

In short order, those suspected of having Communist associations—or who might even have belonged to intellectual groups critical of society in the 1930s—were blacklisted unless they cooperated with HUAC. The result was that those who did not, who included some of Hollywood's finest talents, never worked there again. At the same time, during a writers' strike, studios fired all employees who refused to toe the mark by cooperating with the HUAC.

All this reached critical mass with the rise of the notorious Senator Joseph McCarthy, a forty-year-old Wisconsin Republican who was about to launch one of the worst assaults against American constitutional rights in the nation's history. Almost single-handedly, McCarthy—with the loud support of millions— expanded the Hollywood witch-hunt, claiming he had the names of known Communists who were working in the highest government offices. The "lists" of these names he never produced, nor could he ever provide a convincing case against a single individual. Nevertheless, capitalizing on the country's anxieties about Korea and Eastern Europe, McCarthy raged on, trampling civil liberties in the name of patriotism. It was, therefore, a short route from the imprisonment of the Hollywood Ten in 1947 (designed to protect America from corruption within) to the inclusion of a new phrase in the Pledge of

---

* The Hollywood Ten: screenwriters Alvah Bessie, Lester Cole, Ring Lardner, Jr., John Howard Lawson, Albert Maltz, Samuel Ornitz, Adrian Scott and Dalton Trumbo; and directors Herbert Biberman and Edward Dmytryk.

Allegiance in 1954: no longer were Americans merely
"one nation indivisible, with liberty and justice for all";
now they were "one nation under God . . ."—in other
words, He is on our side. *Annuit coeptis*, runs the adage
on the dollar bill: He has blessed our undertakings.

McCarthy was finally disgraced in 1954 after his
lunacy led him to attack (of all people) President
Eisenhower as tainted with Communist sympathies.
But by the time the Senate finally censured him,
McCarthy's fantasies had ruined countless lives and
helped to canonize a dangerous ideal of extreme right-
wing conformity—a notion that was itself anomalous
in a nation born in revolution, raised on healthy dis-
sent and encouraged on a diet of rugged individualism. But Senator McCarthy and his species had talked
a lot about God blessing their undertakings, and they
were mighty sure where those undertakings led and
where they were being corrupted. In the entertainment
industry, one of his staunchest supporters was Walter
Winchell, whose reports to "Mr. and Mrs. America"
approved the blacklisting of actors, writers and technicians in radio and television.

Thus the Southern California temperature that
summer of 1949 was more than warm: it was hot with
both rage and fear. No writer or producer who
wanted to work dared to submit a story that was even
vaguely critical of something gone wrong in the
nation, or to imply that the culture was increasingly
blanketed by paranoid delusions. An appallingly narrow, conservative smog darkened the entire landscape of the entertainment industry just when James
Dean arrived in Hollywood in June 1949. And to further complicate the economic and creative situation,

there was the growing threat of television and the financial difficulties of the studios after the war. Fewer films were being made (and more cheaply) than ever before, and even established actors were often begging for work.

In such a society, it would certainly not have been a good idea for Jimmy Dean to tell his family about his dream of acting in California. The reason for his secrecy—why "he pulled into himself and didn't share," as his uncle said—is, therefore, not hard to understand. The Winslows and the Dean grandparents, good country people, believed role-playing was fine for high-school theatricals, but as a career it was unthinkable for any decent person. To put the matter plainly (as they usually did), actors were strange, immoral, no-account people, especially in California, where acting meant movies. Newspapers told you all you needed to know about the antics of Lana Turner or Bette Davis, Mickey Rooney or Errol Flynn. Movie stars, as Louella Parsons and Walter Winchell implied on the radio, were not always nice people. Sometimes they drank too much and got arrested; they had extravagant homes and wild parties; worst of all, they got divorced and remarried as often as normal folks have birthdays.

Just look at Ingrid Bergman, a hardy American might have said, expressing the sentiments of millions. Everybody loved her so much as a nun in *The Bells of St. Mary's*, and then she had been St. Joan on stage and screen. Now what do you think: she had left her husband and daughter to go off with some Italian movie director—by whom she was already pregnant! "People saw me in *Joan of Arc* and declared me a saint," Bergman said. "I'm not. I'm just a woman, another human being." Well, that was no excuse. The puritan public disgrace heaped upon Ingrid Bergman was so virulent that on the floor of the United States Congress there was a motion to revoke her passport and to bar her from ever returning to America lest her shameful behavior pollute the country. And how about Robert Mitchum, who had been arrested and jailed on charges of marijuana possession? That's what actors are like!

It was, therefore, more prudent for Jimmy to say he would go to college and embark on a respectable career—law, perhaps. (Earlier, he had told a reporter from the *Fairmount News* that he was going to study art and drama at the University of California at Los Angeles [UCLA]. When the newspaper published a social item about his farewell party in June, they ignored a retraction he had announced in the presence of the Winslows: he had no idea which school he would enter, nor what would be his field of study.) And so, after a flurry of letters between Fairmount and Los Angeles that spring, Winton Dean agreed to board Jimmy so he had an official address, could establish state residency and could obtain a driver's license. Then he could enroll, free of charge, in a public school.

Within days of arriving at Winton and Ethel Dean's two-bedroom cottage, at 1527½ Saltair Avenue, West Los Angeles, Jimmy was eager to start classes— somewhere, he said; just about anywhere would do. His eagerness was not related to a sudden desire for the academic life: he felt profoundly dislocated, uncomfortable with his father (who was not a warm, welcoming man in any case) and a complete stranger to his stepmother. Ethel was nervous around her moody stepson, and Winton's only advice to him was to become a lawyer if he wanted to be rich or a basketball coach if he wanted to have fun. For the present, a decision was delayed, but Winton bought him a cheap used car for the daily trip to Santa Monica City College.*

Founded in 1929, Santa Monica City College had an enrollment of just over sixteen hundred students in programs designed to supplement high-school education with courses required for transfer to a four-year baccalaureate program. Officially, Jimmy registered as a pre-law student, which required courses in English and American history; he also elected two drama courses (acting and theater history), joined the Jazz Club, and played on the basketball team.

"Dean was very conscious of his presence on the court, more so than his teammates," recalled coach Sanger Crumpacker. "He had bad eyesight that greatly influenced his playing ability—he developed an almost acute sense of balance, timing and agility. At times, he didn't wear his glasses while playing, just because he didn't like the way he looked when he had them on." Crumpacker's memories highlight several aspects of Jimmy's personality at eighteen: his need to succeed, his desire for attention, his sense of displacement and his discomfort with his appearance. The shortest member of the team, he compensated in speed and an almost ferocious determination to be noticed; teammates and opponents alike knew by the fire in his eyes that here was a short, bespectacled, absolutely determined player.

---

*In 1949, the school (later known as Santa Monica College) held classes at Santa Monica High School, 601 Pico Boulevard, while new facilities were under construction at 1900 Pico.

At Santa Monica, his grades were unremarkable, but in an effort to socialize—which never came easily to him—he volunteered to help at registration, ushered at performances and took tickets at dances. By spring 1950, he was appointed to membership in the Men's Honor Service Organization. Limited to twenty-one students each term, this society loaned its fellows a royal blue sweater with an embossed emblem. Jim Dean is identified in the yearbook wearing eyeglasses and a shy smile, proudly sporting the club's distinctive garb.

He was not always known as Jim Dean, however. During August of 1949, he rushed from daytime classes to evening rehearsals with the Miller Playhouse Theatre Guild, a traveling summer stock company in repertory at UCLA. For *The Romance of Scarlet Gulch*, he did not have a role: he painted scenery and billed himself with the company as "Byron James." This bit of artistic affectation was abandoned after four performances of the pallid little playlet, which was neither reviewed nor described in any historic record. His constant presence at rehearsals, although not required, indicated his true country.

There is, however, record of his development as a performer during the autumn of 1949 and the spring of 1950 with the Drama Club at Santa Monica City College, where he appeared in scene studies as Iago and Hamlet, as well as in more fragile works (*She Was Only a Farmer's Daughter* and a student musical revue called *Iz Zat So?*). His drama teacher, Gene Nielson Owen, recalled that

his articulation was poor, he mashed his words and he was somewhat difficult to understand.

In an interpretation class, someone pointed this out and blamed it on his Hoosier accent. Later, when we were alone in my office, Jimmy protested and removed the upper plate [that is, his two false front teeth]. Obviously it made some tongue positions difficult for certain sounds.

The bridge was also responsible, as Mrs. Owen learned that day, for Jimmy's unwillingness that his teeth be seen when he smiled for a photograph—a hesitation common in the lives of those who, like himself, had sustained a dental accident. More to the point, his youthful insecurities and lack of strong self-confidence clashed with his desire to act; the result was a combination of eagerness and equivocation, manifest in a certain unfortunate muddy diction from which he would never be freed. During his career, directors and fellow players were driven to distraction by an idiosyncratic acting style that apparently prevented him from speaking clearly.

To refine Jimmy's enunciation, Gene Owen suggested to him that they work privately several hours each week on an oral interpretation of *Hamlet*: "I told him that if anything would clear up funny speech, it would be the demanding soliloquies of Shakespeare." Well, yes, perhaps—but one might ask if such utilitarianism was quite the right introduction to Shakespeare for a young man whose high-school English courses had been restricted to reading a few scenes from *The Merchant of Venice*. Within days, he was floating in what seemed the inexplicably murky depths of Renaissance poetry.

But within a month it was as Ralph Waldo Emerson wrote:

> *When Duty whispers low, "Thou must,"*
> *The youth replies, "I can!"*

If his diction had only somewhat improved, his comprehension was remarkable—he had studied notes to the entire text as well as given it multiple readings—and the actor and the role, however briefly and embryonically, blended. Jimmy understood confused sentiments about parents, the admixtures of love and resentment, of yearning and loss.

In a way, Gene Owen was like Adeline Brookshire: sympathetic but demanding, a mentor but also a woman in her late thirties who was drawn to nurture the talent and so to relieve the adolescent bewilderment of a sensitive but inarticulate young man. When Jimmy came to the words,

> *O God, O God,*
> *How weary, stale, flat, and unprofitable*
> *Seem to me all the uses of this world!*

there was just the slightest catch in his voice, the briefest caesura that left Owen breathless. "He established a deeply disturbed young Hamlet who touched my heart," she recalled, "a vulnerable and troubled Hamlet that was artistry."

Few dramatic situations are so moving as the appeals of a handsome, distraught young man who, on the brink of destruction and nearly in tears, reaches out for help. Gene Owen was not his first audience, but she was present at a moment of growth in his talent. Jimmy was, however unwittingly, emotionally accessible to the character—hence the natural, deeply felt performance; hence, too (when she congratulated him), his realization of a certain power he had to manipulate the emotions of others.

"He was shy and awkward," according to a classmate, "and he peered through big horn-rimmed glasses at a world that baffled him. But somehow he knew exactly what he wanted, and he was learning quickly what strings to pull to get it." What he wanted was the applause, the success, the acceptance that to a certain type of actor endorses his very humanity and justifies his existence.

Which is why, with the summer troupe and at Santa Monica, Jimmy openly defied his father's expressed repugnance for dramatics. When Winton learned of the plays and the roles, and that his son's passion was for neither law nor athletics, there was a quietly seething confrontation. "This is my house," ran the drift of his father's ordinance, "and as long as you're living here . . ." Such discourse is not the best way to deepen a bond between parent and child. That winter, Jimmy began to spend more time away from home with his schoolmates—even to the point of not returning for a night or two. Ethel and Winton declined to inquire; they may not have cared.

If they interpreted his absences as a time in which this junior college boy was sowing wild oats, they could not have been more wrong. Needy as he was of comfort and recognition, James Dean was apparently, by spring 1950, still virginal, and not at all comfortable, even in the most general social atmosphere, with women his own age.

Fortunately, in light of his uneasiness and lack of social grace, this was a time when young men and women were not expected to prove anything to themselves or others by accumulating sexual experience. In 1950, casual sex among college students—not to say pregnancy outside marriage—was not the commonplace it later became. Birth control pills were unknown and simpler devices were not easily available to the unmarried (in fact, they were still officially illegal under the Pure Food and Drug Act of 1933). There was also terror about venereal disease, for the antibiotics that could remedy such a catastrophe (and so it was considered) were only just then becoming available to the general public after the war.

Most of all, however, the culture was still resoundingly puritanical, and those who hoped to finish high-school (much less college) and compete in the job market might admit to sexual experience—but very quietly, and only to trusted confidants; loss of virginity had no social cachet. Furtive kisses on a back porch at night or necking in a car at a drive-in movie: this was the extent of sex for the vast majority of young, unmarried Americans until the late 1960s. This situation of widespread heterosexual frustration was, of course, enormously difficult for some, but there was not much expectation that it would be otherwise; and for anyone who was shy, nervous or homosexual, such proscriptions were a blessing.

A diffident, socially insecure young man like Jimmy
Dean, who still had hayseed in his hair, was not
expected to prove he was "normal" by attempting a
seduction, and a young woman could say no without
losing her reputation. By all accounts, Jimmy's dates
for dances, picnics and Sunday afternoons at the beach
in Santa Monica or Malibu were girls he knew from
one campus club or another. There is no evidence for
any serious romance (as there is none for any sustained
friendship), and one co-ed's recollection was typical of
many:

> A boy I had dated invited him to join our
> crowd for a beer at The Point—a small café
> overlooking the Pacific, where the younger
> crowd could go to drink beer, look at the ocean
> and talk. But Jimmy wasn't in the talking mood
> that evening [or ever, according to others]. He
> contented himself with watching the waves
> breaking on the shore. He had no use for small
> talk.

By June 1950, Jimmy had made two decisions, both
of them because he was restless at Saltair Avenue and,
despite the attention of Gene Owen, bored at Santa
Monica City College—as he often became bored with
people and places when he felt he had exhausted their
benefits.

During his brief tenure as a scene painter on *The
Romance of Scarlet Gulch* at UCLA, he had seen Royce
Hall, the performing arts theater on campus; he had

also obtained the school bulletin and learned about the many dramatic presentations each term—a far more impressive enterprise than anything Santa Monica offered. He decided, therefore, to transfer to UCLA, which charged only nominal fees for courses. His second decision was to leave Winton and Ethel, but to do that he needed cash. Through coach Crumpacker, he landed a summer position as athletic counselor at a day camp just over the Santa Monica Mountains, in what was then becoming familiarly known as "the Valley." There he worked six days a week from late June to mid-August. He then completed the enrollment forms for acceptance at UCLA in early September, and in the intervening two weeks (very likely to escape Winton and Ethel) he knew where he could have a reasonably undemanding and inexpensive intermission before the start of classes: back home in Indiana.

"Jimmy told none of his friends he was back in town," according to Marcus Winslow. "He just worked from sunup to sunset with me. Never said much, drove his bike up to the cemetery, tended his mother's grave and took one trip into Marion to see a movie." The movie, as it happened, had been publicized for months before its release, for it had a controversial plot and an even more controversial leading man.

The Men, a film about the physical and emotional dilemmas faced by war veterans whose wounds left them paraplegics—with all the attendant physical, emotional, psychological and sexual problems—marked the film debut of Marlon Brando. Produced by Stanley Kramer and directed by Fred Zinnemann, *The Men* moved Jimmy, as he later often told friends, more than any movie he had ever seen.

Kramer's *Champion*, released the previous year, had been a fable about the moral corruption of a prize-fighter (played by Kirk Douglas). "One night shortly after it had opened," the producer recalled, "Kirk and I took it to show to the patients at a Veterans Administration Hospital. It was then and there that I got the idea for a film about the problems these para-plegic veterans faced." Soon after, Kramer, screen-writer Carl Foreman and director Fred Zinnemann returned to the hospital and interviewed some of the men and their physicians. "It soon became clear," Kramer continued, "that this would be a very special film and would require a very special talent."

At precisely this time, a bidding war was being waged among producers to sign twenty-five-year-old Marlon Brando, who had shot to fame on Broadway in Elia Kazan's production of Tennessee Williams's prize-winning play *A Streetcar Named Desire*. Kramer won the bid with an offer of $50,000, Carl Foreman's script (which intrigued the actor) and the announcement that Brando's co-star would be the very appealing Teresa Wright, whose achievements for (among others) Alfred Hitchcock and William Wyler had earned her enor-mous popularity and an Academy Award.

Brando prepared for the role in a way that many considered revolutionary. "He went and actually lived for a month with the paraplegics," according to Kramer. "He lived like them, he stayed in the wheelchair, he exercised like paraplegics. He went out to local haunts at night and drank with them when they were able to find such accommodating locales." In addition, Brando encouraged Kramer and Zinnemann to have patients in the film, and forty-five of them are. All during preproduction and rehearsal, he continued in the ward, practicing the exercises, enduring the semimobility, learning to manipulate braces. He also knew how to defuse a difficult moment with his own style of humor. One day, when Brando and some of the patients went to a local bar, a religious fanatic turned from her stool and, urging them to heroic faith, assured them they would walk again if only they would believe. The men said nothing; the drunken "preacher" droned on.

Then everyone noticed that Brando was clutching desperately at the armrests of his wheelchair, agonizingly trying to push himself up. He fell back exhausted, then tried again. Finally, rising on tottering legs, he took a few hesitant steps and suddenly broke into a leap. Sprinting from the bar, he returned in seconds with a bundle of newspapers that he hawked wildly: "Now I can make a living again!" The patients howled and applauded the performance. "But the drunk," recalled Zinnemann, "was instantly sober and very resentful at being the victim of a practical joke."

Such bravado was absent during filming. "Marlon Brando was terribly insecure when he did this picture," added the director. "He had never been before a camera, and he didn't trust people. He was completely enclosed within himself, so totally identifying with Stanley Kowalski [the character he played in *A Streetcar Named Desire*] that he approached the part of the paraplegic veteran as Stanley." Still, Brando's sullen tenseness is nearly always right. In *The Men*, he conveyed quiet bitterness and inchoate longing with unsentimental poignancy. The scene of his wedding night, when at last he is left alone with his bride (Teresa Wright, in a marvelously controlled performance), is almost unbearable as his anxiety causes reflex spasms in his leg. Because Brando moved not a muscle in his face, the detachment comes across as humiliation, and the quivering that otherwise might have been seen as a bit of over-the-top Freudianism was instead frightening and heart-wrenching.

Kramer had brought Brando to Los Angeles late in 1949, and Brando astonished the community—and got himself almost daily press coverage—by being as much a nonconformist in Hollywood as he had been in New York. A T-shirt and jeans, a motorcycle, a scorn for mere good manners and a wild (some might say occasionally calculated) disregard for the ordinary forms of politeness—as well as an aura of sexual threat and confusion—all these made him an entirely new kind of masculine personality, a new kid on the block who was going to shake things up. Thanks to the movies and the magazines, sexual energy radiated to the whole world from Brando (he was, after all, both a serious actor and a pinup).

Like Dean, Brando was a Midwesterner who had been transplanted to California; like Dean, Brando had an unhappy relationship with his father (who thought acting was only for "faggots and fairies"), and his mother had died. After an unhappy and peripatetic youth, Brando had followed his sister to New York, where he learned two different approaches to acting from two types of classes—Stella Adler's, at the prestigious Dramatic Workshop of the New School for Social Research; and Lee Strasberg's, at the Actors Studio.

After his celebrated performance in *Streetcar* and his equally celebrated term of psychoanalysis, Brando spoke often and openly about both experiences, summarizing them by saying that he was trying to use everything that happened to him in his life to create characters. His sexual ambivalence, the subject of much gossip (and later confirmed by himself and his biographers) and his dark intensity onstage were both alarming and awe-inspiring for colleagues and audiences, and in *The Men* he dug brilliantly beneath the script to find the truth of a bitterness beyond pathos. As Ken, he was in several ways a middle-class variant on Stanley Kowalski, his circumstances once again defining a deeper resentment against society.

Brando had been very much in the news since 1947; now he was on the screen, and so even more touted in the press as the emblem of a new style of acting and a new type of star. In Greenwich Village, he had wandered into cafés and haunted bars, had ridden around the city in his leather jacket, torn shirt and carpenter's jeans. Brando studied passersby with almost clinical precision, becoming a brilliant mimic, picking up accents as well as lover after lover. He studied not only acting but people, languages, art, religion, dance and fencing. In 1950, he was twenty-six, inscrutable, dangerous, irresistible—a fresh aggregation, somehow all physique and all inner complexity, just as he was a disciple of both Strasberg and Adler.

Simply stated, the former stressed the necessity of one's own affective memory, of improvisation, of emotional truth in acting based on one's own personal history; the latter emphasized technique, the accumulation of external details from which a character emerges, and the primacy of conveying the meaning of the playwright's text (not, she objected, one's personal emotional history). Both Strasberg and Adler drew on the principles of Konstantin Stanislavski and the Russian school, variously represented in America by (among others) Michael Chekhov and Maria Ouspenskaya. All this was very much in the air among theater and movie folk in 1950, as Brando streaked his way upward in celebrity and (for a time) the admiration of millions. He never appeared on Broadway after *Streetcar* (but was directed by Kazan in three films), and those whose financial and emotional attachment was only to movies took this as a sign of the times: serious dramatic art arrived in Hollywood, it seemed to many, on the back of Brando's motorcycle.

Jimmy Dean spoke often, over the next five years, of that night at the movies; for him, it was a moment of revelation. He had never conceived of acting such as he had just seen, of stillness and apparent serenity conveying anguish and confusion, of a minimalism that delivered so much. The Brando trademarks—the apathetic gaze, the granite moodiness—were carefully calculated, timed to the second (or so it seemed) so that every flicker of emotional variation surprised viewers. It is no exaggeration to say that James Dean's future was fixed that hot summer evening when he zoomed his motorbike to Marion. He would become a serious actor—not merely to play roles and to win contests and applause, but because of what he had seen and admired in Marlon Brando.

In September, classes began at UCLA. Jimmy gathered his few belongings and modest wardrobe, left Saltair Avenue and asked to pledge loyalty with Sigma Nu house, at 601 Gayley Avenue, on the fringe of the university in Westwood. A room in a campus fraternity was much less costly than living in a dormitory or apartment—but there were still expenses, and so he worked part-time as a department projectionist.

History and anthropology supplemented Jimmy's drama classes, but to those academic courses he gave scant attention. Several plays were going into rehearsal for fall and winter production, and auditions were held in early October. Convinced that Gene Owen's training had prepared him for Shakespeare, he won the role of Malcolm in *Macbeth* after the director perceived a certain wily intensity—which did not, alas, survive into the production. "He needed glasses to read his script," according to Dick Eschleman, a classmate, "but he hated wearing them"—and so was constantly fumbling for the glasses, taking them off, putting them aside, losing them.

As it happened, that was the least of his problems. Gene Owen's tutorials may have been enjoyable, ego-stroking exercises that opened up the text to him, but the old problem of diction still sabotaged the final result. Harve Bennett Fischman, who reviewed the performances (presented in Royce Hall from November 29 through December 2) found them "void of exciting movement, actor thought processes and overall conception." Of Malcolm, Fischman lamented that the young actor "failed to show any growth and would have made a hollow king." Another student in the theater arts program, William Bast, recorded that Jimmy "made no impression at all. His acting was not good, and his Indiana twang" came dangerously close to transforming the play into a comedy.

As usual, he did not take criticism easily, and when

other players and some of his housemates tried to point
out flaws in the performance, Jimmy argued or withdrew irritably. Before the Christmas recess, he refused
to join the parties at Sigma Nu, and when everyone
returned in the new year 1951, his mood had not
improved. When he fell behind in payments on his
house bill, got into arguments with the fraternity brothers and goaded one into a fistfight, a council was
called. James Dean was asked to quit Sigma Nu and
find another residence.

For blind partisans, it would perhaps be comforting
to demonstrate that Jimmy's conduct was justified; that
he was defending a principle or his honor in some matter; that he had been wrongly accused of misdemeanors; or that he simply lacked patience and certain
social skills. "I wanted to be a professional actor," he
said later, trying to account for this time. "I couldn't
take that tea-sipping academic bull. So I busted a couple of guys in the nose and got myself kicked out." But
his conduct was scarcely professional, much less
socially acceptable or even polite. The men at Sigma
Nu, it must be added, were hardly tweedy Ivy
Leaguers: beer was more to their taste than tea.

In fact, all accounts of his behavior at UCLA indicate
that Jimmy could be insufferably immature. Resentments against his father, guilt and loneliness for his
mother, a feeling of social inferiority and a longing to
refine his natural acting skills: these were battles he
conducted outside, in fights and arguments and ornery
demeanor, rather than inside, in reflection and thought
about his past or present. Thus he had blamed Adeline
Brookshire when he lost the forensic contest; winning
medals was the only proof of his superiority; excelling

on the basketball court was a way of showing others
the value of a self in whom he had little confidence.
"He was the kind of guy who had to win," said classmate James Bellah. "He had to be the best at everything
he did." But his refusal both to accept criticism and to
practice ordinary acts of politeness canceled out whatever admiration he may have won; the result was that
James Dean, as he turned twenty, was quite friendless.
"He had a scary, unpredictable quality," said racing
champion Phil Hill. "He had too much to prove to the
world."

In fact, he may have felt that he was already proving
something, despite his bad notices as Malcolm. Before
Christmas, he had made his first professional appearance on film.

chapter five

> Don't let young people tell
> you their aspirations. When
> they drop them, they will
> drop you.
>
> LOGAN PEARSALL SMITH

Unpredictable in his moods—yes, that was James Dean," agreed Isabelle Draesemer, his first agent. For years, admirers claimed that she saw the talent beneath the follies of his Malcolm at UCLA, that she went backstage after the last performance of *Macbeth* on December 2, handed Jimmy her business card and within a week signed him to a contract. That is an appealing scene from a movie like *Broadway Melody of 1940*, but the reality was far less numinous.

"An advertising agency needed some young people for a Pepsi-Cola ad," recalled Draesemer, who managed a talent agency in Los Angeles and, to get the right look, telephoned a friend who worked at UCLA. Next day, a notice was posted for student actors who wanted to earn $10 for an afternoon's work on a television commercial. Hundreds flocked to Draesemer's office on Hollywood Boulevard, and a dozen attractive students were selected. So it happened that on December 13, 1950, James Dean took the bus to his first movie location, in Griffith Park. "We rode on the carousel all afternoon, drinking our Pepsi-Colas," recalled Beverly Long, who was also in the commercial. "The next afternoon, a few of us were called back for the studio shot, to dance around a jukebox for the second scene of the commercial. Jimmy was very noticeable in it."

Jerry Fairbanks, the producer, had been told to emphasize all-American teenagers in the close-ups, and no one looked more down-home than Jimmy Dean. "He had the advantage of being older but looking younger," said Draesemer. "He had a softness one minute and a rebelliousness the next," and it was just that sort of lively appeal, combined with a certain hint of the unexpected, that remains nearly fifty years later in this black-and-white commercial. There is James Dean, riding the wooden horses and reaching for the gold ring, then snapping his fingers, leading the group in a record hop and merrily passing out bottles of Pepsi-Cola.

The $10 payment seemed like a thousand; more to the point, it was salary for acting. Jimmy received the money just after Christmas, when he needed to find a new residence, and after he had quit his job as a campus projectionist: everything, he vowed, would be subordinate to his career. But an apartment was not possible for $10. At precisely that time, he happened to meet Bill Bast on campus—the drama student and apprentice writer who had been so unimpressed with Jimmy's acting in *Macbeth*. Bast, also a transplant from the Midwest, disliked the noise and expense of dormitory living; Dean, in one of his expansive, smiling moods, said he understood, that he disliked fraternity living. "I didn't like Jim all that much when I first met him," Bast said years later. "But, necessity being the mother of hysteria, we ended up sharing digs together." So began, as usual for James Dean, a mercurial, unpredictable and finally tortured and embittered relationship.

At first, nothing augured ill. Moving to a small place on Comstock Avenue, just over a mile east of campus, the roommates learned how devoted they both were to the theater. Bast was certainly the more sophisticated and intellectual of the two, and Dean admired his bookishness, his good manners and his catholic tastes in the arts. Over morning coffee, they pored over the papers for news of the New York theater world, for news of local readings and auditions, for every opportunity to supplement their limited experience.

From Bast, Jimmy learned the value of constantly reading plays as well as reviews of them; he also saw in action, but did not emulate, the virtues of discipline and application. For his part, Bast liked the freshness and excitement that his roommate brought to activities he suddenly took up—drawing and clay sculpting, for example, for which Jimmy had an evident talent, and making whimsical mobiles to decorate the sparsely furnished flat. Together they improvised sketches for possible tryouts, just as they invented fresh uses for oatmeal at dinner: budgeting, for two unemployed students whose meager savings had dwindled, required all their ingenuity—even to the point of borrowing from classmates to repay other classmates from whom they had borrowed so they could borrow a second time. The round robin of debt encircled the times they shared.

There were, they quickly learned, some ways to have an admiring audience and get a free meal: they had only to invite one or two solvent drama co-eds to their apartment, warning them in advance that after their little scene study ("We're awfully sorry, but . . . ") they could not offer dinner. This little foray into *Scenes de la vie bohémienne* was invariably successful: the boys acted for their supper, the girls cooked for the price of their entertainment.

Sometimes the entertainment was unexpected, even for Bast. Jimmy had somehow read portions of a smuggled copy of Henry Miller's erotically explicit novel *Tropic of Cancer* (which was not sold legally in America until 1961), and he thought a brief dramatic reading would impress two girls one Sunday evening. But enthusiastically detailed descriptions of sex organs and their various (and often, in the case of Miller's characters, bizarre) uses were not quite what the young ladies expected to hear as they set down a tureen of tomato soup, platters of meat loaf and bowls of Jell-O. Were they not going to discuss T. S. Eliot's mystical verse play *The Cocktail Party*? Yes, but not before Jimmy had his chance to shock, perhaps to titillate: causing others shock and embarrassment is, after all, a method for those who imagine themselves inferior to exert control; they remain calm and in charge while others are reduced to anxiety.

A variant on such moments was for Jimmy to mention that he had been working on some "sporting sketches." Asked to show his artwork, he calmly passed around the table an artist's pad he had filled with drawings of matadors (whose confrontations with death dazzled him). The figures he had drawn were remarkable not so much for fluid action as for unusual details—especially the care with which the artist had rendered the contours of clothing: it was impossible for a viewer not to focus on the unnaturally bountiful contents with which the artist had endowed the subjects' trousers. To Jimmy, this was bold and amusing conduct; to his guests, the drawings were childishly crude, the sort of folk art normally found only in public toilets.

But on at least one occasion, Jimmy surpassed risqué cartoons, ghoulish illustrations of dancing skeletons and estimable sculptures of figures in anguish or ecstasy. He certainly went too far when he proudly displayed, one quiet spring evening, his latest piece of craftsmanship: a candleholder whose base was obviously the form of female genitalia. Into this, Jimmy calmly inserted a candle, lit it and watched gleefully as white-hot wax dripped suggestively over the candleholder's "thighs." One poor girl left the room in tears of embarrassment.

"He was cocky and arrogant," said Bast later, "and he was pushing his limits as much as he could. He knew what he was doing most of the time. He was not an extraordinary person in real life; if anything, he was rather bothersome." Certainly so much could be said of that unfortunate evening at Comstock Avenue. The minds of some undergraduates may often be crowded with such fantasies, but they are not ordinarily presented graphically at the supper table.

Late that mild Southern California winter, Jimmy

received a note from Isabelle Draesemer, who had been contacted by Jerry Fairbanks. Not limited to soft drink commercials, the producer had been hired for an Easter episode of *Father Peyton's Television Theater*, a religious program sent out to American markets unconcerned with dramatic subtleties and unoffended by treacly pieties.

In early March, Jimmy sped again to Draesemer's office, where Fairbanks was settled into a chair, turning script pages. The teleplay was "Hill Number One," which began on the Korean War front and proceeded, through a chaplain's sermon, to flash back and draw parallels between the plight of the beleaguered American soldiers trying to capture an enemy hill and the plight of Christ crucified on "hill number one." With the announcement of the Resurrection on that first Easter Day, the action reverts to Korea, where— voilà!—the soldiers are rewarded by the news that the enemy hill has been (miraculously?) taken.

The role offered to Jimmy was small, Fairbanks explained—a few lines in only two brief scenes. But it was an appealing one: the boyish apostle John, whose innocence had to be obvious and whose enthusiasm passionate. His audition was acceptable, he projected the appropriate wide-eyed wonder, and he was hired.

James Dean's television debut in this dramatic role (broadcast on March 25, 1951) was certainly inauspicious. First of all, he arrived for the filming with a wretched cold. Then, as the camera rolled for his scene, he lowered his eyes demurely to show humility, then declaimed piously to the fearful apostles who were considering disbanding after the death of Jesus: "Was it for this we left our nets to follow the Master," he asks, as if he were imitating a country preacher from Fairmount, "just to go back to our boats again now?" In his second scene, on Easter morning, he exclaims with bogus astonishment, "He will bring us enlightenment! Come! We must spread these good tidings quickly!" The performance was altogether too grand and sweeping, but in fairness it must be added that the script (as usual in American religious programs) was rubbish. Never mind: Jimmy pocketed the princely sum of $150 and awaited the next development in his career.

As it happened, a kind of local fame blazed immediately. The senior girls at Immaculate Heart High School, Los Angeles, had been required to watch the teleplay. Their class president wrote to Jerry Fairbanks, who passed the letter on to Isabelle Draesemer. Would Jimmy honor them with his presence at the first meeting of the James Dean Appreciation Society? He would. They made a cake and poured tea for him, they stood around shifting uneasily from one foot to another, twirling their hair and smiling shyly, they giggled when they asked for his autograph. Bill Bast, who went along, noticed that Jimmy loved every minute of it, as what twenty-year-old aspiring star would not? Prudently, he left his racy artwork and the candleholder at home and was on good behavior. But as is the way of such hastily established fan clubs, it did not survive the girls' graduation, and they never met their hero again.

One evening in April, Bast returned home with some exciting news. He had just met James Whitmore, the thirty-year-old actor who had made an estimable Broadway debut in *Command Decision* in 1947 and then made half a dozen movies (one of which, *Battleground*, earned him an Oscar nomination). Bast complained to Whitmore that there was no substantial instruction at UCLA—productions, yes, but no serious classes in theory, improvisation and discussion, of the sort Bast knew were practiced at the American Theatre Wing or the Actors Studio in New York. Would Whitmore, an articulate actor and an alumnus of the Yale Drama School, be willing to meet with a group of earnest students? Whitmore agreed—somewhat reluctantly at first, for he had never been a teacher, and on condition that he receive no fee and the "classes" be in the style of discussion workshops.

Later that April, Bast and a few friends found a large upper room at the Brentwood Country Mart, a pleasant shopping area at San Vicente Boulevard and Twenty-sixth Street, at the Los Angeles–Santa Monica border. Once or twice weekly that spring, Whitmore met the group, which ranged from nine to twenty students. "We did sense-memory exercises and improvisations," Whitmore recalled years later,

> and we worked on scenes they wanted to polish. It was all very casual—much discussion and self-criticism, that sort of thing—but there was no doubt of everyone's seriousness. At first, Jim Dean [who had been allowed to attend only because of Bast] made absolutely no impression on me, and probably not on the others, either. He seemed very shy, very hesitant to volunteer.

Working with Brookshire and Owen had the comfort of a kind of maternal nurturing, but Whitmore was serious business. Jimmy would not embarrass himself, nor would he readily risk rejection.

Then one afternoon Jimmy and Bill were asked to improvise a scene. Whitmore spoke to each separately: Bast was to act the part of a jeweler who had repaired a stolen wristwatch brought to him by Jimmy, a petty thief. The scene was to proceed with Bast struggling to detain Jimmy until the police arrived. To Jimmy, Whitmore gave instructions that he was to get the watch back at any cost, fleeing the scene to avoid capture. The two apprentices tried several times, but the class was restless with boredom: nothing the pair did generated excitement. Either Bast finally gave up the watch, or Jimmy departed without it. No drama, no tension, no revelation of character. Whitmore interrupted the dull proceedings to discuss concentration and character motivation, to explain how a character's history might be revealed through gesture and intonation, and how mood could be heightened through carefully placed pauses and implications of unexpected violence.

That was all Jimmy needed. The two began again, and (thus Bast) "the noticeable change that came over Jimmy was almost frightening." Nothing mattered but getting the watch back, and his insistence fueled Bill's. Finally, the two actors were so involved in their respective character dilemmas that they were throwing punches. Whitmore had to shout a halt to the scene. "From that moment on," Bast concluded, "everything he heard, everything he read, everything he did seemed to have new meaning for Jimmy. Until then, he had understood everything, but now he was able to apply it."

He had, in other words, gone deeper through an exercise in imaginative identification. For a few moments, he had been freed from mere intellection. He had found something of his own experience, something truthful about himself in the role, and so he had been able to lose himself in it. He had discovered an essential principle of what they had discussed theoretically, the so-called Method school of acting, the very same theory that was much discussed with especial regard to Marlon Brando and his mentor, Elia Kazan. "I owe a lot to James Whitmore," Jimmy said later. "I guess you can say he saved me when I got all mixed up. He told me I didn't know the difference between acting as a soft job and acting as a difficult art. I needed to learn these differences."

There is a curious phrase lurking in this self-description: what precisely did James Dean mean when he admitted to being "all mixed up"? In context, he may simply have been referring to his lack of appreciation for the complex and arduous aspects of the actor's craft—the reflection, the preparation, the hard inner work that precedes any credible performance.

But there is perhaps an allusion to something darker here. "Jim was never honest with himself," Bast said twenty-five years later. "He felt that he was above having to kiss anyone's ass in order to get a part, and whenever he saw his friends in this situation, he put them down for it, said he lost respect for them. The truth, though, is that Dean kissed a lot of asses, and he hated this about himself. That's why he took it out on others."

But there is still a lack of clarity: "ass-kissing" is an insinuating, provocative vulgarism that can encompass anything from exaggerated and hypocritical flattery to gift-giving to outright sex-for-favors; all this is par on the Hollywood course. Several chroniclers, without a shred of conclusive or firsthand evidence, have gone so far as to claim that Dean in fact was known to be a homosexual hustler—that prostitution was, for a time, his means of making both money and his career.

But such assertions have no irrefutable proof and so are impossible to sustain. Very likely they derived from the fact that later that same year, Jimmy did have a sexual relationship with an older man named Rogers Brackett who helped him financially and professionally. This seems, however, to have also been an affective relationship, with real sentiment on both sides—hardly a "deal." In addition, Dean's conduct throughout his short life indicates that he was not entirely heterosexual, as even his girlfriends confirmed. "He dabbled in everything," said Bast. "He wanted to experiment with life."

But bisexual conduct is not prostitution, and bisexuality is as much as William Bast affirms—and very likely as much as he knew, for the single motif threaded through his recollections is Dean's reticence and solitude. Had he known more, it would of course have been much to his advantage to include the most incandescent and shocking revelations when he wrote and produced a film years later about Dean's life, for he has never been so protective as to alter any other truth. But there is nothing from Bast about prostitution, and no one else has stepped forward to claim either fellowship or patronage in that common market.

It is also important to understand that becoming known as a hustler was a short route to wrecking a serious career in just about anything except pornography. People of influence are ordinarily slow (for all the obvious reasons) to advance the careers of those with whom they sexually barter, for discretion is not usually the strong suit of prostitutes. Just like the fisherman's wife, hustlers tend to return for more business when their fortunes need reinvigorating. Nor should it be ignored that in his efforts to establish himself as a serious actor, James Dean would have been destroying himself very quickly. In a short time, he had done a commercial and a teleplay, and now he was studying with a bona fide stage and screen actor. There would have been no reason for him to pitch himself into a dangerous and sometimes lethal job. Racing motorbikes and cars was about as risky a business as he undertook.

Finally, if Jimmy was trading sex for cash, it is hard to understand why, in early April, he prevailed on Bill Bast—who worked as a part-time usher at the CBS radio studios in Hollywood—to recommend him for a job there. Bast did just that, although Jimmy quit after a week of ushering. This he did not only because he was impatient to get on with his career, but because he had a crack at a good role in UCLA's leading spring festival play, and he wanted to prepare full-time for it, alone and with Whitmore.

The part was that of the eerie Witch Boy in *Dark of the Moon*, Howard Richardson and William Berney's adaptation of the Barbara Allen legend, a Broadway success in 1945. The plot concerns a fantastic spirit who takes on human form and weds the beautiful Barbara,

who bears him a child; it ends tragically with the revelation of her infidelity, her death and the Witch Boy's
return to the ghostly world.

According to Joe Brown, who competed for the same
role, Jimmy moved beautifully and his speech was
absolutely clear during auditions. The director and the
other members of the drama department attended the
final readings, when Jimmy chose his climactic scene,
and his performance was astonishing. Just as for "A
Madman's Manuscript" two years before, he built a
chilling sense of loss, lunacy and death. "I've lost my
baby," he whispered—and then his voice rose in a wail:
"My baby is dead"—until he was nearly crazed with
grief: "I've lost my child!" The rehearsal hall was absolutely still; Jimmy's intensity gripped everyone. After
he withdrew, the stunned silence was maintained—
and then there was raucous applause.

But he did not win the role, which was given to a
third candidate—a chap who was tall, lean and pale,
and (so the director believed) more likely to be
accepted as an otherworldly creature. Jimmy stormed
out of the hall in silence and spoke to no one of his disappointment. Two weeks later, before final exams and
advisement for the next term's courses, he simply
stopped attending UCLA.

From that time, Bast found Jimmy difficult as a
roommate and unreliable as a friend. Sullen, moody
and withdrawn, he neglected his share of household
duties, defaulted on his portion of expenses, refused to
keep his things in any semblance of order and was generally grumpy, uncommunicative and disagreeable.
The source of his disaffection could not have been
merely the loss of the role at UCLA; rather, all signs

point to a deep sexual conflict, for although he loved to shock and tease, this was mostly from a naughty-boyishness and the concomitant desire to be thought a young rake. In this case, the rake made little progress and the sexual fantasies remained on the level of jokes, books and crude artifacts.

But in this as in all things, he was no less competitive. At the time, Bill was dating an attractive young actress named Beverly Wills, whom he had met at CBS; she was the co-star of a radio comedy series called "Junior Miss" and Jimmy—idle from the end of April—was not to be socially isolated. He arranged double dates for Bill and Beverly, with himself and Jeanetta Lewis, a brunette from UCLA's drama program.

Very quickly, things became thorny. Beverly was the daughter of comedienne Joan Davis, star of the television series *I Married Joan*, and the Wills family lived in Bel-Air, that parcel of expensive estates tucked on winding streets and rising glens north of Sunset Boulevard, between Beverly Hills and Brentwood. Often she invited her friends for pool parties, barbecues and casual Sunday evenings of records and supper. Jimmy, impressed with the wealth, the servants, the luxuries and the starlets who sometimes showed up at the Willses (Debbie Reynolds, for example), tried somewhat crudely to be the man about town. But his lack of social grace annoyed Beverly's mother, as did his comments on her golf game. He put his feet on sofas and tables, he helped himself to their larder, his language was rather salty, his attitude disdainful.

This, as so often, encouraged Beverly to jump to Jimmy's defense—and one evening Bill Bast was surprised to hear Beverly tell him, "We have something to tell you. It's Jimmy and me now—we're in love." For consolation, Bill visited Jeanetta Lewis, only to learn that Jimmy was sweet-talking her, making promises to her, keeping her on the proverbial string, just in case (Jeanetta now learned) the wooing of Beverly collapsed. As it did. Mother and Father Wills whisked their daughter off to their Malibu beach house for the summer, and absence did not make her heart grow fonder. In Beverly's mind, Jimmy faded like a watercolor exposed to the California sun. Reflecting from a distance, she realized that for reasons other than her mother's disapproval, Jimmy was troublesome. "He was almost constantly in a blue funk," she wrote a few years later.

> He couldn't get an acting job and he was growing increasingly bitter. When he was happy, there was no one more lovable, but when he was depressed, he wanted to die. These low moods became so violent that he began to tell me that he was having strange nightmares in which he dreamed he was dying. I soon learned that it was nothing for Jimmy to run through a whole alphabet of emotions in one evening. His moods of happiness were by now far outweighed by his moods of deep despair . . . He was a hurt and misunderstood boy, he thought.

To these moods Beverly was unwilling and unable to subordinate herself, and so she permitted the summer to separate them forever. They never met again. Beverly Wills was killed in a tragic house fire at the age of twenty-nine, several years before her mother's death.

To no one's surprise, Jeanetta slammed down the telephone when Jimmy, lonely and begging for understanding, rang to ask for her company. Neither of these young women could sustain the mercurial moods that, at their root, very likely sprang from a lack of trust in people. Once he had moved toward people, felt an affection for and reliance on them, he pulled away, afraid of being abandoned again as he had been by those on whom he had counted in childhood. To prevent rejection, he would withdraw first. He would play the rascal, the truant, the delinquent manqué; the problem, however, was the conviction and success of this act.

Jobless, impatient, directionless and forlorn, Jimmy could turn only to Bill Bast, to whom he tearfully apologized, pleading for patience and offering to do any kind of work to bear his share of expenses. "I'm so tense," he said. "I don't know how anyone stays in the same room with me. I wouldn't tolerate myself." This admission was so pathetic that Bast (for no other reason than that he was touched by the attractive defendant), gave Jimmy one more chance. They had to vacate the Comstock apartment, and Bill had found a small duplex in Mar Vista, at 12623 Green Avenue, about two miles from the ocean.

They began the summer of 1951 in two cramped rooms, and life was bearable only when Bill's mother visited, stocked the refrigerator and cupboards and cooked lavish meals for them. While Bill went to class and to work at CBS, Mrs. Bast was left alone with

Jimmy, who was so taciturn and ungracious that the
poor woman was convinced she was unwelcome and
ought to depart as quickly as possible. But a telling
moment suggested that just the opposite might have
been true—that Jimmy envied Bill his attentive mother,
that his silence betokened not resentment or disapproval but a very deep sadness. When the two men
delivered Mrs. Bast to Union Station for her return
train journey, Jimmy excused himself, dashed off to a
kiosk and returned with a box of chocolates and a
spray of flowers. This and a gray envelope he pressed
into the lady's arms. As the train left Los Angeles, Mrs.
Bast opened the folder to find a photograph of himself:
"To my second mother," he had written in a firm, clear,
round child's hand. "With love from Jimmie."

Now things happened quickly.

By mid-July, Bill's patience ran out.

> Jimmy became subject to more frequent peri-
> ods of depression and would slip off in a silent
> mood at least once each day. If I had thought it
> difficult to communicate with him at other
> times in the past, I had never known such lack
> of communication as existed during his fits of
> depression. He sat in the room and stared off
> into space for hours. I made several attempts to
> get through to him, but rarely got more than a
> grunt or a distant stare for a response.

As would soon be clear, Jimmy was trying to plan a
future, attempting to find the place he belonged in a

world that always discomfited. But a gift for friendship was short-circuited by a terrible self-absorption with his unspent talent and by inner conflicts he seemed unable to resolve.

When Bast told him they would probably both be happier living separately, Jimmy seemed not so much anxious as determined to relocate as quickly as possible. He contacted a young married man named Tex Avery, a lanky, friendly soul with whom he had a few laughs during his brief tenure at CBS. As it happened, Tex's wife was about to depart for a journey to visit her family, and Jimmy was welcome to the living room sofa in their tiny apartment at 1216 North Edgemont, Hollywood, just on the border of seedy. Within days late that June, Jimmy moved his meager sackful of possessions and clothes and, through Tex, landed a part-time job parking cars for executives and visitors at a lot adjacent to CBS.

And then, just before the Fourth of July holiday, Jimmy met a man named Rogers Brackett, who drove his car into the lot one morning to supervise the recording of a radio commercial. Thirty-five, tall, slim, sophisticated and solvent, he was a successful account executive for the Foote, Cone and Belding advertising agency. When Brackett drove away three hours after his arrival, he and Jimmy Dean had exchanged telephone numbers. Two weeks later—when Tex's wife returned to Los Angeles—Jimmy accepted the expedient offer of moving to the chic little apartment Brackett kept on Sunset Plaza Drive, just north of the so-called Sunset Strip in West Hollywood. A California native, Brackett maintained his primary residence in New York, but business often brought him to Los Angeles.

In both cities, he had interesting friends, important professional contacts and a colorful social life that included a large portion of the very closeted Hollywood gay community. "My primary interest in Jimmy was as an actor," Brackett said after Dean's death. "His talent was so obvious. Secondarily, I loved him, and he loved me."

"He said we could have twin beds," Jimmy told a skeptical Isabelle Draesemer when he gave her his new address and number; that detail of cohabitation she could never verify for herself, but in fact they shared the same bed. "I wasn't so easily fooled," Draesemer commented years later. "And then, before I knew it, they were living together—in Hollywood, Chicago and New York." That the relationship was sexual is beyond question: both men confided the matter to women friends years later. That it was beneficial to Jimmy is also not disputed, for within weeks he had a string of jobs and introductions to people who could help him. That Rogers doted on him, showed him off to friends and colleagues and provided him with tutorials on everything from manners to Maupassant was also evident. But this is very different from keeping a hustler, as many have described the relationship. That was certainly not the case.

The truth is that Rogers Brackett was as generous with Jimmy as he was besotted by his youthful good looks, his dependence and admiration and his childish antics. As for Jimmy, he certainly saw the older man as a kind of father figure and paternal provider; in this regard, each appreciated the attraction of the other to himself. And if sex went with the new territory—well, that is not uncommon in such arrangements, and there are worse ties with which to bind. There is no evidence that Jimmy was kidnapped or forced into sexual enslavement against his will—much less that he was hurt in any way by the relationship.

Quite the contrary: more than anyone in his career thus far, Brackett introduced him to a wide array of people who enabled him to work. It also needs to be said (and later Jimmy said so to more than one confidant) that Jimmy was not simply flattered by Brackett's patronage. He learned very quickly that he responded to sexual intimacy with men: it troubled him, and he wondered whether it was good for his name, but he could not deny the truth of it. Rogers Brackett did not, then, seduce an innocent victim. Twenty-year-old James Dean was primed for a sexual relationship with a man he trusted. Few things so stroke the ego of an ambitious young man as the blandishments of a respectable older man, whether or not the bond is overtly erotic. In this case, Dean was gratified to be with such an intelligent and worldly man, while Brackett preened in the company of so attractive and docile a companion. But because it was 1951, Jimmy had to act out the charade of being a boarder in the house at Sunset Plaza Drive.

Immediately, Brackett fulfilled his promises. In July, Jimmy was engaged for minor roles on radio dramas broadcast live from Los Angeles ("Alias Jane Doe" and "Stars Over Hollywood," among a few others); neither recordings nor transcripts of these survive. He also did a radio commercial for Toni home permanent, in which he told his "wife" how lustrous and silky her hair looked while violins swooned romantically in the background. Jimmy refrained from laughing only by avoiding the glance of the woman on the other side of the microphone, a witty woman who sounded much younger than her fifty-four years and made clownish faces at him. For a few minutes of work he received a one-time fee of $56.99.

More promising—but only briefly—were the movie jobs he got through Brackett's efforts. Around Labor Day, at Twentieth Century-Fox Studios, he worked uncredited for a day in Samuel Fuller's war drama *Fixed Bayonets*, playing a nameless soldier; his only line ("It's a rear guard coming back") was excised from the final version. Three weeks later, on September 28, he was identified on a call sheet as "First Sailor #210," a wordless, momentary bit in a Dean Martin–Jerry Lewis comedy first titled "At Sea With the Navy" (and eventually released as *Sailor Beware*), directed by Hal Walker. Then, on the afternoon of October 9, he played an unnamed lad in "Oh Money Money" (later *Has Anybody Seen My Gal?*), a mildly amusing piece of family nostalgia whose only distinction was the smooth pacing by the noted immigrant director Douglas Sirk. When the film was released in July 1952, James Dean was seen and heard in an American film for the first time. Wearing white trousers, a straw boater, bow tie and collegiate sweater, he calls to Charles Coburn (who is behind a soda fountain), "Hey, Gramps! I'll have a choc malt, heavy on the choc, plenty of milk, four spoons of malt, two scoops of vanilla ice cream, one mixed with the rest and one floating." The three roles, all dispatched between July and October, netted him a total of less than $300.*

---

* His paychecks were sent to the Avery apartment at 216 North Edgemont, which he still used as a mailing address.

These three roles did not advance his career at all, and by early October Brackett had to agree with Jimmy that there seemed to be more work in the new television market than in the foundering movie studio system. That was the opinion of a new friend, too—Dick Clayton, a former child actor who also had a walk-on in *Sailor Beware*, and who later became Jimmy's Los Angeles representative. "He seemed very vulnerable in Hollywood at that time," according to Clayton, "and very impressionable. People wanted to reach out and hug him, he had such a lost-puppy look. But something in him made him pull back. He wasn't the hugging type."

In 1951, most television drama was broadcast from New York, where the networks had headquarters. In addition, the most prestigious acting classes were, quite naturally, in New York: among others, the Actors Studio, the Neighborhood Playhouse School of the Theatre, the American Academy of Dramatic Arts and the seminars at the American Theatre Wing.

"I remember Jimmy tracking me down one afternoon that autumn," James Whitmore remembered. "'What should I do?' he asked me, as if he were looking for a father's advice. I told him he couldn't do any better than to go to New York, where all serious actors had to study at some point." Until he died, Jimmy never forgot the direction Whitmore indicated: "There's always somebody in your life who opens your eyes. In my life that somebody was James Whitmore. He encouraged me to go to New York, and that's when things began to happen."

The relocation, however, would require funds he did not have, and so Jimmy asked Rogers Brackett and the Winslows for help. As it happened, Brackett was also en route to New York, but first he had business in the Midwest. Just as well, said Jimmy, who was hesitant to go alone to New York. Together, they left Los Angeles and drove east in early October. But after spending several idle days at the Ambassador Hotel in Chicago, where Brackett had important appointments, Jimmy became restless. Brackett sensed his boredom and eagerness for the future, bought him a train ticket and telephoned his old friend Alec Wilder, who composed incidental music for theater and film. Yes, promised Wilder from his suite at the Algonquin Hotel, he would be happy to welcome the new boy in town and look after him.

After a brief visit to Fairmount (and to Indianapolis, where Reverend De Weerd gave him an envelope containing $200), Jimmy arrived in Manhattan in mid-October.

"New York overwhelmed me," he said later. "For the first few weeks I was so confused that I strayed only a couple of blocks from my hotel [the Iroquois] off Times Square. I saw three movies a day in an attempt to escape from my loneliness and depression—spent $150 of my limited funds on movies alone."

And when the cash got low, he began a habit of running up tabs and establishing credit. Louis Fontana, haircutter at the DuMont Barber Shop, recalled him as "a nice boy but moody—always looking for work and angry when he didn't get the job. He had no money to pay me, but as soon as he got a job he did."

Among the movies he saw was *A Place in the Sun*, with Montgomery Clift and Elizabeth Taylor. Clift he adored, developing a fixation to meet and know of his moody, reticent acting technique just as he longed to meet and know Brando. The film of *A Streetcar Named Desire* was also playing to great crowds that autumn. Marlon Brando, on the big screen, was astonishing moviegoers with the role of his career, that of Stanley Kowalski, the raw, primal measure of macho. Jimmy, according to Alec Wilder, saw *A Place in the Sun* and *Streetcar* five times each in four days and inevitably brought the films and their male stars into conversations over a beer at the Algonquin bar. "He seemed almost obsessed with Brando," agreed photographer Roy Schatt, who soon became a kind of surrogate father as well as photography teacher. "Occasionally, for no apparent reason, Jimmy would begin quoting from *A Streetcar Named Desire*. One time, during a discussion of Method acting, he took off his shirt and ripped his undershirt to shreds, yelling 'Stella!' in imitation of Marlon Brando as Stanley Kowalski. He was always 'on.'" But Schatt recalled him as essentially "a loner—he was a loner in every possible way."

Did he see himself as the next Brando? "Well," he said when the question arose, "I had a motorbike before he did."

Of his idolatry of Clift and Brando, James Dean made no secret. "In one hand," he told actor Dennis Hopper some time later, "I offer them something like Brando saying 'Fuck you!' and I have Clift in the other, saying, 'Please help me!'"

Before autumn turned to winter, he had managed to locate the unlisted home telephone numbers of both Brando and Clift in New York, and he routinely rang them in hopes of a meeting. Neither one of them was interested in an unknown, gushing young fan.

chapter six

> Hope is the feeling you have
> that the feeling you have
> isn't permanent.
>
> JEAN KERR

Rogers Brackett finally arrived in New York just before Christmas 1951, and Jimmy quit the Iroquois Hotel and moved in with him to Brackett's apartment on West Thirty-eighth Street. On Jimmy's behalf, Brackett at once rang an old acquaintance, the television director Ralph Levy—who in turn called his friend, James Sheldon, then supervising commercials for the advertising firm Young & Rubicam. One of the clients was Maxwell House Coffee, sponsor of the memorable television series *Mama*, inspired by the play *I Remember Mama*. Sheldon, after meeting and hearing Jimmy, saw a certain stylistic resemblance to Marlon Brando, who had appeared in 1944 in the Broadway production as the son Nils. As it happened, Dick Van Patten, the young actor then playing that role on television, was about to be drafted into military service, and Dean might be the perfect replacement. But Van Patten, for health reasons, was not drafted and stayed with *Mama*.

Sheldon, however, continued to champion Jimmy's talents, befriended him and generously loaned him cash without question. He found Jimmy likable, sometimes moody and full of fiery ambition for his career. He also felt that the novice ought to have New York representation, and so he sent Jimmy off to his friend Jane Deacy, who had been a switchboard operator at the Louis Shurr Agency on East Forty-second Street and had just graduated to the status of theatrical agent on her own. A warm, motherly lady, she evoked the sobriquet "Mom" from several of her clients. Henceforth, that was how Jimmy addressed her.

Year's end, Mom explained, was not the best time to be sent out for auditions. But she did call casting director Elinor Kilgallen (sister of columnist Dorothy) at CBS, who sent him over to producer Franklin Heller. There was a job available immediately behind the television cameras, Heller said—as a rehearsal stuntman for the weekly game show *Beat the Clock*. Hosted by a genial ringmaster named Bud Collyer, this zany program required contestants, in a race against time, to perform outrageous slapstick stunts—juggling plates while standing on one foot; or transferring water from one glass to another by siphoning through a straw, for example; or passing plates from one person's neck to another's; or tossing pudding at a bull's-eye painted on a contestant's forehead—the possibilities for messy silliness were endless. Meantime, the studio audience and home viewers watched the contestants make idiots of themselves. But the stunts had to be carefully tested and rehearsed prior to showtime, and this was James

Dean's responsibility. It was not exactly a featured role in *Death of a Salesman*, but it paid $5 an hour, which gave Jimmy about $60 a week.

With the new year 1952, Jimmy knew he needed to make friends. Brackett traveled a good deal of the winter, and his New York friends were older and, Jimmy thought, did not warmly welcome him into their circle. One evening, a young woman who worked with him at *Beat the Clock* took him to her hotel nearby to offer him a meal; she lived at a place called the Rehearsal Club on West Fifty-third Street, a residence for young women in the arts.

> She brought him there just to give him a good
> meal, because he looked so hungry, he looked
> lonely, he looked like he needed a friend. Later
> I found out that he always looked that way.
> And at first he certainly didn't impress me.

Such was the recollection of another Rehearsal Club resident who met Jimmy that evening—an attractive, bright-eyed woman with long hair, a warm smile and a quick wit. Within minutes, she and Jimmy were talking animatedly, discovering that they shared common interests, a similar sense of the absurd, a love of theater and dance, a hunger for success—and, of all things, a fascination with the dangerous art of bullfighting.

Her name was Elizabeth Sheridan, but friends called her "Dizzy," a family nickname since childhood. Daughter of a concert pianist and a singer, Dizzy had been raised in the village of Larchmont, in Westchester

County. A gifted modern dancer and an engaging singer, Dizzy was two years older than Jimmy, quick-witted, intelligent and utterly without affectation. "We became friends quickly," she recalled years later.

> He heard I was a dancer, and he wanted to come to a rehearsal with the two men I had in my trio. We danced in the country, we danced in Harlem—all over. And then, all of a sudden, Jimmy seemed to be with me everywhere. Jimmy watched us rehearse and we became close—fast. Then, before we knew it, we had spent so much time on the phone that we decided to move in together, to a room in a hotel on West Eighty-ninth Street.

As it was for all the youngsters struggling in New York in the early fifties, life was, as Dizzy said, "scary and terrific at the same time. We were having enormous fun, but half the time we seemed on the edge of starvation." Late that January, Jimmy and Dizzy were in love, sharing the room just off Central Park and, because it was all they could afford, eating Shredded Wheat for dinner most evenings. "He was completely captivated by her warmth, charm and alert mind," recalled Bill Bast, who arrived in May and renewed his friendship with Jimmy. "She had a wonderful sense of humor and was easy to know. It was understandable that she and Jimmy got on so well." As for Bast, he was happy to forget the thorny past, for he knew no one but Jimmy in New York, and there he, too, hoped to advance his career. "No longer was I the one with my feet planted firmly on the ground," Bast admitted. "No longer was it Jimmy who turned to me for the answers, as it had been in the beginning. Now I was following Jimmy's lead."

But things became difficult when, after only a few weeks, Franklin Heller had (to his disappointment) to dismiss Jimmy from *Beat the Clock*—not because he was incompetent at the job, but because in fact he was too dexterous and athletic. "He could do anything," according to Heller. "He was the best coordinated human being I've ever known, and of course we needed to know which stunts wouldn't work, which were too hard for the contestants. Because Jimmy could do everything and make it look easy, he was no good to us!"

Jimmy had dated before, of course, and there had been long drives and quiet evenings with, most recently, Beverly Wills. But Dizzy Sheridan was the first woman he loved; she was certainly the first with whom he lived. "We had a lot of fun," she said.

> We were poor and uncertain of the future, but somehow when we were together we didn't care. It was "you and me against the world." It's hard to remember why, but we were both very sensitive about things. We felt separate from the rest of the world, like the brother and sister who live in the attic in *Les Enfants Terribles*.

They encouraged each other, they laughed, they read aloud to each other, everything from poetry to art history; they danced up Broadway and walked along

Central Park West at four in the morning, and Jimmy insisted on teaching Dizzy to sketch. "We clung together that year, for a lot of reasons—not the least being that it was the first time both of us were really falling for someone." Jimmy, she thought, was very like a kind of urchin: she had the impression that he was restless and rootless, drifting from person to person and home to home without any emotional stability; in important ways, this was on the mark. "And he felt very strange and sad about his mother, whom he missed terribly." Of his father he said practically nothing.

Jimmy liked Dizzy's family immediately, and they welcomed him on visits to their suburban home. His manners with her mother and sister, she remembered, were impeccable. With the Sheridans he did not, as so often otherwise, resort to the practical joke of dropping his false front teeth into someone's drink, and he displayed a remarkable gentleness that was new in his personality. Dizzy found a cabin near a country lake, and there she and Jimmy nested on several long weekends, preparing simple suppers over a fire in the hearth, singing along with a wind-up record player, or reading and discussing *The Little Prince*, the allegorical fantasy by Antoine de Saint-Exupéry that Jimmy had first read in high-school and with which he now very much identified. For the rest of his life, he never moved anywhere without his copy of *The Little Prince*.

Saint-Exupéry's short, gossamer-thin fable charts the adventures of the title character, a visitor from outer space, as he searches for and discovers the nature of true friendship. There are talking flowers and animals in the book, which is peppered with the author's naive drawings; what Jimmy caught, however, was the clash between the child's world of imaginative sensitivity and the adult world of speed and cruelty—a hoary, comforting contrast that has often won over children and been a boon to confused older readers.

"You talk just like grownups!" cries the Little Prince. "You mix everything up together. You confuse everything!" With quiet intensity, Jimmy read the lines aloud to Dizzy Sheridan. "Only the children know what they are looking for . . . It is only with the heart that one can see rightly; what is essential is invisible to the eye." The phrases became like mantras to James Dean, who often repeated them to friends and strangers. In a way, he considered himself a Little Prince—a lonely outsider, needy of friendship but an instant hero to the world just because of his isolation and his instant epiphany about the necessity of inner vision. Jimmy liked, he said, "the writer's escapist attitude, his refusal to adjust to anything earthbound"—and, no doubt, the celebration of childhood and of perilous physical adventures as one's highest aspiration.

The bohemian lifestyle of Jimmy and Dizzy was not endlessly carefree, however, and without work the young lovers were short of cash for food and rent; eventually, they had to quit the hotel room. While awaiting news of a choreographing assignment for the summer, Dizzy took a part-time job and an apartment with her friend Sue Height just off Eighth Avenue in the theater district; sometimes Jimmy and Dizzy spoke of living together again when their finances allowed. As for Jimmy, he wrote to the Winslows, who sent him enough cash to pay for a tiny room at the Iroquois Hotel. Meantime, he waited for Jane Deacy to call about his big chance at a television, stage or film role.

Then there was the matter of Rogers Brackett. He could provide financial and professional help, but how could Jimmy finesse Dizzy in one part of his life and Rogers in the other? When Brackett returned from Los Angeles in early February and tracked down Jimmy through Jane Deacy, things were perhaps destined to be awkward.

"He told me everything about his relationship with Rogers even before I met the man," Dizzy said years later, although what Jimmy told her about Brackett was not entirely truthful.

> He told me he met Rogers in a parking lot, that they had lived together and gone to Chicago together. Then he told me he was extremely unhappy about what he'd done—that he had "succumbed" to Rogers because he thought [Rogers] could help him. Then he said he didn't want to see Rogers anymore, but that he had to, to break it off—and that's when he dragged me along to Brackett's apartment and presented me as his girlfriend. And he just hung on to me the whole time. I remember that it pleased him so much that I was very calm and presentable and stoic in front of Rogers Brackett.

But the fact is that although Jimmy was grateful for her moral support, the scene was perhaps concocted with two goals in his mind: to make Brackett jealous, and simultaneously to convince Dizzy that he really meant to end that relationship when in fact he did not.

The truth, of which she was unaware, is that Jimmy did not stop seeing Brackett, and in fact when Dizzy worked in New Jersey that summer, Jimmy spent most evenings and weekends with Brackett, whose company was enormously beneficial. Brackett was entertaining and protective, he introduced Jimmy to the right people. He also had money, he paid for dinner and for the theater. This caused James Dean enormous conflict, not to say the necessity of maintaining a delicate social balancing act, and from this time forward he was very careful to keep clear separations between most people in his life, lest one of them trip him up in the presence of another. Henceforth, people wondered why Dean was so extraordinarily secretive, why he seemed to have so much to hide. Only a very few knew the reason.

The disunity in James Dean was, indeed, enormous—and clearly, as Dizzy realized years later, it was something he hated and could not resolve. "He did not want to be gay, whatever that meant at the time or whatever it might have meant to him. And of course that was not a part of his life that I knew about apart from this one meeting. Jimmy never seemed to me a sexually driven or sexually obsessed young man. My experience of him was as a gentle, tender, complicated young heterosexual." But her experience was not, of course, the entire story. In this regard, the introduction of Dizzy to Rogers that cold winter evening had precisely the effect Jimmy may have intended: to defuse the concern of both these two good people and to enable Jimmy to sustain both relationships to his best advantage. Dizzy believed that Rogers was out of the picture, and Rogers believed the same of her.

On the one hand, there is no question that James

Dean loved Dizzy Sheridan—for herself, for her talent
and wit and encouragement. Alec Wilder, among others, saw what a good influence she could be on him.
"He was a neurotic, mixed-up kid who tried to con
everybody to death," said Wilder. "There just wasn't
an ounce of maturity in that boy." Nor, some would
argue, would there ever be.

On the other hand, Jimmy needed more than Dizzy—
he needed from Rogers Brackett both the career counsel
and the material assistance Brackett was willing to provide—as well as whatever emotional support Jimmy
derived from their intimacy: all this he was unwilling to
renounce. But neither could he have been comfortable
with thinking of himself as a kind of hustler, and some
such doubts must have occurred to him, for he lived
the rest of his life as if he was hiding some dark and terrible secret: he seemed to everyone shrouded in a moodiness and misery that betokened terrific guilt. With Rogers
Brackett, he had elegant meals, sophisticated companionship, helpful professional introductions and a standard of
living far superior to anything he had ever known.

He had, in other words, a dilemma not uncommon to
many men in bisexual relationships: unwilling or unable
to make any sort of commitment, he was true neither to
Dizzy nor to Rogers. He was leading a double life worse
than that of a married man with a mistress, for his was
complicated by the social stigma attached to homosexuality. Doubtless Dizzy was correct: he "did not want to
be gay," if for no other reason than if this were known,
his career could collapse at once. He might be able to
lead his own quietly closeted life when he was a terrific
success, but while he was on the way up—well, it was
1952 and this was unthinkable.

Movie and television studios were very strict in enforcing their so-called morals clauses, and homosexuality was regarded as wicked, and almost as treasonous as espionage. Many public figures had to suppress or conceal their homosexual or bisexual lives (even to the point of marrying and raising a family) or they risked the blacklist and an immediate end to their careers—a situation that, alas, had not much altered almost fifty years later, under the threat of censure not by studios but public opinion.

Nevertheless, Dean socialized with Brackett and his crowd, who sometimes, after a few drinks, frequented some of the less attractive and more dangerous waterfront bars in the West Village. Of this part of his life nothing is known for certain, and therefore imaginative writers have concocted lurid tales of James Dean, masochist hustler; or James Dean, the male whore of Greenwich Village; or James Dean, who consorted sexually with anyone who would provide a meal and a bed for the night; or James Dean, who earned money by appearing in pornographic films. These anecdotes provide trashy diversion only for readers unconcerned with evidence. Since there is not a single scrap of it, no one should take these tales seriously.*

It is true, however, that Jimmy was fascinated by unconventional behavior—he practiced it himself, after

---

* Just so for a singularly prurient but blurry photograph that circulated for years, of a young man of indeterminate facial features. This picture, purporting to be of James Dean proudly masturbating for the camera, is yet another fraud. Alas for the gossipmongers: the younger brother of a man named Richard Laselle recently admitted that it was a crude and cruel snapshot taken in 1957, of the Laselle brothers' mentally handicapped cousin, who has since died.

all. As he once told actress Ella Logan, "I like you, Ella. You're good. But you know, I like bad people, too. I guess that's because I'm so damn curious to know what makes them bad." Perhaps after all he did not consider them or himself bad, but so polite society judged them. "People with odd viewpoints and strange modes of existence always intrigued him," according to Bill Bast. "He probably used 'bad' in the sense of 'different' or 'unusual.'" From his upbringing, he had learned to associate nonconformist behavior with "bad conduct." In this regard, he could not have been more typical of his times.

Jimmy may, indeed, have disliked the sexual "obligations" of life with Brackett, but whatever his deepest feelings about such intimacies, they went with him to the grave. In any case, everyone who knew him sensed, for the rest of his life, that Jimmy was a deeply divided personality—a character torn between optimism and gloom, between the desire to trust and to love and the refusal ever to confide completely in anyone. This certainly derived in part from the disaster of effectively losing both parents when he was nine.

Professionally, things got off to a slow start that winter. In February, Franklin Heller remembered his agile former assistant on *Beat the Clock* and gave him a role in a live television drama, "Sleeping Dogs," an episode of the CBS series *The Web* that was broadcast on February 20, 1952. Back home in Indiana, the Winslows bought their first television set for the event. Ortense thought he looked so thin that they at once shipped off tins of food and a check, with instructions to go shopping. Heller thought he looked worse than underfed: "He came to the first rehearsals very badly dressed—a mess, unkempt, uncaring—and he was absolutely impossible to work with, arrogant and uncooperative. Elinor Kilgallen and Jane Deacy had warned me I'd hate him, and I did. He was an absolute horror until he went on the air—and then he was absolutely brilliant." Alas, this judgment cannot be appreciated, for without the benefit of tape or the occasional kinescope copy, "Sleeping Dogs," like thousands of early live television shows, has vanished.* Twelve days later, CBS used Jimmy again, in the walk-across-the-screen role of a hotel bellboy in "Ten Thousand Horses Singing." He was all but invisible and had only a few inconsequential words, just as in "Forgotten Children," for which he was dressed as an antebellum Southern swain, one of a crowd in an early party scene.

That mixed bag of entertainment known as early live television was surely more of a brass than a golden age,

---

*Of James Dean's thirty dramatic roles on television between March 1951 and May 1955, there are (up to autumn 1995) no extant prints of the following sixteen, which therefore cannot be treated in this book (nor were they reviewed at the time): "Sleeping Dogs" (February 20, 1952), "The Foggy, Foggy Dew" (broadcast March 17, 1952), "Prologue to Glory" (May 21, 1952), "Hound of Heaven" (January 15, 1953), "The Case of the Watchful Dog" (January 29, 1953), "The Capture of Jesse James" (February 8, 1953), "No Room" (April 14, 1953), "The Case of the Sawed-Off Shotgun" (April 16, 1953), "Something for an Empty Briefcase" (July 17, 1953), "Death Is My Neighbor" (August 25, 1953), "Rex Newman" (September 11, 1953), "Life Sentence" (October 16, 1953), "The Little Woman" (March 30, 1954), "Run Like a Thief" (September 5, 1954), "Padlocks" (November 9, 1954) and "The Dark, Dark Hour" (December 12, 1954). Some sources, without documentation, cite minor appearances in other television shows.

for when "Marty," "The Miracle Worker" or "Amahl and the Night Visitors" is mentioned in odes to nostalgia, it is important to remember what egregious exceptions they were amid the nightly array of crudely written, overlong, badly acted and hastily produced shows, most of which could easily have narcotized an army of amphetamine addicts. Television did not pay well, either—late in his career, Dean received nothing more than a hundred dollars for a leading role—but the advantage was the exposure, for Hollywood and Broadway scouts watched the new medium constantly for new faces available cheaply.

But sometimes James Dean fared better than a mere cameo. On a *Westinghouse Studio One* production of John Drinkwater's "Abraham Lincoln" that May 26, he appeared briefly but to great effect as William Scott, a Vermont soldier scheduled to be court-martialed for falling asleep on night watch during the Civil War. In a deeply affecting scene with Robert Pastene as Lincoln, Dean breaks down, weeping quietly—not out of fear for his trial and death sentence, but out of shame for his widowed mother, who will be disgraced by his fate. Lincoln, seeing the boy's sense of honor and rightly sensing that the mishap was due to simple exhaustion and not laziness, pardons him. Dean's humble gratitude is expressed with admirable calm, and the performance demonstrated for producers at CBS that he was a young actor who was untrained but whose on-camera emotions and gestures were never overstated, always natural. In rehearsal he was, as before, uncooperative, ungracious and withdrawn, but once the show began he came to life as the person in the story.

At "home"—and he had many of them between

May and December 1952: almost a dozen, none of
them for more than a few weeks at a time and always
on his own—he was so worried about his future that
he became insomniac. Jane Deacy was worried when
he arrived at her office one day to collect his mail and
a few paltry checks. Jimmy had dark circles under his
eyes, he smoked too much and drank too much coffee
in an attempt to energize himself after a sleepless
night.

He was, according to Dennis Stock, "the worst
insomniac I've ever met—so at odd times and in odd
places he would simply pass out, for a few minutes or a
few hours, then wake up and start out again." He had,
according to several who knew him then, no hesitation
in sitting all night at a bar, or all afternoon at a sandwich counter, initiating conversations with strangers.
"He did not hesitate to try to procure fans," according
to Christine White, whom he met that year. "Many
times I saw him turn around to address people he
didn't know: 'Hey, I was on television! Did you see my
show?' It might have been only a walk-on, but he
wanted to be known. I thought he was the kind of person who was going to burst if he didn't get the attention he needed."

Christine White, an educated, cultivated young lady
from Washington, first met Jimmy Dean that June of
1952. White was an aspiring young actress, blond, wil-
lowy and earnest, and although she was in New York
to pursue her career as an actress, she was also writing
a play. One afternoon, she was at Deacy's office, borrowing a friend's desk and trying to work on her play
when Jimmy entered—"sloppy," in White's description, "constantly pushing his glasses back onto the

bridge of his nose. He did not look like a matinee idol."
Curious about her work, he tried to engage her in conversation, but she was too busy and brushed him aside.
Leaving the office shortly after, she met him in the
outer waiting room and turned to apologize for her
earlier impatience. When he suggested they go out for
a cup of coffee, she felt "trapped—I had apologized
and I didn't want to be rude again, but I thought to
myself, the last thing I want to do is walk down the
street with this guy who looks this way!"

Two hours later, they were still at the Blue Ribbon
Deli near Forty-second Street, talking about their pasts,
sharing their thoughts about the theater. Jimmy, she
recalled, was all over the booth, slouching on one end,
then animated and sliding across to the other end. By
the time they left, she found his candor and his wide
range of interests rather attractive. He might, she
thought, be a friend. What was his name? "James
Byron Dean," he replied.

"Byron? Like the poet? Don't you think James Byron
would look better on a marquee?"

"Well, whatever they want."

That same day, in the delicatessen booth, Jimmy
confided to Christine that he was eager to find a way to
join the Actors Studio—as was Christine. What was
that play she was writing? he asked. Would some
pages of it be suitable for him to use as an audition
piece for the Studio?

They read her pages, talked some more, then parted
at the corner bus stop—forever, she thought. But next
morning she was surprised to receive his call. "I think,"
he said, "that you and I ought to do your play for the
Actors Studio."

"I don't think so," she said. "I'm going to do a scene from *The Master Builder*."

"No, you play the girl in your play and I'll be the boy."

He was impossible to deny, and within the hour he was at the apartment she shared with a few other girls at Madison Avenue and Ninety-first Street. There, on a tiny balcony, they rehearsed her scene, about young lovers trying to sustain a painful, difficult but loving relationship. "Something told him," White said years later, "that I was his ticket to win a place in the Studio, and I was going along with him. It was really impossible not to yield to him. He had this sense that he wanted to play somebody trying to get free of something, and that's just what the scene was about." Nor was it hard to understand why such a scene would appeal to him, for he was himself trying to be free—of his past, his memories, his father, his compromised relationships. The desire to be free, to break a sense of entrapment, to allow some elemental sadness to emerge before his heart breaks—this is the conjunction of feelings that is at the root of every first-rate scene James Dean ever performed on film or television.

In July, Christine White had the good fortune to land a role in a film, and she sped off to Hollywood to make *Man Crazy* at Fox, with Neville Brand as her leading man. When she returned six weeks later, two of her roommates were about to marry and so she required new lodgings. Jimmy was passionate to know everything about her experience, everything about working in the movies, and so he arranged for her to book a room at the Iroquois Hotel, just below the one he occasionally inhabited with Bill Bast. Chris and Jimmy renewed their friendship—and their preparations for the Actors Studio audition.

The action of Christine White's scene, revised and rewritten by her and Jimmy together that August, is set on an island about to be pummeled by a hurricane. A young girl, eager to flee her domineering parents, meets a boy lying in the bullrushes near the sea.

SHE: There are no stars tonight.

HE: They went behind that big black blanket, but they'll peep out again.

SHE: I'm sure I'm nuts! People were evacuatin' the other way and we just roared off into the darkness . . . wind . . . and unknown. What are you thinking about? What have you been doin' most of your life?

HE: Ripping off layers to find the roots. How about a beer? Do you mind it out of the bottle? . . . I'm thinking you're in despair. You've come to me with the emptiness of your world.

SHE: I know, I know. What can I do? I need your freedom. You've been running away all your life and knocking the world down with your fist. But what a warm and tender hand you have . . .

HE: Come inside with me. You're new at running away.

(Afraid, she runs into the darkness and leaves him.)

HE: (alone, tossing the empty beer can in the air, then tossing it away): You see, you can toss your whole life away, and nobody will care. We . . . all of us . . . are alone . . .

Of one hundred applicants for a dozen new places at the Actors Studio, Elia Kazan and Lee Strasberg selected a dozen as finalists that August—and of the twelve, only James Dean and Christine White were chosen for membership. "I have made great strides in my craft," Jimmy wrote to the Winslows in a letter thanking them for a small check.

> After months of auditioning I am very proud to announce that I am a member of the Actors Studio. The greatest school of theater. It houses great people like Marlon Brando, Julie Harris, Arthur Kennedy, Elia Kazan, Mildred Dunnock, Kevin McCarthy, Monty Clift, June Havoc and on and on and on. Very few get into it, and it's absolutely free. It's the best thing that can happen to an actor. I am one of the youngest to belong. If I can keep this up and nothing interferes with my progress, one of these days I might be able to contribute something to the world.

He knew what Ortense and Marcus needed to hear so that they would soften their attitude toward how he was spending their stipend.

And then a very odd thing happened and indeed interfered with his progress.

For his first solo presentation piece at the Actors Studio, Jimmy adapted from a novel called *Matador*, by Barnaby Conrad, a scene about an aging bullfighter's last contest. When he had finished, Strasberg virtually tore the act apart, criticizing the text and the actor and describing exactly what was untrue, what unconvincing. That, of course, was the method of the Method, and thousands believed it was Strasberg's genius as a teacher.

But James Dean simply would not accept the critique. "He never went to Mexico," he said of Strasberg to Christine White. "I did. He never fought a bull and neither did any of those other actors—none of them ever stepped in front of a two-ton bull. I don't have to take that."* And, as he told Christine and Bill, he did not. He never appeared again in an exercise at the Actors Studio. "He just came in a few times, slouched down and never again participated in anything," according to Kazan, who regretted to say that Jimmy was "a surly mess. What any director who worked with him should have done was to tell him off." Less than two years later, however, Kazan would use the insolent conduct to good advantage.

Of the few times Dean visited the Studio, actress Carroll Baker recalled that Jimmy seemed "a sad-faced, introverted oddball [who sat] alone in a corner by himself even when we all gathered together." Strasberg was also disappointed in Jimmy's behavior, for he, too, had recognized his potential, as did Cheryl Crawford, a co-founder of the Studio, who lamented his lack of application and bizarre behavior, judging him to be "as a human being, too sick." For Strasberg, "His behavior and personality seemed to be part of a pattern which invariably had to lead to something destructive. I always had a strange feeling that there was in Jimmy a

---

* The apparent journey to Mexico cannot be documented.

sort of doomed quality." He also recalled that Jimmy's every manner seemed to be "a gesture of defiance from within."

When Jimmy was not working with Christine or in one of nine television dramas that year, he roamed the streets of Manhattan, scoured bookstores, sat at Cromwell's luncheonette counter or at Louie's Tavern on Sheridan Square in Greenwich Village. He talked to strangers or friends of being out of work, he spoke of his recent show, he wandered. Sometimes he met Christine or Dizzy or Bill, or a combination of these, and they had spaghetti at Jerry's Bar and Restaurant on Fifty-sixth Street, or beef stew at Dinty Moore's on Eighth Avenue, or a bowl of soup at Riker's on Fifty-seventh Street, or cheese blintzes at Ratner's on Second Avenue, or chicken sandwiches at Cromwell's, in the RCA Building at Rockefeller Center. For these culinary excursions, the little band had what they called a "floating twenty." Whoever was working during a particular week loaned $20 to someone who was unemployed, and this was passed back and forth, round and round to whoever needed it, from week to week. "I'm doing okay this week," one would say. "Who needs food money?"

An odd combination of exhibitionist and isolate, Jimmy longed, at such gatherings, to be noticed, to be the center of attention, and yet to hide from the public. He finally quit patronizing Louie's in the Village, for example, because he said the lighting was too low, and he feared no one would recognize him; then he often withdrew into a moody silence if someone did. Photographer Roy Schatt recalled that Louie's attracted an astonishing number of actors and artists, "and that made him uncomfortable, too. Even an inkling of competition was difficult for him." To counter it, Jimmy sometimes went so far as to bring his bongo drums to a restaurant; that guaranteed him an audience.

During the summer of 1952, Jimmy visited Dizzy Sheridan when she was working as a choreographer in Ocean City, New Jersey; she recalled that he seemed miserable being around people working in the theater because he was not. Back in Manhattan, where all activities in the arts and entertainment ease off in July and August, Jimmy was no happier. Christine White tried to cheer him, but to no effect—and sensing his confusion and emotional poverty, she gently but firmly turned aside his romantic advances. "It was I who kept saying no," she recalled. And so, prudently, they remained friends.

Then, as if on cue, Rogers Brackett again came to the rescue. Among his friends was Lemuel Ayres, a brilliant thirty-seven-year-old stage designer (for, among other productions, *Oklahoma!*, *Kiss Me Kate* and *Out of This World*) who also often co-produced. Tall and lean, handsome and stylish, Ayres was quietly gay despite his friendly marriage. These details would be of only academic interest but for the fact that Brackett knew Ayres would like Dean, and hoped that Ayres would be of some benefit to the morose young man.

And so, in late August, Jimmy was aboard the Ayres yacht, sailing up and down the Hudson River, along the coast of Long Island and, in another voyage, as far as Cape Cod. At once Jimmy, who knew the value of such a connection as Lemuel Ayres, ingratiated himself, and Ayres promised to keep him in mind as he prepared to cast a new play by N. Richard Nash called *See the Jaguar*. Jimmy had heard polite pledges like this before, of course—most recently from the offices of Irving Jacobs and Guthrie McClintic, the producer and director of Mary Chase's comedy *Bernardine*, for which he had unsuccessfully auditioned for a supporting role as a truculent teenager.

By September, Dizzy was back in New York, where she took a part-time job as an usherette at the Paris movie theater on Fifty-eighth Street, just west of Fifth Avenue. As autumn arrived, Bill had an unpromising job at CBS, but Jimmy was completely indolent. Having angered and alienated Rogers Brackett by being undependable, unpredictable and emotionally inaccessible, he was also now virtually indigent, and for several weeks his meals were the coffee, doughnuts and candies Dizzy slipped him when he passed the Paris. At this time, they and Bast were living together in rooms uptown, and one evening Jimmy said he needed to go on an errand. From the corner phone booth, he telephoned Dizzy and, to her astonishment, asked her to marry him. Very politely, she deferred the question. "We must get married," he begged, "before we get caught up in all this"—by which, she knew, he meant (as he considered) the inevitable stardom, celebrity, the pressure of successful careers. Still, she declined and told him to come home.

"And then suddenly, late one night, Jimmy announced that the only way we were going to have a good meal was to visit the Winslows!" They awakened Bill and told him to pack: they were going to hitchhike to Indiana, and at dawn, the three set out, rode a bus to New Jersey and there began the trek westward. As it happened, the first driver to stop on the highway was the professional baseball player Clyde McCullough, who welcomed them aboard and even bought them meals at roadside diners. McCullough's Nash Rambler was comfortable but cold, and while Bill sat with the driver, Jimmy and Dizzy huddled under a blanket in the back.

The Winslows and the Deans welcomed the refugees and, for a week, fed them enormous meals and treated them like visiting dignitaries. The young guests rode motorcycles and horses, aimed rifles at tin cans, strolled through the town and visited Fairmount High, where Jimmy coached a drama class, Dizzy performed a modern dance and Bill wrote a clever skit for Adeline Nall's students. What Jimmy and Dizzy did not do that week, however, was to share a bedroom: "I remember our conversation," she said years later, "about whether or not we should creep from one bedroom to the other in the middle of the night. We decided against it because the Winslows were very stern and strict about such things." Just so, this would not have gone down well with Winton, who happened to be visiting his parents that same week, and who fitted his son with a new dental bridge.

His friends saw a new aspect of Jimmy's personality that October—his gentleness and sweetness with young Markie; his tenderness with Aunt Ortense, now suffering painful arthritis; his concern for Uncle Marcus and the farm; his rapport with children and animals. A fundamental simplicity of spirit shone forth, something they had no opportunity to see amid the

dither of New York or the allure of Los Angeles.
"Acting and farm folk, animals and simple things,"
said Dizzy years later, "these were the things that mattered to Jimmy. He never talked about government or
politics or the world order or any issues like that. He
didn't care at all about anything except the small world
he was in—but when he was in Fairmount he was at
his best." From this visit came a labored, awkward but
deeply felt attempt at poetry:

> *My town likes industrial impotence*
> *My town's small, loves its diffidence*
> *My town thrives on dangerous bigotry*
> *My town's big in the sense of idolatry*
> *My town believes in God and his crew*
> *My town hates the Catholic and Jew*
> *My town's innocent, selfistic caper*
> *My town's diligent, reads the newspaper*
> *My town's sweet, I was born bare*
> *My town is not what I am, I am here*

"Here" was New York, where he wrote the lines on
the endpaper of a book on Lorca.

Just as the trio was about to accept the Winslows'
invitation to extend their visit, a call came from Jane
Deacy: Jimmy was to return immediately, for he had
been asked to read for the part of Wally Wilkins, a tortured seventeen-year-old social outcast in *See the
Jaguar*. More than eighty young men had auditioned
already, Jane cautioned, but Ayres would make no
decision until her client returned. There was a round of

hasty farewells at the farm and in town, and then Jimmy, Dizzy and Bill were back on the road—this time with a truck-driving cowboy who had no business on a long drive, for after every meal along the route he became violently ill.

See the Jaguar was a play filled with noble ideas but gravely lacking dramatic structure and credible characters. The story, gravid with portentous dialogue and turgid symbolism, concerns Wally Wilkins, confined under lock and key since childhood by his neurotically overprotective mother (played by Margaret Barker) in an effort to spare her son the brutality of the modern world. Released just before her death, he wanders into the world with only a rifle and his childlike wonder intact within a young adult's body. Wally is tracked by the town storekeeper and bully (Cameron Prud'homme), who captures wild animals for display in a clumsy rural zoo ("See the Weasel," "See the Fox" and so forth). Hell-bent on snaring a jaguar (for which he has prepared a cage and a sign), he comes on Wally—who, he believes, has his cash inheritance in his pocket. But Wally is befriended by the storekeeper's unmarried daughter (Constance Ford), who is also an outcast—she is pregnant by her schoolteacher boyfriend (Arthur Kennedy). The play ends tragically when Wally shoots the jaguar and is forced to replace it, confined in the cage.

Ayres, playwright Nash and director Michael Gordon were not, at first, sure that Jimmy was right for the role. For the first audition, he arrived with one lens of his eyeglasses cracked, and this badly hampered his reading. Nash told him to have the glasses repaired, and when Jimmy replied he had no money the play-wright handed him $10 and told him to return two days later. When he did, Jimmy still wore the broken glasses but with the help of Dizzy and Bill he had committed the entire part to memory. When Nash asked why the glasses were unrepaired, Jimmy drew from his pocket a hunting knife: "I just had to have it," he said, "but I figure I couldn't betray you entirely so I memorized the script." His manner and tone were naive, credulous and potentially vicious—just what the role of Wally required.

And so Jimmy was given a second chance, and this time there was no doubt. Nash and Gordon felt he was the only candidate who could manage the strangely pathetic, half-demented creature. Gordon, who believed that Dean was the only actor in the play who understood its deepest significance, saw through the young man's curious, concocted bravado. "He claimed, among other things, to have been a novillero in various bullrings south of the border, and I often saw him make daring passes and farinas at onrushing taxicabs while crossing Broadway or Seventh Avenue." Jimmy's battles and contests, in other words, were still being fought outside himself—the challenges engaged to prove himself to a world he distrusted but whose applause he required.

During out-of-town previews prior to the Broadway opening of *See the Jaguar*, Jimmy was for the most part a cooperative member of the cast, except for one occasion when, backstage after an argument, he pulled his knife on another player. Arthur Kennedy intervened, snapping the blade in two and warning Jimmy, at once the image of repentance, that violence would not be tolerated. The complexity of the play's character—part transplanted farm boy, part noble savage—had gotten under the skin of his exponent, who bore a less hysterical but real resemblance to Wally Wilkins. Kennedy in fact tried to befriend the unpredictable Dean, and took him for a walk one afternoon. Look at what Kazan has done for Brando, said Kennedy: who knows what Dean's own future might be? "What's Kazan ever done for me?" muttered Jimmy, as if he were owed something based on his passing connection to the Actors Studio.

The play, alas for Nash, Ayres and Gordon, was demolished by the critics and closed on Saturday, December 6, after just five performances at the Cort Theatre. "*See the Jaguar* accomplishes nothing but noise and confusion. [It] is verbose and says nothing," wrote Brooks Atkinson in the *New York Times*; his opinion was shared by colleagues and audiences.

But judgment on the actors was generally favorable, and the newest of them all made a stunning impression documented in the press on Thursday, December 4:

- "James Dean adds an extraordinary performance in an almost completely impossible role" (Walter Kerr, in the *New York Herald Tribune*).
- "No show is complete without a character actor who thefts the show [*sic*]. This has two, Roy Fant as Grandpa Ricks and James Dean who impersonates a weird young man" (Lee Mortimer, in the *New York Daily Mirror*).
- "James Dean achieves the feat of making the

childish young fugitive believable and unembar-
rassing" (Richard Watts, Jr., in the *New York
Post*).

Jimmy's favorable notices derived from a won-
drously subdued combination of pathos and terror: to
Wally Wilkins he brought a kind of dreamy wonder, so
that his most plaintive lines—emerging from the forest
to ask, "Am I lost?" for example—were never arch or
cloying. Alternately feral and vulnerable, Wally sprang
to life as much from the imagination of James Dean as
from the pen of N. Richard Nash.

Henceforth, every role assumed by James Dean
capitalized on variations of Wally Wilkins in *See the
Jaguar*: he invariably portrayed a youthful variant on
the unleashed animal, sometimes sleek and tame, at
other times dangerous—but always acting according
to nature. He was forever the not yet mature boy confused by his fate, wrapped in uncertainty, mistrust-
ing himself and a world perceived as hostile to any
shade of individuality. That the variations on a theme
occurred with astonishing frequency owed not to the
deliberate intention of producers, directors or writers
creating according to Nash's model, but because as a
type Wally Wilkins was James Dean. From December
1952 to August 1955, he, perhaps more than any actor
in Hollywood history, assumed roles that were tai-
lored to his experience and his personality, made his
own by himself and set before audiences with a brutal sensitivity that was fresh and free of stereotype.
His was a limited talent, but within the borders of
those limitations there was something of both the

perplexed refinement of Montgomery Clift's image and the cool contempt of Marlon Brando's. With good reason could he sign occasional notes to friends—"From James-Brando-Clift-Dean."

The company's sense of doom about the future of the play had taken root out of town, even before the New York critics came to the Cort, and there was no false bravado at the cast party at Sardi's after the opening on Wednesday, December 3. As Dizzy and Bill recalled, it was a shining night for Jimmy, who was much the center of adulation that evening, for he was that perennial cause for excitement, the attractive unknown apprentice whose debut, everyone sensed, would be trumpeted as the arrival of an important new talent. Jimmy thrived on the attention, the congratulations, the requests for autographs and photos, as if he were making a thousand a week as a major star, not the total of a mere $75 he received for the four days of performances.

But as so often happens, there were losses accompanying the excitement. From that evening, he saw little of Bill Bast and even less of Dizzy Sheridan. "He sort of disappeared after that," she recalled with some regret: it seemed as if he had been in some way apotheosized by fame. "And I felt very sad about it all—happy for him, of course—but I knew nothing would be the same. I saw him a few more times, but he wasn't at all warm and open as he used to be. There was something too guarded, too casual." It was, in other words, just as he had feared when he asked Dizzy to marry him: he got caught up in it all, too deeply, too fast, and his subsequent ascendancy to fame when he was transplanted to Hollywood had, as so often, unfortunate consequences. "It's hard for Jimmy to trust a person," wrote the sagacious columnist Sidney Skolsky, who knew little of Dean's early years, "and it's easy for a person to rub him the wrong way." This was a sentiment echoed many times over by those who tried to befriend James Dean—and one with which he sometimes concurred. "I'm a serious-minded and intense little devil," he admitted, "terribly gauche and so tense I don't see how people stay in the same room with me. I know I wouldn't tolerate myself." It was one of the rare occasions he revealed the tendency to self-analysis and the gravity of his self-disgust.

"In the beginning," Dizzy continued,

when we first met, I felt he was afraid, he clung to me so. Then it was I who was afraid, and I started to cling to him, and he didn't want the responsibility of anyone doing that because he was going up, too fast, and anyone would be just extra added weight. Yet from that time on, he had a lousy attitude about working. It seemed like he didn't care about rehearsals. He didn't care about the way he dressed. Sometimes he didn't even care about whether he was decent to people or not, as long as he was acting . . . When I went to visit him at a hotel, he seemed in even a worse condition, more hard and bitter than before [when he visited her in New Jersey the previous summer]. I

wished we could have been back in Indiana,
where I saw how completely serene he could be.

Shortly after, Dizzy Sheridan's work took her away
from New York. She did not see Jimmy for two years,
and their reunion was not happy. "He was complex
and he was troubled, but I will always remember the
little-boy side of Jimmy—his high giggles, his love of
animals, his sweetness with children and old people,
his passion to learn everything quickly, before it was
too late to learn anything. And I remember his need to
be loved—an infinite need, I remember thinking. He
was like a bottomless well. No matter how much anyone or everyone offered, no love was enough."

Jimmy had tried to sustain the relationships with
both Dizzy and Rogers, but then he made no effort to
sustain either one. For the rest of his life he fought battles with his past, his parents, himself, his sexuality, his
career the only way he could—in brawls, arguments,
moodiness or races against time. Had he been able to
deal with his demons internally, where they festered
and poisoned him; had he been able to mature to the
point of some kind of emotional or psychospiritual
assistance, he would perhaps not have been so filled
with self-recrimination.

By the end of 1952, he had enough money to keep
the room at the Iroquois Hotel when Bill Bast left for a
writing job in Los Angeles. Jimmy offered his friend a
parting gift, a copy of the works of André Maurois
which he knew Bast liked and in which he had
inscribed "To Bill—While in the aura of metaphysical
whoo-haas, ebb away your displeasures on this. May

flights of harpies escort you on your winged trip of violence." If the rather muddy sentiment was genuine, the words, which doubtless Dean thought sophisticated and poetic (he was not subtle enough for literary satire), are virtually meaningless. There is, indeed, something both immature and sad about the feeble attempt to sound enlightened and erudite.

Jimmy also bought himself a Christmas present, the flutelike woodwind instrument known as a recorder. The Winslows offered to bring him home for Christmas, but he declined. During the holidays, he sketched, loped around Broadway and slapped his bongo drums with a few Greenwich Village acquaintances. Then, as winter's gray light hung over the city, Jimmy found a new interest. To increase his physical flexibility and lose some of the stiffness that resulted from limited exercise, he enrolled in classes with the dancer and choreographer Katherine Dunham. But as with all his interests, it was fleeting, and initial enthusiasm soon turned to indifference and withdrawal. "He was a dabbler," according to photographer Dennis Stock.

Late in the long, cold winter evenings, he often sat alone at his hotel window. When he was sleepless, he often rose from bed and played long, sad threnodies on the recorder. "Being an actor is the loneliest thing in the world," he said that season. "You're all alone with your imagination, and that's all you have." Jane Deacy passed along to him a stack of holiday cards and admiring letters from fans of his Wally Wilkins, but he left the envelopes sealed until the new year.

chapter seven

> Homosexuality is neither a
> vice nor a degradation, and
> it is certainly nothing to
> be ashamed of. It is a great
> injustice to persecute homo-
> sexuality as a crime—and a
> cruelty, too.
>
> SIGMUND FREUD

He did not stay long at the Iroquois. Early in the new year 1953, Jimmy rented an apartment at 19 West Sixty-eighth Street— one miniature room, once a maid's chamber, to which he had to climb five flights of narrow stairs. There was space only for a daybed, a built-in desk and a hotplate. Light entered through two round porthole windows, and for decoration a pair of bull's horns and a mata- dor's cape were affixed to one wall. Usually, as friends recalled, the place was a disastrous mess of empty beer cans, half-eaten food, unsleeved recordings and some books on theater.

The reason for Jimmy's move from the hotel was

uncomplicated. In 1952, Manhattan hotels did not permit unmarried men to invite women to their rooms. He had met a tall, slender, lively young apprentice actress named Barbara Glenn. Their erratic affair, alternately passionate and detached during much of 1953, was far more volatile than the one with Dizzy Sheridan. Barbara found him "insecure, uptight, trying very desperately to make conversation, badly." They had, she recalled "a lot of fights."

Jimmy and Barbara were, in the final analysis, emotionally mismatched: Barbara spoke her mind, while Jimmy "wouldn't communicate." She retained images of friends approaching him at a restaurant or at a social gathering, and he often simply turned away:

> It was as if suddenly you ceased to exist and he couldn't care less. You were an annoyance. And it was something, when he did it to me, that I just couldn't cope with. He wasn't a very social human being, or a nice person to a lot of people. Jimmy was not good at reaching out, [and] he was so frightened of letting people in. He'd show you some of himself, you'd really share something, and then you'd feel him backing off. He sensed his isolation, though he often caused it.

Finally, Barbara Glenn wearied of the outbursts and the silent treatments when Jimmy refused to answer his telephone or to reply to her letters. The romance (if

such it can be called) cooled long before Jimmy
departed New York in early 1954.

He was, however, good at "reaching out" to those he
admired or from whom he hoped for favors. One of
these was Montgomery Clift, whom Jimmy had
revered ever since he saw *A Place in the Sun*, and whom
he now pestered with telephone calls put through to
his East Side residence. According to Clift's biographer,
Patricia Bosworth, the conversations were remarkably
one-sided, with Dean usually muttering something
like: "Uh—hello, man—uh—this is Jimmy Dean—uh—
how are you?" The calls were (thus Clift) "mainly to
listen to the sound of my voice."

"He's a punk but a helluva talent," Elia Kazan told
Clift (whom he had directed in *The Skin of Our Teeth*)
when asked the theater gossip about the importunate
Dean. "They say he likes racing cars and bikes,
waitresses—and waiters. They say you're his idol."
Clift, doubly cautious when theater world gossip carried accounts of Dean's bisexual adventures, was terrified of having his own private life publicly disclosed.
He was even more wary of having to finesse an
amorous advance from Jimmy, who seemed almost
obsessed with getting to know him. At the same time,
Jimmy was trying to contact Marlon Brando, another
Kazan protégé, in New York and Hollywood. Brando,
in full leather motorcycle gear, roared onto the nation's
screens as *The Wild One* in December 1953, a character
who, when asked what he was rebelling against, muttered the quickly legendary reply, "What have you
got?" From that time, the James Dean adulation of
Marlon Brando reached fever pitch. In frank imitation,
Jimmy first rented and then purchased a motorcycle;

the image was then completed with a black leather jacket, jeans and white T-shirts.

He also tried to pattern his career on that of Brando, whose Broadway credits had included a 1946 production of Shaw's *Candida* with Katherine Cornell. Mildred Dunnock, who was planning yet another revival, met that year with the distinguished critic, author and playwright Eric Bentley. Longing to play Brando's role of the sensitive but fierce poet Marchbanks, Jimmy asked for a meeting with them, but Bentley and Dunnock agreed he was inappropriate for the role. "He arrived wearing the sort of ill-fitting, secondhand clothes one could buy from a sidewalk salesman," according to Bentley. "He was earnest, but this role was, we thought, beyond him." Said Mildred Dunnock, after Dean had departed, "He looks more the part of a gas station attendant than an English poet."

There were no classic plays for him, but during 1953 Jimmy had roles in sixteen television programs. Many of these were negligible walk-ons—as, for example, the minor assignment as a laboratory assistant to Rod Steiger, a mad scientist in an episode of the *Tales of Tomorrow* series. But other roles were more substantial. Dick Dunlap, who directed him in Rod Serling's "A Long Time Till Dawn," thought him undisciplined, rumpled, dirty and invariably late for rehearsals, as if Jimmy cared not at all about his career and would blithely have it sabotaged by his own indifference. Dunlap was on the mark, for there was indeed something deeply unhelpful to himself in Jimmy's character—a clash between the longing to succeed (for success would win him applause, approval and acceptance) and the hatred of success (which he felt he did not deserve and distrusted for its attendant fame). Nevertheless, Dunlap was like the other television directors: they had to admit that when the airdate arrived, Jimmy sprang to the performance with invariably apt technique.

As Joe Harris in "A Long Time Till Dawn"—a curious variant of *See the Jaguar*—Jimmy played an ex-convict who accidentally kills an old man. He flees to his family, and his embrace of them is hungry with desire and the need of protection. Rejected by his rigid, suspicious father (shades of Winton Dean), he seems to crumple, to shrink in stature as if reverting to childhood; and when he begs his wife for understanding, he seems to address a lost mother. In these scenes, the emotional truth certainly derives, however unconsciously, from Jimmy's connection with his own history. "He's a poet and he's a gangster," says one of the characters about Joe/Jimmy. "He's a sensitive kid. He's got brains, but he has the logic of a little boy."

Before the police track down Joe Harris and shoot him dead, he crawls into bed, cradling his high-school football like a doll, alternately weeping and laughing hysterically. The image of James Dean as vulnerable renegade was thus reinforced for an audience wider than that on Broadway. At the same time, to Barbara Glenn and others, he began to speak of writing a television story about Billy the Kid. Violent, crude, defined by primal instincts—Billy was Jimmy's alter ego in life as he would be made to conform to him in death.

More was the pity, therefore, that "A Long Time

Till Dawn," very like the majority of Dean's television appearances, was so badly constructed. Much of live television in the 1950s had no third act: even with an hour's time, scripts often seemed to plod aimlessly, overburdened with a surfeit of ideas yet poorly written characters. In a story that went nowhere, James Dean gave a convincingly naturalistic performance, scratching his head, tripping on words, cutting himself off in mid-sentence just like an uneducated, hapless crook. Cornered in his bedroom in the position of a wounded, frightened animal just before he is shot dead by police, Jimmy broke down in tears. He was remembered, after such performances, for his strengths, not for his weaknesses—nor for those of the vehicles that paradoxically served him so well. He may have suspected that Hollywood talent scouts were watching television.

Andrew McCullough also directed Jimmy in 1953, in "Glory in the Flower," an offering of the famous *Omnibus* series. The author was William Inge, famous that year for his Broadway hit *Picnic*. (The program's genial host, Alistair Cooke, introduced the teleplay "by the same gifted writer who gave us that fine play, *Pickwick*.") Years later, McCullough had clear memories of Jimmy's talent and his intractability. Inge himself, who had seen *See the Jaguar*, recommended the actor for the role of (what else?) a troubled adolescent, one of a group of rude teens who upset polite adults at a roadside inn; mainstream authors and producers were beginning to capitalize on the contemporary waves of adolescent rebellion.

Inge had warned McCullough of Dean's reputation, but believed he had a real talent that might be tapped and tamed. When Dean came in to read for McCullough and Inge, according to the director,

> He was wearing boots and brandishing a pocket knife, which he threw onto the tabletop. I told him that was enough, and then he settled down and read very well. Bill Inge rolled his eyes to heaven, as much for surprise as for pleasure.

Rehearsals proceeded with the swiftness typical of live television in the 1950s, Dean his usual quiet, sometimes sullen self, ignoring a small team of admiring young girls who had small roles in the teleplay and who buzzed around him like moths at a flame. He assiduously ignored them, McCullough recalled, and never tried to charm or attract them. "I never saw any young actor with more magnetism, and no matter how he turned, Jimmy was perhaps the most photogenic person I ever directed—he had no bad angle."

As for Jimmy's performance, it was as memorable as those of the two established stars of the piece, Hume Cronyn and Jessica Tandy, and he stood out in the minimal role of Bronco. He drinks, smokes dope and generally makes himself disagreeable to his elders. Then, when he and his cronies dance too wildly and generate a dust-up with proprietor Cronyn, Dean whines, "Everybody blames me!" There would be a straight line from "Glory in the Flower" to *Rebel Without a Cause*, and Jimmy's slouched, disaffected antihero was nothing so much as an unwitting preparation for that film's Jim Stark.

Hume Cronyn, a thoroughbred professional with major stage and screen credits, deeply resented Jimmy's spontaneous improvisations during technical and dress rehearsals, both of them crammed into a day's work and running right up to live airtime. He thought Jimmy's manner said, "I'm here—pay attention—and I don't give a damn what you think." For a scene in which he was to find a forbidden bottle of whiskey brought to the bar by one of the underage teens, Cronyn was to rummage briefly before finding it in the hip pocket of the nearest actor. But at the technical run-through, the bottle was not to be found, and Cronyn fumbled angrily.

"Where is it, Jimmy?" Cronyn asked.

"Why don't you just find it?"

"Is it worth it? I think I can act hunting for it."

McCullough raced down from the director's control booth and asked Jimmy for the bottle, which he naughtily withdrew: it was the rude bulge protruding from the front of his trousers.

As the clock ticked toward airtime, the cast and crew raced through a dress rehearsal. The brawl scene between two teens occurred, and Cronyn, as the nervous innkeeper, had to push Jimmy away from his challenger. But when he got to the ruckus, Jimmy could not be found. He had left his cue marks and was so far away that Cronyn had to rearrange the blocking to find him, and with that the older actor lost his temper. "See that?" he said, indicating the studio wall clock as he grasped Jimmy's arm and whirled him to the right spot. "It says twenty-two minutes to air time, and we haven't yet finished the dress [rehearsal]. For Christ's sake be where you're supposed to be!"

"I was trying something new," Jimmy replied. "I wanted to confuse you—you should be confused."

"I was! I am! But I can act confused. Keep that experimental shit for rehearsal or your dressing room! You're not alone out here!" With that, Jimmy apologized, but when they happened to meet several weeks later, Jimmy embraced Cronyn and said with a shy smile, "I forgive you, Mr. Cronyn. You were nervous." Cronyn, to his own astonishment, was speechless.

As was Andrew McCullough: he found Jimmy amazingly considerate when he directed him again the following year in the television drama "The Little Woman," which referred not to a housewife but to a little girl. Casting executive and author Joe Scully was concerned about Jimmy's growing reputation as a difficult colleague, so he warned him that the slightest misconduct would mean dismissal. Jimmy seemed hurt, explaining that his habit of deep exploration into roles angered producers and directors—which indeed it did, for so little time was available. Nevertheless, Jimmy promised to cooperate—and so he did, almost certainly because his co-star was an eight-year-old girl.

As a delinquent on the run who takes refuge in a child's playhouse, Jimmy was (thus McCullough)

> the consummate professional. His acting was not only tremendously fluid. He became egoless—he was just wonderful with the child actress, Lydia Reed, and because of him they both gave touching performances.

Not for the first time, Jimmy became gentle, considerate—even fatherly—in the presence of a wary child; in a way, he was nurturing himself in his kindness with young Lydia. But such quiet grace during "The Little Woman" was anomalous.

Despite the frequency of his uncollegial gaffes and his growing reputation for defiant behavior, Jimmy was making an impression in the hasty, confused and uneven world of New York live television—although the range of roles was usually limited to variations on a theme of disaffected but vulnerable youth. In "Keep Our Honor Bright," he portrayed Jim Cooper, summoned by college fraternity brothers for cheating on a senior final examination. Because his father and grandfather are due to arrive any moment from California for commencement exercises, Cooper pleads not to be expelled; in this scene, his voice becomes strangulated with embarrassed remorse. But the fraternity recommends to the dean that he be expelled—and with that, Cooper swallows an overdose of sleeping pills. He recovers, however, and exposes forty other cheaters. George Roy Hill's script, full of good intentions about honor and commitment, then stops flat. All cheaters are expelled, and television audiences were perhaps uncertain how they were to feel about James Dean's role.

Never mind: viewers knew quite clearly how they were responding to the actor, and letters poured in to NBC's *Kraft Television Theatre*, many of them from heartsick girls eager for a date and concerned mothers who confused the role with the actor and offered James Dean good home-cooked meals and a room in a safe home. Nor did television watchers object to more sentimentalized roles—that of Joey Frazier in "The Bells of

Cockaigne," for example, in which he played a young husband with an asthmatic child who works in a factory shipping department. Appearing stripped to the waist, Jimmy exhibited not the strapping, toned physique some viewers may have imagined, but the unformed, somewhat flabby body of a pre-adolescent boy. He was no longer playing basketball, no longer racing around the bases or jumping hurdles. But at that time no one seemed to mind, and of course this was irrelevant to a touching performance as a worried father.

Equally moving was Jimmy's performance as a young man wrongly accused of murder, in "Sentence of Death." Hours before the scheduled execution, he is visited by arresting officers seeking confirmation of fresh doubts of his guilt. Affecting blithe unconcern, Jimmy makes a swift, credible dramatic transition when he thinks of his lost family and the girl he will never love again. As he had done with the role of the lad in "Abraham Lincoln," the poignancy was achieved by understating both fear and grief—the small catch of breath, the stifled sob, the sudden welling of tears, just as quickly checked.

He was equally effective in two shows directed by James Sheldon, who was eager to help his friend's career. The first was "Harvest," for *Robert Montgomery Presents*, in which Jimmy was an awkward country bumpkin who falls in love with a slick city girl, is rejected, and joins the Navy. There was not much drama here, but Jimmy drew all eyes to himself with his understated agony, his character's apparent lack of self-understanding, and the haze of pain that washes across his face when he realizes that his love is unrequited. When no letters arrive from his girlfriend, for example, he rests his chin lightly on the mailbox, and slowly lowers his gaze to one side. With each television performance, he learned the value of subtlety during close-ups, of toning down reactions, of conveying inner turmoil without any exterior sign of anguish. It was, in other words, a perfect rehearsal for working in feature films. In "Harvest," Sheldon recalled years later, "Jimmy was wonderful to work with—malleable and cooperative, and everybody loved him."

The situation was different in the next drama Sheldon directed with Dean—the aforementioned "The Bells of Cockaigne," broadcast in March 1954. The date is significant, for by this time Jimmy had been cast as Cal Trask in Elia Kazan's forthcoming film of John Steinbeck's *East of Eden*, "and with this role in his pocket [thus James Sheldon], Jimmy was more difficult, with a certain independent attitude that made things rough for me and the cast. For one thing, he kept everyone waiting at expensive rehearsal time—which of course increased the budget, because we had a live orchestra in the studio, and the musicians were paid by the hour!"

But tardiness was not the worst offense. Veteran actor Gene Lockhart, the star of "Cockaigne," complained to Sheldon during rehearsals that he found Jimmy "impossible—he never says the same line twice the same way, or even with the same words! Won't you please talk to him and try to get him to be more professional?" Sheldon did, gently but firmly scolding Jimmy and warning him that such carelessness would lose him the goodwill of his colleagues and might well jeopardize his career; he ought to check this unfortunate tendency to be difficult.

"Difficult?" Jimmy replied, affecting surprise. "Why everyone on this show loves me! Everyone enjoys working with me —just ask Gene Lockhart, he's crazy about me!" This was scarcely close to the truth, and Jimmy's conduct did not improve. Moments before they were to go live on the air the following week, Jimmy could not be found, and Sheldon had to seek him at a local drugstore, where Jimmy was calmly sipping soda. Then, during the live performance, Jimmy—in a gesture not rehearsed—bit into an apple during some dialogue with Lockhart.

"Why did you do that?" Lockhart asked when they were off-camera.

"Because I felt like it."

"Why didn't you feel like it during rehearsals?" asked Lockhart, rightly annoyed at Jimmy for an unprepared bit of business that had only one goal—turning the viewers' attention to himself. "On 'Harvest' he was an angel," according to Sheldon. "But on 'The Bells of Cockaigne' we had trouble. He was changing, trying new methods for his own benefit." Nevertheless, Sheldon stood by Dean, sustaining in a generous and delicate balance his unpredictable moods, his orneriness, his surprising acts of friendship—and always encouraging him to stretch his talent.

Producer Franklin Heller (who had known him from his stint with *Beat the Clock*) recalled Jimmy's work with Betsy Palmer and the veteran stage actor Walter Hampden (then seventy-four) in "Death Is My Neighbor," in which Jimmy portrayed a psychotic janitor. Jimmy was invariably late for rehearsals and, without a shred of respect for Hampden or the other players and crew, arrived scruffy, used foul language and generally made himself disagreeable. Dismissing the script as "a piece of shit," Jimmy threw it on the floor and stormed off to sulk. Heller remonstrated with him, reminding Jimmy that he was working with the great Hampden and ought to show more respect. Jimmy insisted he had never heard of Hampden; Heller begged for more cooperation and better manners. Later, Jimmy's foul language was heard again—and after a third time, Heller threatened him with dismissal and Jimmy was saved only when Hampden took the producer aside. "He's untutored but talented," said the older actor to the producer, "and I think it's wrong for us to retard him." And with that act of patience and generosity, the show continued and Dean's job was saved.

As it happened, Hampden was on the mark and the performance gained Jimmy one of his rare television notices. "James Dean stole the spotlight," wrote the reviewer for *Variety* on September 2, 1953, praising his "magnetic performance that brought a routine [melo-drama] alive. Dean's performance was in many ways reminiscent of Marlon Brando's in *Streetcar*, but he gave his role the individuality and nuances of its own which it required. He's got quite a future ahead of him."

In an odd way, Jimmy helped to secure this future by refusing, in 1953, ever to discuss anything political with anyone—which was not difficult, since he had no such interests. But he had to be careful of his company and more careful of an idle remark. The Communist witch-hunt was sending waves of fear and repression throughout the television industry as it did in Hollywood, and the effect of having one's name listed in a weekly newsletter called *Counterattack: The*

Newsletter of Facts on Communism was too terrible to contemplate. "Communist actors, announcers, directors, writers, producers . . . should be barred from working," urged the newsletter, founded by three former employees of the Federal Bureau of Investigation. Their dangerous vigilante group ran American Business Consultants, Inc., which had the goal of purging the media of anyone who read the *New York Post* (a liberal newspaper with a Democratic editorial policy), who admitted to living in Greenwich Village or who had a history of helping war refugees, fighting racism, opposing censorship, criticizing HUAC and favoring good relations with the Soviet Union. Jimmy did not want his name added to the list of 151 people considered worthy of blacklisting—a virtual catalogue raisonné of some of the most gifted people in the arts at that time.*

But because he was resolutely apolitical, it did not follow that Jimmy was not interested in controversy; in fact, it is no exaggeration to say that his most enjoyable form of social intercourse was controversial conversation, and the occasional descent into shock for its own sake. In this regard, he used his friends for reactions, just as he depended on bright, creative people to supply what he felt was lacking in his education.

---

* Among those who suffered—many of them simply for sending a congratulatory telegram to Russia on the anniversary of the Moscow Art Theater—were Vera Caspary, Lee J. Cobb, Aaron Copland, Olin Downes, Alfred Drake, José Ferrer, John Garfield, Ruth Gordon, Uta Hagen, Lillian Hellman, Judy Holliday, Lena Horne, Langston Hughes, Burl Ives, Garson Kanin, Arthur Laurents, Joseph Losey, Burgess Meredith, Arthur Miller, Edward G. Robinson, Pete Seeger, Artie Shaw, Howard K. Smith and Orson Welles.

One amiable and loyal friend from this time was Jonathan Gilmore (later the writer John Gilmore), a handsome man five years Jimmy's junior with a lengthier list of credits as an actor. Raised in Los Angeles, he had appeared as a child in small roles and worked consistently in films, television and radio. He decided to be an art major but never lost his interest in acting, although he resented the sexual pressures often put on virile and dapper young actors. In 1953, at the urging of his friend, the actress-director Ida Lupino, Gilmore went to New York to pursue his career, and in the spring of 1953 he met Jimmy through a mutual friend. An easy camaraderie soon emerged, for Jonathan and Jimmy were both devoted to their careers, interested in the art of bullfighting and willing to experiment with life at all its various levels.

"There was something solid and focused about Jimmy," Gilmore said years later, "but I remember sensing that he needed to see things through to a point where they related to himself. He worried everything into a relationship with himself—and then, just as suddenly, he would drop the issue or the person. He seemed to me someone who could become as obsessed with people as he did with sculpture or poetry or a role, and then—presto!—he lost interest."

In 1953, Gilmore was eighteen—not naive, but certainly no opportunist: he had, after all, broken a professional relationship with a powerful agent (representative of, among other gay actors, Rock Hudson) because Gilmore was vexed by the agent's sexual pressure. Precisely at this time, with rumors circulating of the bisexuality of Marlon Brando and the confused, closeted homosexuality of Montgomery Clift, Jimmy longed to experiment with gay sex for its own sake—not, as with Rogers Brackett, because there were identifiable perquisites. Jonathan Gilmore—handsome, savvy, congenial—seemed the perfect partner. And Jimmy, to cement the friendship, inquired about the details of Gilmore's own early years, which were in some ways as unhappy as his own. "He asked me a great deal about myself," according to Gilmore, "but he gave little in return—and then he seemed to regret sharing anything at all, as if to share was to give part of himself away."

The sexual innuendo was not long in coming. "His intense interest in gay sex seemed as intense as his passion for the heroics of bullfighting or sculpture," Gilmore continued. "He wanted to fool around, to do the forbidden thing, to be artsy, a renegade and an outsider. But as for being a hustler or a whore—well, I don't know anyone who had an indication that was true. He never had to hustle, and he certainly was not some promiscuous madman." Yet—perhaps partly out of adulation for his heroes Brando and Clift, as for the writers and artists he admired whose lives were resoundingly unconventional—Jimmy became known as something of a dabbler in the varieties of sexual experience; even in the repressed 1950s, it seemed, sex could have a political subtext. There was no question that Gilmore and Dean had a strong attraction to each other, but (contrary to more imaginatively lurid accounts) the intimacy between them was, they discovered very quickly, sexually awkward and unsatisfying ("Frankly, it just didn't work" was Gilmore's forthright summation)—and they did not attempt it again. Rightly, neither of them tripped over into a paroxysm of anguish, guilt or gloom.

Nevertheless, Jimmy liked to do what Gilmore called "weird things," such as prevailing on Jonathan to attend a wild Greenwich Village party as his date— in drag, which was in itself not so outrageous even in 1953. But then Jimmy staged an elaborate fight in which Jonathan was revealed (to Jimmy's "surprise") to be a man in costume—and then an equally elaborate scene of kissing and making up would ensue, doubtless devised to further shock the guests. At such times, no one could be quite sure just what James Dean wanted—a pliable man, a strong woman, a man who cradled him like a woman, a woman who acted like a man . . . It was all very confusing, perhaps most of all to Jimmy himself.

But what became clear to Gilmore (as it did to Bast, Sheridan, White and others in the months to come) was that Dean needed people absolutely committed and devoted to him, people of unquestioning loyalty who would invariably be present to him—until he decided to drop them. None of this, in light of his childhood trauma, is difficult to understand. Terrified of losing anyone's affection, he often fell into the habit of attracting men and women, becoming obsessed with the veracity of their attachment to him—and then, precisely because he disbelieved in the permanence of any love, he rejected before he could be rejected.

The matter of James Dean's bisexual conduct should not, however, be neatly categorized as simple manipulation, much less as a desire to attract and achieve pleasure wherever he could find it. In the world of young actors in the 1950s, sexual experimentation was, for many, part of a renegade posture. To be unconventional sexually was a variant of political or social liberalism.

Sometimes, to be sure, liberalism became libertinism.
But there are many stories, some told, others carefully
guarded, of women and men both inside and outside
the arts who made no great puritanical fuss about
moments in their youth when they wandered along sexual byways they later abandoned.

Besides, as Gilmore recognized, whatever Jimmy's
personal or sexual pastimes, he was most of all obsessed
with himself and his career. Yet except for a brief, wordless role in *The Scarecrow* that June, based on a Nathaniel
Hawthorne story, there was no theater work for Jimmy
until late in 1953. (He coveted the role of the sensitive
young man in *Tea and Sympathy*, but playwright Robert
Anderson and director Elia Kazan realized he was not
right for the part, which was superbly acquitted by John
Kerr.) Eli Wallach, Anne Jackson and Patricia Neal
appeared in leading roles in *The Scarecrow*, and there
was a small stipend. Jimmy wrote to Barbara Glenn,
then out of town, that he hoped to learn from the other
players, and from director Frank Corsaro. Barbara,
meantime, was sending him small checks, as were the
Winslows. "Got a new pair of shoes, honey," he wrote to
Barbara after receiving some money from her.

> Shit! I'm so proud of them. Got a pair of pants,
> too. My uncle sent me $30.00 and besides I
> deserved it. Made me feel good just to go in
> and get something. I would like to see you
> very much. I miss you too. Didn't figure on
> that too strong. But you just can't tell always, I
> guess. I'm getting sleepy. You write me real
> soon. You hear? Then I'll write again.

She did write, and he responded, with a typical amalgam of ornery distrust and literary affectation, seasoned with a little gin:

> I never suspected one could know as few nice people as I know. My own damn fault. Lamas [sic] and scientists may fume and quander [?]. Everything is not just illusion. You are my proof. You have gone to Israel but you have not. I am very lonely for you. I am alone. Thoughts are sweet, then wicked, then perverse, then penitent, then sweet. The moon is not blue. It hangs there in the sky no more.
>
> Please forgive me for such a sloppy letter, I'm a little drunk, drink quite a bit lately. You see, I don't know what's going on any more than you do. Remarkable lot, human beings. I care too.
>
> In antiphonal azure swing, souls drone their unfinished melody . . . When did we live and when did we not? In my drunken stupor I said a gem. I must repeat it to you loved one. Let's see "great actors are often time pretentious livers. The pretentious actor, a great liver." (Don't get a headache over it.) God Damnit!! I miss you . . . You're terribly missing. Come back. Maybe I can come up and see you. You think you need understanding? Who do you think you are? I could use a little myself. You're probably running around up there with all those handsome guys. When I get my boat, you'll be sorry.

> Hope you're ok up there. Working pretty
> hard I guess. More than you can say for us
> poor thespians back here in the city.
>
> Got to move out of this crappy old apart-
> ment. Can't get along with nobody I guess.
> Makes you feel good when you're not wanted.
>
>   Love, Jim

With reason did Barbara have the impression that she was often dealing with a schoolboy.

Such was the impression, too, of many who came to know and work with James Dean that winter of 1953–54—especially the producer and entire company of *The Immoralist*, his second and last Broadway appearance. As a wily young Arab blackmailer who preys on a married homosexual's fears of exposure, Dean had a role smaller than that of Wally Wilkins in *See the Jaguar*; it was also a pivotal, controversial part full of character possibilities and bound to be discussed by critics and audiences.

Adapted by Ruth and Augustus Goetz from André Gide's autobiographical novel *L'Immoraliste*, the play traces the lives of Michel, a handsome, wealthy but physically frail young archeologist, and Marcelline, whom he marries in a doomed attempt to suppress his homosexuality. Set in Normandy and North Africa in 1900 and 1901, the action centers on the attempts of the couple to love each other yet remain true to their very different needs. As the play opens, Michel has just buried his father, whose will stipulates that the son's inheritance be placed in trust against the possibility of his scandalous conduct. The father's reservations, it turns out, were based on Michel's expulsion from school at the age of eleven for "a sin of the flesh with another boy." Stunned by his father's distrust and eager to disprove the suspicions, he accepts a marriage proposal from a childhood friend, Marcelline.

To improve Michel's health, the newlyweds travel to North Africa; their marriage, much to Marcelline's frustration, is still unconsummated after two months. There, surrounded by the easy carnality of Arab boys eager for quick cash or easy sex or both, it is impossible for Michel to deny his true orientation any longer. A hired houseboy and alluring con artist named Bachir taunts the couple and provides his master with access to the local gay scene and an array of possible lovers. Marcelline slips quietly into alcoholic despair, and Michel, driven by Bachir's taunts, forces himself to bed with his wife. This one night effects her pregnancy, but she is so bereft by knowledge of her husband's true nature that she decides to leave him and return to France alone, there to await the birth of her child. Michel follows her, determined to share his parental responsibilities. The play's final lines set forth the uneasy chart of the couple's marital journey as they attempt to negotiate the dangerous waters of compromise.

MARCELLINE: Tell me how to accept it [that is, his homosexuality] or to ignore it—to say to myself, this is only a fraction of him . . . How would we live together?

MICHEL: There are many kinds of marriages, and people sacrifice many things to hold on to them . . . We must promise nothing—except to like each other as we are.

MARCELLINE: You want me to accept all of you.

MICHEL: That's what our child will want.

MARCELLINE: I can do it for him.

MICHEL: Can you? Can I? And what will happen to him if we don't [accept all of me]?

MARCELLINE: We must learn, Michel. A good way will be to practice on each other.

The Immoralist was not the first Broadway play to deal with homosexuality (it had been variously treated as a principal or as a subordinate theme in, for example, plays by Lillian Hellman, Tennessee Williams and Robert Anderson), but the adaptation of Gide's novel by the Goetzes seemed astonishingly forthright for its time. Yet the adapters only suggested (and did not develop) the real concern of the book: that the protagonist is immoral not for being gay but for insisting on avoiding the consequences of his self-awareness, for insisting simultaneously on being true to self and conforming to the prudish demands of polite society. They wrote, in other words, in a spirit of what critic Eric Bentley called at the time "a kind of liberalism which is safely conservative, [carrying] all the soft and self-congratulatory motion of reformism without running the risks."

The Goetzes found the right producer in Billy Rose (who had brought to Broadway such controversial works as *Clash by Night* and *Carmen Jones*) and, they thought, the right director in Herman Shumlin (who had staged Lillian Hellman's plays *The Children's Hour* and *The Little Foxes*). Geraldine Page, who had recently triumphed in Viña Delmar's *Mid-Summer* and Tennessee Williams's *Summer and Smoke*, was signed for the role of Marcelline, and the French screen actor Louis Jourdan was to make his Broadway debut as Michel.

A dozen young actors auditioned for the part of Bachir, but from the start Shumlin favored Jimmy, whom he had seen in *See the Jaguar* and on television and whom he invited to read before Rose and the Goetzes. Wearing torn blue jeans and boots, Jimmy arrived at the producer's office one cold afternoon in November and, with Shumlin reading Marcelline's lines, acted the scene in which lazy Bachir tries to avoid housework. Ruth Goetz, whose first impression was that Dean's red-blond hair and pale skin made him woefully inappropriate for the part of an Arab, was quickly convinced he could handle it brilliantly. He had, she said, "the quality of sweetness and charming attractiveness, and at the same time a nasty undercurrent of suggestiveness and sexuality." Her colleagues agreed, and a contract was settled with Jane Deacy; Jimmy was to receive $300 a week for the run of the play—generous compensation, at the time, for a supporting role by an actor with only one previous Broadway credit. Billy Rose was, for the moment, content to go along with the director's and authors' choice.

But from the start there was trouble with *The Immoralist*.

Very early during December rehearsals, Jimmy established a strong rapport with Shumlin, serving the director as both filial acolyte and seductive protégé, and gaining him as ally while alienating many members of the company. "Herman was intrigued by Jimmy," recalled the play's assistant stage manager, Vivian Matalon, later a highly respected director in England and America. "And Jimmy recognized it. He was careful to wrap his arm around Herman's shoulder, as if he wanted his director to be also his father." For his part, Shumlin found Jimmy "a remarkable and unusual personality whose endless variety in experimenting with his role fascinated me—up to a point."

But the estimable Shumlin turned out to be the wrong choice as director. Terrified of the subject matter, he could not decide whether he wished to treat it boldly or timidly. In addition, the other cast members felt Shumlin was not sufficiently stern with Jimmy, who often appeared late for rehearsals and then stumbled on his lines. Paul Huber (the play's Dr. Garrin) complained that Jimmy was so intent on improvisation that he threw off the other players and centered attention only on himself; Adelaide Klein (as Sidma, an African servant) found Jimmy difficult to rehearse with; and everyone was annoyed when he parked his motorcycle backstage, thus creating a logistical nightmare.

Six days before the Philadelphia opening in January 1954, Shumlin was replaced by Daniel Mann, who had staged *Come Back, Little Sheba* and *The Rose Tattoo*. At once, Jimmy's attitude changed. Mann had no time (much less the inclination) to give a young supporting player the constant attention and support he craved, and Jimmy's behavior had turned uncooperative and unprofessional—even more so when his role was reduced. "I had this strange young man who

was defying the whole company," recalled Daniel
Mann. "I would ask him to do what he had to do, try
to communicate with him, but it was extremely difficult. He was a rebel." According to Mann, Jimmy
decided to play a scene differently each time he
rehearsed, acting only what came to his mind.

Losing all interest in the play and nervous about
being identified with the role of a seedy homosexual,
he lost all common sense about his career, and all sense
of collegial responsibility.

"Reason you didn't get a call Sat. morning," he
wrote to Barbara Glenn,

> was because (as usual) I just made the train [to
> Philadelphia]. Rehearsals are quite confusing
> at this point. Lighting etc. Can't tell much
> about the show yet. Looks like a piece of shit to
> me. Stereophonic staging and 3-D actors.
> Probably be a monster success . . . Hate this
> fucking brown make-up.

"The little son of a bitch was one of the most
unspeakably detestable fellows I ever knew in my life,"
said Ruth Goetz bluntly. "The little bastard would not
learn the words, would not really try to give a performance, would not really rehearse. He drove us up the
wall. The only person he made a connection to was
Geraldine Page, because Gerry was an artist he could
understand and she had great fellow feeling for him."
Page also rehearsed privately with Jimmy as the script
went through a flurry of revisions.

Jimmy did not even respond to Mann's critical notes, and in the end the director found him destructive to himself and the play—despite occasional flashes of real brilliance. Mann resented Jimmy's childish notions of what constituted real adult manhood, his habit of carrying a knife, of roaring his motorcycle: "I thought," said Mann, "that he was a very, very disturbed, very compulsive young man." The Philadelphia opening in late January was ragged, shot through with poor pacing and uncertain rhythms, largely due to the tension surrounding Jimmy Dean. "The company was divided between those who thought Jimmy was right to be offended at Shumlin's dismissal, and those who considered Jimmy a bastard," recalled Vivian Matalon. "In any case, his behavior was really awful, and he became too burdensome for the entire company."

Producer Billy Rose, ordinarily patient and content to let the director manage temperamental stars, lost his temper just before the New York opening. Mann was giving a recalcitrant and uncooperative Dean several points about playing a particular scene, and finally Rose interrupted. "Okay, Dean, this is Billy Rose talking! Shape up or ship out of here!"

With a slow turn of his head and a bored expression, Jimmy replied, "What did you say your name was?"

Rose stormed away, muttering about impertinence and afraid that, a moment later, he might indeed fire Dean—which would, of course, only cause serious trouble for the production.

Why would James Dean sabotage his own best interests at such an important time in his career? Why would he so alienate the company of *The Immoralist* that Ruth Goetz told Matalon to learn Bachir's lines in preparation for assuming the role if Billy Rose could finesse Dean's run-of-the-play contract and fire him?

The reason for his odd behavior was not merely Shumlin's dismissal, Mann's refusal to coddle Jimmy, or Jimmy's diffidence about playing a gay pimp (especially after his success as the sympathetic bumpkin in *See the Jaguar*). James Dean felt he had to find a way of quitting *The Immoralist*: creature of the moment as always, he had prospects for a far more exciting career, and despite Jane Deacy's counsel, he had quickly lost interest in the play and its other players.

His hopes were based on something that had happened on December 15, 1953, while the cast of *The Immoralist* was still rehearsing in New York. Executives of Warner Bros. were considering dozens of young actors for roles in *Battle Cry*, a war film to be directed by Raoul Walsh. William Orr was Jack Warner's executive delegate in New York, testing new young actors from Broadway and television, and every agent in town was sending clients for consideration. "Jimmy was the last one to be auditioned," Orr recalled years later. "He came in unshaven, wearing a cap, boots and full motorcycle regalia. I told him we were going to do a gentle love scene between a soldier and his girlfriend, whose father doesn't like the boy. And without a bit of preparation, Jimmy Dean gave a reading that was the best I'd ever heard."

Next morning, Orr—convinced he had found a talent to recommend to the executive offices in Burbank—tested Dean for another role in *Battle Cry*, and that afternoon he dispatched a letter to studio headquarters:

James Dean is a young man who is gaining quite a reputation as a fine young actor. We tested him today for [the role of] Ski, even though we didn't think him right for the part. There is a trace of the Marlon Brando school in his work. But he is not a conventional actor and brings much more ability to the scene than either of the two other [actors competing for the role].

Jimmy received neither of the roles in *Battle Cry* for which he read. But he had impressed William Orr, one of Warner's most intelligent, experienced and trusted executives, and he knew it.

Unhappy in *The Immoralist*, he hoped it would soon close and that he would be free to test again for a movie role. As it happened, the play had a three-month run after its New York premiere at the Royale on Jimmy's twenty-third birthday (February 8, 1954). But he was free of this assignment long before the final curtain rang down on May 1. By that time, he had left New York and was on the way to fleeting stardom but enduring celebrity.

chapter eight

> Transport of the human voice
> and of flickering pictures:
> in this century our highest
> accomplishments have the
> single aim of bringing us
> together.
>   ANTOINE DE SAINT-EXUPÉRY

No doubt about it: James Dean was the most controversial character in *The Immoralist*, and his performance as the corrupt Arab houseboy Bachir had, in the apt phrase of critic Brooks Atkinson, an "insidious charm." In a provocative scene with Louis Jourdan as Michel, for example, his diction—limpid, almost hypnotic—was both innocent and seductive:

BACHIR: Soon the warm season will come and I can spend the nights in the orchards.
MICHEL: The orchards?
BACHIR: Yes, sir—the trees are filled with fruits; dates,

figs, oranges, everything grows in the orchards. Many boys tend the crops, the earth, the goats. They are very beautiful, those places.

MICHEL: Where are they?

BACHIR: Which one, sir?

MICHEL: I don't know—the one you seem so poetic about.

BACHIR: They are all out there beyond the walls. It is always green and cool and they live like a thousand years ago.

MICHEL: And do whole families live there?

BACHIR: There are no families. Only men and boys. Beautiful men. They live without women.

MICHEL: Oh. That is not very interesting.

BACHIR: You asked me, sir.

MICHEL: You misunderstood me! And you eat disgustingly, Bachir!

BACHIR: Yes, sir. I think so. I am very healthy and disgusting.

Moments later, Jimmy kept the audience motionless, almost breathless—some of them shocked with his languorous dance of seduction around Louis Jourdan. Snapping his fingers over his head, moving like a sleek animal in native garb as suggestive as a thin robe, he wove a spell like a dark, dangerous angel of doom.

Despite its fetid candor, *The Immoralist* earned several respectable reviews for its poetic gravity, many excellent accounts of Geraldine Page, and a few laudatory comments for James Dean. His role was very brief, but several critics noted his "realistically unpleasant" performance as a "colorfully insinuating scapegrace" who "clearly and originally underlines sleazy impertinence and amoral opportunism." The consensus of New York reviews was, in fact, that he was "especially good." Critic Daniel Blum, editor of the *Theatre World* yearbooks, listed each year a number of "promising personalities" who struck his fancy. For the 1953–54 season, James Dean's name was among them.*

In the audience one February evening was the playwright and screenwriter Paul Osborn, who went home convinced that James Dean was perfect for a major role in a movie he had just written for Elia Kazan to direct—a free adaptation of portions of John Steinbeck's sprawling but undistinguished novel *East of Eden*. Next morning, Osborn telephoned Kazan, advising him to rush to the Royale to see James Dean. The director did not in fact see the play, but he agreed to meet Jimmy at Warners' New York offices. At first, Kazan was unimpressed by Dean: having directed Marlon Brando in the stage and screen versions of *A Streetcar Named Desire* and in the films *Viva Zapata!* and *On the Waterfront*, Kazan had Brando in mind for *East of Eden*—to play the role of the confused young man abandoned by his mother and starved for the love of his rigid, puritanical father.

"James Dean came to my office looking surly and unresponsive," recalled the director years later.

---

* The others: Orson Bean, Harry Belafonte, Joan Diener, Ben Gazzara, Carol Haney, Jonathan Lucas, Kay Medford, Scott Merrill, Elizabeth Montgomery, Leo Penn and Eva Marie Saint. James Dean did not win the Tony award, as so often has been claimed by fans. Nor was he the recipient of a Daniel Blum Theatre World Award as Best Newcomer of the Year.

He slouched on a sofa and, for no reason that I could fathom, he looked resentful and impatient. We tried to talk, but conversation was not his gift, so we sat looking at each other. He asked me if I wanted a ride on the back of his motorbike, so I went with him—and after that I wished I'd never met him! He was showing off—a country boy not impressed with big-city traffic.

But a second, equally casual meeting convinced Kazan that Osborn was right; Jimmy was sent along to meet John Steinbeck. "He didn't like him any more than I did," Kazan continued. "Dean was guarded, sullen, suspicious and vengeful. He seemed to me to have a great deal of concealed emotion."

Osborn and Steinbeck kept making favorable comparisons between Dean and Brando, but Kazan caught a crucial difference. Dean, he sensed, was in some fundamental way "twisted and sick—a very hurt person. He was suffused with self-pity and the anguish of rejection, and the main thing I sensed was [that he had been] hurt, which was also the main thing everybody else felt. You wanted to put your arm around him and protect him and look after him." Jimmy was, Kazan reckoned, the ideal person to play Caleb Trask in *East of Eden*. Since 1954, very many people maintain that this eventually became James Dean's finest performance, not to say the clearest portrait of himself.

Saying nothing about the meetings to anyone in *The Immoralist*, Jimmy made a test for Kazan and Warner Bros. at a Manhattan studio that February—a dramatic

Age four, 1935. (*Culver Pictures*)

(*Left*) At Fairmount High School, 1946. (*Culver Pictures*)

(*Below*) Front and center, Fairmount High, 1947.

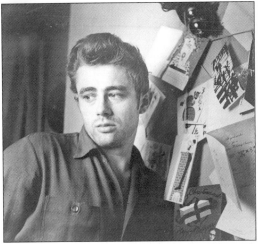

Christmas 1952, in New York. (*Culver Pictures*)

New York, 1953. (*Dennis Stock/Magnum Photos*)

Reading the Indiana poet, James Whitcomb Riley.
(*Dennis Stock/Magnum Photos*)

Test for *East of Eden* (February 1954), with Paul Newman.
(*Culver Pictures*)

As Cal Trask in *East of Eden*. (*Culver Pictures*)

With Julie Harris in *East of Eden*. (*Culver Pictures*)

In *East of Eden*. (*Culver Pictures*)

With Elia Kazan and Julie Harris, welcoming Marlon Brando
to the set of *East of Eden*.

New York, 1954. (*Roy Schatt*)

As Jim Stark, with Jim Backus, Edward Platt and Ann Doran, in *Rebel Without a Cause*, 1955. (*Culver Pictures*)

Preparing for a shot of *Rebel* with director Nicholas Ray. (*Courtesy of Joshua Smith*)

With Sal Mineo and Natalie Wood, in *Rebel Without a Cause*.
(*Culver Pictures*)

In Texas with director George Stevens, filming *Giant*,
summer 1955. (*Academy of Motion Picture Arts and Sciences*)

Diverting Elizabeth Taylor on the set of *Giant*
(with Rock Hudson).

At the Winslow farm,
Fairmount, 1955.
(*Dennis Stock/
Magnum Photos*)

The pose of a rebel.
(*Academy of Motion Picture Arts and Sciences*)

With his cousin Marcus Winslow, Jr., 1955.
(*Dennis Stock/Magnum Photos*)

Warner Brothers
publicity still.
(*Academy of Motion
Picture Arts and
Sciences*)

As Jeff Latham, in "The Unlightted Road" (television), May 1955. (*Culver Pictures*)

With Steffi Sidney, at the Villa Capri restaurant in Hollywood, August 1955. (*From the collection of Steffi Sidney*)

September 30, 1955. (*Culver Pictures*)

With his Porsche Speed-ster, 1955.
(*Culver Pictures*)

The first pilgrimage. (*Culver Pictures*)

(*Academy of Motion Picture Arts and Sciences*)

scene in black-and-white that presented the new stars, James Dean and (as his brother) Richard Davalos, who was a movie theater usher when discovered by Kazan. This remarkable test has survived, and it is startling testimony to the emotions Kazan could evoke from Dean. In a scene eventually excised from the final script, Dean, clad in pajamas and playing a lament on his own recorder, puts the instrument aside to ask Davalos why their father cannot love him, too. "It's because you haven't tried to love Dad," Davalos replies.

"I don't know how, Aron," Jimmy says in a choked whisper, the faintest sob trembling in his throat.

"It's easy, Cal—you just have to try."

A haze of pain washes over Jimmy's face, on which the camera remains in unflinching close-up. He tries to smile, tears glisten, and he nods. "I know—I know." Fade out.

Seldom has a swiftly produced screen test been so affecting, seldom has it promised so much for the final product. Kazan was vindicated by the enthusiasm of Jack Warner and the casting office in Burbank.

The tradition of a pro forma announcement from the studio, by means of a national press release, required a temporary but absolute silence from everyone about Elia Kazan's new film, with its new faces. But word got around that Kazan was burnishing a new young talent. "You're going to need all your patience," Hume Cronyn said a few days later when he met up with his old friend Kazan. "But he's very talented," was the reply, "and we've hired him."

As for Davalos, he had not been Kazan's first choice for the role of Dean's brother. Paul Newman, then a supporting actor on Broadway in *Picnic*, tested with

Dean and Kazan—not a rehearsed scene, but spontaneous dialogue so they might simply be photographed and recorded together. During the first half of the test, Jimmy—affecting casual machismo but appearing like a factious teenager—constantly toyed with his opened switchblade. Newman wore a white shirt and bow tie, Dean an open shirt and jeans.

KAZAN (off-camera): Okay, Paul—tell us, which of you guys are the girls going to go after? You or Jimmy?

Newman, caught off-guard, tries to come up with an answer, but is interrupted by

DEAN (smiling slyly at Newman): Kiss me.
NEWMAN (grinning): I didn't hear that.
KAZAN: Okay, you two, now face the sound man.
NEWMAN (laughing): He's a funny-looking bastard, too.
KAZAN: He's just doing his job.—Okay, now you two swap places.

They change places, and as they do Newman pinches Dean's bottom.

KAZAN: Okay, now turn towards each other.

They do so, and there is a moment of awkward

silence. Then they both smile slightly as Jimmy gazes deeply into Newman's eyes.

NEWMAN (as if being challenged): Oh yeah?
DEAN (so close that he can speak in a low, seductive whisper): Yeah.

Kazan then calls "Cut!" and the improvisation ends—but not before James Dean revealed a magnetic attraction for his partner, who seems slightly bemused yet somehow flattered. (Newman returned to *Picnic* and made his film debut the following year in *The Silver Chalice*.)

Meantime, restless and bored, Jimmy had to appear each evening at the Royale and go on as Bachir—a role, on at least one occasion, that he seemed to assume off-stage as well as on. Recalled Vivian Matalon, "He could be the most charming—even seductive—person in the world, as he had been with Herman Shumlin. But I liked him enormously. We played chess and listened to music together, and I often visited his small apartment on West Sixty-eighth Street."

And then an odd thing happened.

One cold February night during a week of New York previews and just before the formal premiere, Matalon accompanied Dean home and stopped in for a drink. When he rose to go home, Jimmy invited him to spend the night—but there was only one bed in the room and Matalon, not at all eager to subject himself to an awkward and compromising situation, politely declined and departed. This situation recurred perhaps four or five times over the next several weeks, and finally, on one particularly frosty night, Matalon agreed. Jimmy put a recording of Pergolesi on the phonograph, dimmed the lights and set up what his friend knew was a classic seduction scene. When they crept into bed, however, Jimmy was perhaps astonished to hear his friend murmur, "If you think anything's going to happen you're wrong. Now turn over and go to sleep." That was the extent of their intimacy.

Two days later—for no apparent reason—Jimmy picked a fight with Vivian, who chose not to rise to the bait. For opening night and because it was Jimmy's birthday, Vivian then offered him a gift copy of the book *Los Toros*, which he knew would please an aficionado of bullfighting. Jimmy was touched by the thoughtfulness and asked Vivian why their friendship had seemed to cool.

"That's an easy question to answer," said Vivian calmly. "That night I stayed with you—I didn't make a pass at you, as you expected, because I didn't want you to say, 'I'm not queer!'" The moment, Vivian admitted quite frankly, would have been too painful to endure.

"But," Jimmy replied, "you must remember what I told you about Rogers Brackett." Vivian said he certainly did remember. "Well," Jimmy continued, "you remind me of him."

The nature of the resemblance was not clear, but Vivian felt that Jimmy had set up a seduction scene that he needed to control—very like the situation with Jonathan Gilmore. According to Matalon, "I had the impression, much as I was fond of Jimmy, that he needed people to love him, never mind that he didn't love them in return." It was a perceptive comment, quite similar to

Dizzy Sheridan's observation that Jimmy's need for love was "like a bottomless well," and Jonathan Gilmore's, that Jimmy "latched on to people he liked, took what he needed and was quick to drop them before they might drop him." All these people retained enormous affection and admiration for James Dean, but they also knew that his dire emotional poverty could, quite unwittingly, hurt them. In their comments, one hears a wistful melancholy, as if for a lost child. Like Bachir, James Dean practiced but could never master the fine art of seduction, and often his attempts left him dejected and isolated.

On February 20, just two weeks after opening night of *The Immoralist*, Jimmy—to the astonishment of everyone in the company—tendered his resignation, refusing to offer an explanation. Twelve days later, Warner Bros. announced the leading players in Elia Kazan's forthcoming production of John Steinbeck's *East of Eden*. The Hollywood trade papers noted that James Dean was placed under exclusive contract to Warner Bros. at a salary of $1,200 per week, with a guaranteed minimum of ten weeks, for his work in the picture.

The standard salary escalation clauses were included in the contract, which gave the studio the right to his services for nine films over six years, and a guarantee of ten weeks of work for each film. Jane Deacy negotiated for a clause that allowed him to do guest roles on radio and television and, at the completion of Dean's third picture for Warners, the right to do a Broadway show. He subsequently received $1,250 a week for *Rebel Without a Cause* (total salary: $12,500) and $1,500 a week for *Giant* (total salary: $22,500). These were considered generous fees for contract players at major studios. Marilyn Monroe, for example, was paid $1,250 a week (a total of $15,000) by Twentieth Century-Fox for *Gentlemen Prefer Blondes* in 1952, while her co-star, Jane Russell (not a Fox player but contracted to Howard Hughes), received a fee of $150,000.

"I think Dean is o.k.," Kazan wrote to Jack Warner. "Impress on him—or have someone impress on him again when he arrives out there—the great importance of living an outdoor life, sunshine, exercise, food and fucking. Just all the healthy things, and lots of sleep. He's an odd kid and I think we should make him as handsome as possible."

"Inasmuch as your impression of him is a good one," replied Warner, "we naturally will go along with you. You said he is an odd kid. I hope he isn't too odd, as it is getting to the point now that when we make pictures with odd people, the whole machine is thrown out of order. You know it only takes one odd spark plug to make the motor miss. I, too, am fed up with people who are too odd."

Four nights after he left *The Immoralist*, Jimmy appeared (without fee) in the last stage appearance of his life—at the Cherry Lane Theater in Greenwich Village, a modest space where the Drama Workshop of the New School for Social Research presented a dramatic reading of Ezra Pound's new translation of the *Trachiniai—The Women of Trachis*—by Sophocles. Jimmy accepted the offer for the chance to work with director Howard Sackler and seasoned actors Eli Wallach and Anne Jackson.

The play centers on the efforts of Deianeira, wife of

Heracles, to regain the affections of her philandering husband, who has been absent on one of his heroic missions
and who has shipped his latest concubine, Iole, to live
with his wife at their home in Trachis. The magic
Deianeira uses on Heracles turns out to be poisonous,
and she kills herself in guilt over the agony she has
caused her husband. Heracles commits suicide, too, com-
manding his son Hyllus to take Iole as his own bride.

Jimmy read the roles of Hyllus and of Lichas (herald
of Heracles)—both of them loyal to Heracles—and by
all accounts he was an affecting performer, addressing
the Chorus in Hyllus's sad and angry lament for his
mother's perfidy:

> Let her go, and I hope a fair wind blows to
> carry her far out of my sight. For why should
> she maintain the pointless dignity of the name
> of mother when she acts in no way like a
> mother?

and in a heartbreaking lament, to Heracles:

> In all that she did wrong, she intended good
> . . . So wretched, so helpless am I, no matter
> where I turn.

Unfortunately, there were only two readings of *The
Women of Trachis*, which was soon forgotten in the
annals of Off-Broadway theater lore. But from this

simple production an important friend came into the
life of James Dean, a man who would be a loyal friend
as well as a mentor. A major artist on the brink of a significant career, he had inner resources that were deeper
than Jimmy's; hence he was able to praise his friend
when that was due—just as he was unafraid to repri-
mand him for improper conduct.

In February 1954, Leonard Rosenman had composed, as a favor to his friend Howard Sackler, some
incidental music for *The Women of Trachis*. Rosenman,
then twenty-nine years old and so almost seven years
Jimmy's senior, was born in Brooklyn to immigrant
parents, but was greatly influenced by the tutelage of
his grandfather, a gifted artist who recognized and
encouraged the boy's talents for both painting and
music. After studies at the Art Students League and the
Pratt Institute, Leonard began to study piano
seriously—much to the diffident chagrin of his father,
who emotionally abandoned Leonard much as Winton
Dean left young Jimmy without paternal affection.

"When I finally met Jimmy's father," Rosenman
recalled years later, "I understood how similar our
emotional backgrounds had been. Jimmy's mother had
been very encouraging, but she had married this rigid,
stupid, dreadful man with an infantile jealousy of both
his wife and his son—and of their closeness to one
another. As for me, my father, too, was jealous—of my
close relationship with his father—and I was virtually
abandoned by him from a very early age. This common
background brought Jimmy and me together."

By 1954, Leonard Rosenman had an impressive
résumé, and no one was more fascinated by it than
James Dean. He had studied in America with Arnold

Schönberg, Roger Sessions and Milton Babbitt, and in
Europe with Luigi Dallapiccola; he had written choral
and chamber music and drew enthusiastic praise from
the likes of composer Aaron Copland and novelist
Thomas Mann (who offered to write a libretto for a
Rosenman opera).

At the first rehearsal of *The Women of Trachis*,
Rosenman approached Sackler. "Who's the kid?" he
asked, pointing at Jimmy.

"A very tough guy—James Dean. He sleeps on razor
blades." Rosenman picked up the metaphor at once:
Dean affected a troublesome, brooding and bruised
disposition.

After the public reading, Rosenman was playing
piano at a cast party, and Jimmy turned score pages for
him. Two weeks later, on a cold night at about eleven,
the doorbell rang at the Central Park West apartment
of Leonard and Adele Rosenman. "There was a kid
with a black leather outfit, looking like a storm
trooper," Rosenman recalled—or, one might have
added, a Halloween trick-or-treater, dressed in homage
to Marlon Brando in *The Wild One*.

"I don't think you remember me. I'm James Dean,
and I want to study piano with you." Within days,
Jimmy was frequenting the Rosenman apartment, taking music lessons and, in return, delivering his teacher
to various appointments on the back of his new motorcycle. "As for sleeping on razor blades," said
Rosenman,

the toughness was a pose. The most important
element in his self-image—and, I think, the

singular element in his attraction to the public—
was his almost pathological vulnerability to
hurt and rejection. Enormous defenses on his
part were required to cover it up—hence the
leather-garbed motorcycle rider, the tough kid
having to reassure himself at every turn of the
way by subjecting himself to superhuman tests
of survival, the last of which he failed.

Very quickly, Leonard Rosenman became the object
of James Dean's affection, admiration—and even someone to worship as a culture hero and surrogate father.
Whatever book Rosenman read, Jimmy bought,
although he rarely got past a few introductory pages;
as for the music lessons, he was surprised that after
four or five hours of instruction he could not negotiate
the thickets of Bach and Mozart, and so his interest in
playing quickly cooled. Rosenman sensed Jimmy's
desire to be an intellectual and thus gain respect, but he
was still the distracted Indiana schoolboy impatient
with the demands of formal education.

The music lessons waned, but Jimmy did not cool
toward Leonard Rosenman. The time was approaching
for Kazan to depart for California and the production
of *East of Eden*, and although he had complete freedom
to select everyone in his cast and crew, he had not chosen a composer. With the boldness of a seasoned star,
Jimmy told Kazan that the composer of the score for
The Women of Trachis was a friend and that Kazan
ought to listen to the score. Kazan did, liked the music,
and offered Rosenman the job. But the composer temporized: he had never considered writing for movies,

and, he told his colleague Leonard Bernstein, knew nothing about it. Nonsense, said Bernstein, who had just completed a magnificent score for Kazan's *On the Waterfront*: good music is good music in any medium, and Rosenman could write better than good. Bernstein, Copland and others finally prevailed, and by early March Leonard Rosenman was signed to compose the score for *East of Eden*. "To this day, I owe Jimmy Dean a debt of gratitude. He got me into films." And so began another impressive phase in Leonard Rosenman's multivalent career.*

Kazan and Dean arrived in Los Angeles on April 8. Early that morning, a limousine from Warners' New York office came for Kazan at his home on East Seventy-fourth Street, then proceeded to West Sixty-eighth for Jimmy, who had decided not to give up the apartment; he was, after all, scheduled to return as soon as three weeks later, for a two-day shoot on a television drama ("The Little Woman"). His luggage for the flight to California consisted of two overstuffed paper bags of clothes tied with kitchen string; later, he would occasionally contact Christine White or another old acquaintance to send him books or boots or records.

Very soon, Kazan realized that Jimmy was in some ways, beneath the cool and sullen exterior, something of a naif. That departure day, he told his director that this was his first airplane journey, and Kazan remembered the look of a disheveled immigrant, his nose almost pressed to the window during the entire flight.

---

* Many memorable Rosenman scores followed, including those for *Barry Lyndon* and *Bound for Glory*, for which Leonard Rosenman received Oscars.

The impression he had of a nervous child, eager to please, was reinforced as soon as they landed in Los Angeles, when Jimmy asked to stop at his father's house. "Obviously there was a strong tension between the two, and it was not friendly," Kazan noted. "I sensed the father disliked his son. [He] didn't seem to think his son's future very promising. They stood side by side, but talk soon collapsed, and we drove on."

That short visit to Winton Dean, and the chilly reception he gave his son, were crucial for Kazan's preparation of *East of Eden*, and the emphases he gave those portions of the novel he chose to adapt. In those few moments observing father and son, he saw that the script—which stressed the bitter disconnection between Adam Trask and his son Caleb—was a mirror of Jimmy's separation from his father ("just as it was, in a way, my own [story]," added Kazan). These personal histories would give *East of Eden* much of its emotional impact. "Jimmy was Cal," Kazan added. "He was guarded, vengeful, sullen and he had a sense of aloneness. He was suspicious of everyone. In fact, he looked and spoke just like his character in *East of Eden*." When she saw the finished film, Adeline Brookshire agreed: she noted that many of the movements of Cal Trask were characteristic gestures of James Dean. "His funny little laugh that ripples with the slightest provocation, his quick, jerky walks and actions, his sudden change from frivolity to gloom"—the character onscreen was the boy she had taught in Fairmount.

The new young contract player at Warners required a West Coast agent to work with Jane Deacy, and she chose young Dick Clayton at the Famous Artists Agency. Quite coincidentally, Clayton, once a juvenile and teen actor, had met Jimmy briefly when they both appeared in bit roles in *Sailor Beware*. He understood his new client's anxiety and sensed the nervous bravado beneath the antagonism. "I don't think I ever saw any actor so vulnerable," Clayton said years later.

> You had the sense, if you watched him carefully, that he was absolutely terrified of rejection, that underneath his coldness there was some terrible wound that would never heal. Sometimes I thought we were good friends, but often he withdrew into a shell and clammed up, especially if he thought he had revealed too much of himself. He wanted to be understood and loved for himself, but he was afraid to disclose himself. It was an impossible dilemma.

Jimmy's conduct, too, could be difficult. Arriving in California without money and with no prospect of payment until the first day of shooting *East of Eden*, he had no place to live and was forced to bunk down in a small room at his father's house, now located at 1667 South Bundy Drive, West Los Angeles. This, of course, made Jimmy more than ever a surly malcontent. The more he complained to Kazan of this disagreeable living arrangement, the more secretly pleased was the director. Each day rehearsing scenes between Dean and Raymond Massey (as his *Eden* father), Kazan stoked the bitterness and frustration in the boy's performance. This, to Kazan, was precious, real-life anger, brilliantly exploited and transposed to the film.

In an effort to find his own lodging, Jimmy prevailed on Clayton to get him a salary advance, but with it he made a down payment for a sporty, bright red MG; bought a sleek little European motorbike; and purchased a palomino he kept on the Warner lot. But Kazan had to intervene when Jimmy spent too much time with the bike and the animal. Fearing an accident, he forbade him to speed around the studio; as for the horse, it was shipped out to the Warner ranch in the San Fernando Valley, where Jimmy tended it off-hours.

For the delicate color and CinemaScope process to be used for *East of Eden*, elaborate film tests were necessary, and Jimmy was scheduled to be photographed in full costume with his co-stars. But there was a problem: Jimmy kept such late hours during his first week in Los Angeles, and was so pale and exhausted, that he was not fit for a color test. At once, Kazan dispatched him to Borrego Springs, three hours out into the California desert, to gain some color and lose his peaked, almost haunted appearance. His character was to be intense, after all, not ill or neurasthenic.

The footage, to determine the precise lighting necessary for his costumes relative to his height (five feet, eight inches), weight (155 pounds) and coloring (blond hair, blue eyes, very fair skin), has survived. In it, he seems shy and uneasy—not inappropriate for Cal Trask—but he has also clearly calculated every gesture and grimace. He clowns puckishly with Richard Davalos and Julie Harris (set for the role of Abra, first in love with Aron and then with Cal); she was even then acknowledged as one of America's finest stage and screen actresses.

During March and April, Jimmy was restless in California, as he wrote to Barbara Glenn:

Gadge Kazan and [Tennessee] Williams
[whom Dean had met through Kazan] are nice
but I wouldn't trust the sons-a-bitches far's I
could throw em. They can take advantage of
you like anybody else.

Honey!!! I'm still a Calif. virgin, remarkable,
no? I'm saving it—H-bomb Dean. A new addition has been added to the Dean family. I got a
red 53 MG (milled head etc. hot engine). My
sex pours itself into fast curves, broadslides
and broodings, drags, etc. You have plenty of
competition now. My motorcycle, my MG and
my girl. I have been sleeping with my MG. We
make it together. HONEY.

The picture began shooting in Northern California
locations on May 27, but Leonard Rosenman—by now
Jimmy's best friend—had not yet arrived, and he had
no old acquaintances to contact in Los Angeles. He did
know something about publicity and promotion, however, and so he zoomed his MG or his motorbike to the
appropriate spots on Sunset Boulevard, the better to
be noticed or photographed or both. But apart from the
tests and a brief rehearsal schedule, his life was
remarkably static and empty. "I don't like it here," he
wrote in another letter to Barbara Glenn, hand-written
on Famous Artists stationery:

I don't like people here. I like it home (N.Y.)
and I liked you and I want to see you. Must I
always be miserable? I try so hard to make

people reject me. Why? I don't want to write this letter. I would be better to remain silent. Wow! Am I fucked up! . . . I DON'T KNOW WHERE I AM. Rented a car for 2 weeks it cost me $138.00 I WANT TO DIE . . . I HAVEN'T BEEN TO BED WITH NOBODY and won't until after the picture and I am home safe in N.Y.C. (snuggle little town that it is). Sounds unbelievable but it's the truth I swear. So hold everything, stop breathing, stop the town—all of N.Y.C. until (should have trumpets here) James Dean returns.

Am I fucked up! I got no motorcycle, I got no girl. HONEY—shit, writing in capitals doesn't seem to help either. Haven't found a place to live yet, still living with my folks. HONEY. Kazan sent me out here to get a tan, Haven't seen the sun yet (fog & smog). [He] Wanted me healthy looking. I look like a prune. Don't run away from home at too early an age or you'll half [sic] to take vitamins the rest of your life. Wish you cooked. I'll be home soon. Write me please. I'm sad most of the time. Awful lonely too isn't it. I hope you're dying, BECAUSE I AM.

Love,
Jim (Brando Clift) Dean.

Confusion, frustration, a feeling of disconnection from people, depression and a fundamental distrust of anyone's motives—these characterized James Dean more and more from the spring of 1954. Partly this

concatenation of feelings must have derived from his
own facile approach to relationships and a fear of real
intimacy, partly from an inability or a refusal to face
the fact that he must, to mature, abandon the anger
connected to his childhood losses. In addition, his ability to manipulate the reactions of others—from the
days of playacting on the front porch in Indiana, to
high-school oratory contests and plays, to television
dramas—had found counterparts in real-life relationships with, for example, Dizzy Sheridan, Rogers
Brackett and Jonathan Gilmore.

To set forth this actor's complex character is not to
diminish him; rather, it helps to explain his artless ability to project both disaffection and the desire for love,
both a diffuse pain and an inarticulate longing for love
and acceptance. He was indeed, as Dizzy Sheridan had
said, "a bottomless well—no love was enough."

Working in Hollywood is often a downright wacky
affair under the best circumstances: egos clash with
egos, producers with directors, writers with producers
and, often enough, actors with just about everybody. In
addition, there has always existed in the movie business a widespread belief that it is terribly important—
by its very nature a fine art realized by terribly
important people—an attitude that is perhaps, by
some, an effort to justify inflated salaries and outrageous perquisites.

But it may be no exaggeration to say that only the
strongest personalities can survive the American brand
of stardom, and that the absurd blandishments of mere
fame are always a test of even the noblest temperament. There is a long list of people in the history of
Hollywood who, flattered by moguls and revered by

fans, believed in their own superhuman status. So
many schemes and seductions to achieve success, so little time; so many privileges and pleasures attached to
the eros of celebrity, none of it finally satisfying. James
Dean was not immune to the dangers of Hollywood; in
fact with his unfortunate emotional history and
ungrownup disposition, he was a prime target for the
damaging consequences of movie stardom.

By the end of April, he was passing time scouring
the seedier locales of Hollywood Boulevard, observing
hookers and hustlers, buying marijuana from small-
time dealers, guzzling beer after hours in downtown
clubs or out near Santa Monica Canyon—none of these
activities uncommon (then or later) for a young man in
his situation. Kazan, concerned about Jimmy's
exhausted appearance and late hours wandering the
county, decided to get him out of Winton's house. He
found two rooms over a Burbank drugstore at 3908
West Olive, very near the Warner studios, and there he
installed Jimmy—with, for company and good example, Richard Davalos. But by the time the cast and crew
of *East of Eden* departed in late May for Northern
California, there to begin three weeks of location shooting in Mendocino and Salinas, Davalos (like Bast before
him) was weary of Jimmy's unpredictable moods and
antisocial insolence; he told Kazan he would no longer
be his co-star's roommate after they returned to the
studio in mid-June for two months of interior shooting.

Paul Osborn and Elia Kazan's adaptation of John
Steinbeck's novel greatly simplifies and humanizes the
characters of a prolix and confused literary allegory of
moral dilemmas—an epic modeled on the biblical tale
of Cain and Abel, the sons of Adam and Eve. *East of*

Eden on the screen, far more successful than on the page, concerns the relationship between a father and his two sons on the eve of World War I: Adam Trask (Raymond Massey) is a Salinas farmer with puritanical values but little feeling in relating to his competitive sons, Aron (Richard Davalos) and Caleb (Dean), on whom (unlike the novel) the emphasis of the entire film rests. From the opening of the picture, Cal is shown searching for love—first from his mother, Kate (Jo Van Fleet), who fled her husband's tyranny and has become madam of a bordello; and then from his father. At the same time, Aron and his girlfriend Abra (Julie Harris) plan their future and family together as Cal, jealous, watches.

After the collapse of Adam's new business venture—shipping lettuce eastward in ice-packed trains that fail—Cal borrows $5,000 from his mother and starts a bean-growing business. With the entrance of America into the war in 1917, Cal benefits from wartime profiteering and offers all his earnings to his father as a birthday present, attempting to win love by redeeming Adam's business. But his father refuses the money earned at the expense of others' misery. Devastated by this final rejection and once again compared unfavorably to the favorite son Aron, Cal destroys his brother by forcing him to confront the drugged, degenerate mother he thought was dead. As a drunken Aron goes off to war, Adam suffers a massive stroke. In a redemptive coda, Abra (who has come to love Cal instead of Aron) joins Cal in caring for the stricken Adam, who at last asks for his son's love and devotion.

Unleavened by mercy and undiluted by compassion

(not to say literary distinction), Steinbeck's novel presents a world and its people as ineluctably doomed by irredeemable evil. Osborn and Kazan, on the other hand, are far more realistic: in their hands, *East of Eden* became a tale of generational conflict, not of abstract universal problems. This was, after all, a film conceived and produced during the era of Senator Joseph McCarthy, of *Catcher in the Rye*, *The Wild One*, and *Blackboard Jungle*. Its characters are shot through with dilemmas, to be sure, but they are also capable of transcendence as well as wickedness. In his handling of the script, Kazan (here as elsewhere) emphasized that the paramount issue in all relationships is the pursuit of the truth of one's identity through honesty and, where it is necessary, forgiveness. But above all, *East of Eden* is a film about James Dean as Cal Trask, forever enshrined as the embodiment of the perplexed teenager who wants nothing so much as to be loved by parents from whom he feels forever distant.

"Jimmy wasn't easy, because it was all new to him," according to Kazan. "But when he got the affection and patience he needed, he was awfully good. There wasn't anything he held back. He was loaded with talent, but he had very little training, and he was ready to do anything to be good."

But Jimmy could also be, Kazan continued, "impossible. He was always cutting in on someone's lines or saying the wrong lines. Raymond Massey had studied the script with his wife, had gone over it and knew it exactly. And then onto the set came this little son of a bitch with the wrong lines!"

But Kazan knew that he could make a virtue of necessity, for this was the way to capture the unrelieved

tension between father and son in the story—a tension
Kazan had known with his own father and had recognized between Jimmy and Winton.

So I let Jimmy say his lines the way he
wanted—just because it irritated Massey!
Would I do anything to stop that antagonism?
No—I increased it, I let it go! It was the central
thing of the story. What I photographed was
the absolute hatred of Raymond Massey for
James Dean, and of James Dean for Raymond
Massey. That was precious. No director could
get it in any other way.

According to Raymond Massey, Jimmy was "a rebel
at heart," a boy who approached everything in the picture with a chip on his shoulder, was deliberately antisocial, refused to speak his lines clearly and (so much is
clear from the production schedule and a glance at the
finished film) had to loop (re-record) much of his dialogue after filming was completed. "Simple technicali-
ties, such as moving on cue and finding his marks,
were beneath his consideration," Massey recalled,
astonished that Kazan sustained such antics. "Bear
with me, Ray," the director said to Massey one afternoon while they waited for Jimmy to get in the mood
for a scene. "I'm getting solid gold." To which Massey
replied, "What price gold?" Later, the director whispered to Jimmy, "People will be watching this long
after we've gone, and they'll think it's great." And that,
Kazan recalled, "seemed to please him tremendously."

When Davalos relocated to private living quarters in June, Kazan moved into a dressing room trailer in a soundstage and had one fitted out, just next to him, for Jimmy—the better to keep him "under my thumb all the time." Mentor, analyst, patron and protector to his young charge, Kazan realized that Jimmy's night life and his contempt for speed limits could easily imperil the production, especially because Jimmy's eyesight was so poor. With the actor in residence at Warners, his motorbike and sports coupe were not needed for transfer to and from work.

But Elia Kazan did not, in fact, like James Dean at all.

He was never more than a limited actor, and he was a highly neurotic young man— obviously sick, and he got more so. His face was very poetic—wonderful, and very painful, full of desolation. There are moments when you say, "Oh, God, he's so handsome—what's being lost here? What goodness is being lost here?" Directing him was like directing the faithful Lassie. I either lectured him or terrorized him, flattered him furiously, tapped him on the shoulder, or kicked his backside. He was so instinctive and so stupid in many ways—and most of all I had the impression of someone who was a cripple inside. He was not like Brando. People compared them, but there was no similarity. He was a far, far sicker kid, and Brando's not sick, he's just troubled.

Petulant as ever, Jimmy could not accept criticism, which he invariably took as personal rejection. But he realized what Kazan had done for Marlon Brando and Montgomery Clift, and so, for perhaps the first and only time in his career, he had to take care not to alienate his director.

"Just being in a scene with him could be an unnerving experience," according to Richard Davalos, who found his co-star "dangerous and unpredictable. He had an instinct to disturb." Kazan, for one, was disturbed when he went to Jimmy's dressing room to discuss a point and saw a revolver in an open drawer; this suggested a paranoia that was much more dangerous than the ever-present switchblade, a boy's talisman, suggested.

Much of the violence in Jimmy's attitude and his ornery, self-absorbed demeanor with the production company, were tempered by one whom Kazan called "an angel on our set—I doubt Jimmy would ever have got through *East of Eden* except for Julie Harris. She helped Jimmy more than I did with any direction I gave him." It is easy to understand why. Thoroughly professional and highly respected for her moving portraits on stage and screen, Julie Harris is one of a rare breed—a great actress and the recipient of numerous awards, she is also a woman utterly lacking airs and affectation. Sympathetic to her colleagues, she is also widely known and admired for her generous support of younger apprentice actors.

Ever since they had filmed the test for *East of Eden*, Julie Harris knew she would be working with a talented but idiosyncratic young man. She had rested her face in her hands for a moment as she spoke to Jimmy, and—perhaps in an attempt to dishearten or threaten an established star—he suddenly asked, "Why do you put up your hands like that? Are you covering your face because you think you look too old for me?" In fact, she was twenty-eight, just five years Jimmy's senior.

"I don't think I look a lot older than you," Julie replied (as, indeed, she did not). "But I was never offended by him," she added years later. "I think he loved to be a naughty boy, and he was always looking to irritate others. But I never let it get through to me. He reminded me of Tom Sawyer, always looking for adventure, always looking to mix it up, not wanting things to go smoothly—and no manners, to hell with manners and good feelings." Another woman, whom he met at a director's home, sat on a sofa talking with Jimmy. When she picked up a small cushion and cradled it in her lap, he said, "Can't you have a child of your own?" As it happened, the woman had only recently adopted a child; she left the room shocked and embarrassed.

Unlike Raymond Massey, Julie Harris used for the picture what was natural to Jimmy: "The raw material of our work is people, and I've always thought it's wrong to say, 'Why can't you behave?' If somebody's not behaving, you just say, 'Well, he's not behaving,' and you deal with it. I think of the interviewer who asked Charles Manson why he was so bad! The only answer is because he wanted to be!"

Instead of reacting to his moods, Julie Harris accepted Jimmy's neurotic behavior and never tried to change or educate him—and in so doing, she earned his respect and enjoyed their collaboration. She even agreed to the ultimate test: a white-knuckle ride in his sports car, twisting, turning and whizzing through the Hollywood Hills one evening. Just as when they filmed together, everything was unexpected, everything edged with danger. Their major scenes in the picture (in the field, as Abra and Cal speak of their childhoods; on the Ferris wheel, as her affections are torn between Aron and Cal; and in the great final sequence at the bedside of the stricken Adam Trask) bring the film to life as do no other moments. But off camera, she recalled, "He was desperately lonely and had many problems, so it was hard to get close to him. He was a strange and sensitive young man, and he had tremendous imagination. I liked him very much, but he was not easy to know."

On the last day of shooting *East of Eden* in August, Julie sought out Jimmy in his trailer on the set. After she had tapped at his door a few times, he finally opened. "And there he stood, shaking with grief, racked with sobs," she remembered. "He kept crying, 'It's over! It's over!'"

"But Jimmy, this is just the beginning for you!"

He could not stop weeping. "But this—it's over!"

The film was, she realized, the only family, the only purpose he had. "At that moment, he seemed more than ever to me like a little lost boy. The rebel, the boy who wanted to shock and irritate, was gone, and suddenly there was Jimmy Dean, very vulnerable and very sweet."

Very quickly, news buzzed around Hollywood about Elia Kazan's mercurial protégé, and the studio publicity staff was working overtime to exert damage control and to advance the causes of both the film and the new

player. Reporter Hedda Hopper was invited to the commissary to observe Jimmy at ease. He sauntered in, she
recalled, and slouched down in silence at a table. Then,
with a bare toe, he dragged over another chair and put
his feet up. A moment later, he surveyed the wall of
framed photos of Warners' stars, spat at one, then
wolfed down his lunch.

Hopper, from a safe distance, declined an offer to
meet him, although she reversed her decision after she
saw him in the finished picture. Attempting to justify
his typically bad manners, Jimmy told Nicholas Ray
(his next director), "When I first came to Hollywood,
everyone was nice to me, everyone thought I was a nice
guy. I went to the commissary to eat, and people were
friendly, and I thought it was wonderful. But I decided
not to continue to be a nice guy. Then people would
have to respect me for my work." He saw no lack of
logic in this odd statement, but he may have had in
mind Marlon Brando's affectation of aloof disdain.

During the last weeks of filming, Jimmy unfortunately began to barter in that cheapest of Hollywood
currencies, the belief in one's own importance. Kazan
was dismayed to see him act rudely to the wardrobe
and makeup crew, and he was further annoyed when
Jimmy refused to play a scene with Julie on an inclined
roof. The first misdemeanor he flatly corrected, the second he slyly overcame by getting Jimmy drunk on
cheap Chianti. The scene, with a tipsy James Dean,
works brilliantly in the film; it was a technique Kazan
frequently used with recalcitrant actors, *pace*
Stanislavski.

There was nothing Kazan could do, however, about
Jimmy's swiftly expanding ego. He watched with

sadness and no little fear when he saw Jimmy in front of a mirror, snapping roll after roll of close-up photos of himself, all the while keeping the cast and crew waiting on his pleasure to arrive for a scene. In defense of his increasingly selfish behavior, Jimmy said he was an "objective artist [who] has always been misunderstood. I came to Hollywood to act, not to charm society. And acting is the most logical way for people's neuroses to express themselves." But more mature and serious colleagues in the craft (Julie Harris and Raymond Massey, to name the nearest two) do not consider their profession an excuse for poor conduct, much less an easy outlet for inner turmoil.

As the production moved to its conclusion, the company noticed a definite coolness where once there had been warmth between Dean and Kazan. "In this business nobody helps you," Jimmy told a reporter who asked the major influences and supporters of his career. "You can be grateful to somebody for opening your eyes to certain things, and in return you can open somebody else's. But you do it all yourself." This, many felt, was nonsense—too absurd to warrant a counterstatement. Among others, Kazan, who kept a discreet and dignified silence, may well have been offended by such rank ingratitude.

By this time, in any case, Jimmy felt he no longer needed Kazan's guidance. Leonard Rosenman, who had been present for almost every day's shooting since June, drew the inspiration for his extraordinary musical score from the drama and tension of each scene and the growing separation between Dean and Kazan. Jimmy had anxiously awaited Rosenman's arrival on the picture, as he wrote to Barbara Glenn:

Have been very dejected and moody last two
weeks. Have been telling everybody to fuck off,
and that's no good. I could never make them
believe I was working on my part. Poor Julie
Harris doesn't know what to do with me . . . I
have only one friend, one guy that I can talk to
and be understood [by]. I hope Lennie comes
out here. I need someone from New York.
Cause I'm mean and I'm really kind and gentle.
Things get mixed up all the time [shades of *The
Little Prince*!]. I see a person I would like to be
close to (everybody) then I think it would be
just the same as before and they don't give a
shit for me. Then I say something nasty or nothing at all and walk away. The poor person
doesn't know what's happened. He doesn't
realize that I have decided I don't like him.
What's wrong with people. Idiots.

The letter, with its resonance of adolescent anguish
and self-absorption, also signals that the excitement of
his inchoate stardom under the most auspicious circumstances was not, in the final analysis, bringing him
either happiness or peace. So desperate was he for
acceptance from everyone, and so incapable of trusting
anyone's responses, that even the normal give and take
of friendship was skewed into something almost ego-
maniacal.

Kazan and Rosenman knew how Dean adored
Brando, and so the director invited Marlon, who was
starring as Napoleon in *Desirée* over at Twentieth
Century Fox, to visit the set of *Eden*. Before introducing

them, Kazan told Brando that Dean was obsessed with him, that he was modeling his conduct and style on Brando's character of Johnny in *The Wild One*. For all that, Brando was very gracious to Dean, who (thus Kazan) "was so adoring that he seemed shrunken and twisted in misery."

According to Brando, Dean was very nervous when they met that day. Jimmy said he was learning to play the drums, as had Marlon, and that he, too, was a motorcycle aficionado. From that time, Brando was pestered by calls, and by Dean's attention when they met at parties. "I could see in his eyes and in the way he moved and spoke that he had suffered a lot," Brando recalled. "He was tortured by insecurities [and] said he'd had a difficult childhood and a lot of problems with his father." Brando urged Dean to enter psychotherapy and told Rosenman of his concern. "Len, why don't you get him to an analyst? Your friend is nuts!"

With Rosenman replacing Kazan as patron and confidant, Jimmy said what he thought his new best friend wanted to hear. "He thought that he could ingratiate himself with me," according to Rosenman, "by denouncing everyone in Hollywood as a phony, and Hollywood itself as utterly worthless. But he did everything that was necessary to become a big deal in Hollywood." Rosenman was on the mark: the bad boy pose was carefully calculated, as were the judiciously planned appearances (with starlets for whom he cared nothing) at movie premieres or nightclubs on the Sunset Strip. "He knew all the publicists and reporters and columnists," said Rosenman, "and he was always at the center of things in restaurants, with all the celebrities around him. He knew exactly what to do"—even to the point of seeming to be above it all, to hold everything in contempt. This schizoid attitude must have added to his confusion and, in the final analysis, a contempt most of all for his own disingenuousness.

As for Leonard Rosenman, Jimmy was obsessed with having the attention and affection of the man he so admired, but his means to the end were sometimes poignant. "How about coming out and playing basketball?" he said to Leonard Rosenman one afternoon. That was impossible, Rosenman replied: he had to finish scoring two scenes that day. But Jimmy was insistent, and finally Rosenman asked, "Why do I have to play basketball with you? Why is it so important?"

Jimmy lowered his eyes and spoke almost in a whisper. "Well—it's like—sort of—I—you—want your father to play basketball with you."

This was a transference role Rosenman did not relish. "Look, Jimmy, your father lives here in Los Angeles. Why don't you call him to play basketball with you?" Years later, Rosenman concluded his recollection of this awkward conversation with the comment, "Well, then I met his father and I understood. His father was a monster, a person without any kind of sensitivity. Jimmy was doing everything in his career to get his father to like and approve of him, and his father never took the slightest interest. It was sad, but I could not fill that gap."

The basketball game thus sabotaged, Jimmy turned away in tears—in fact, he cried a good deal, Rosenman remembered, which is why it was easy for him to cry in movie scenes. Julie came to me one day and said, "Lennie, there's something terribly wrong. Jimmy is crying all the time." I told her he was preparing for his scene, which was not entirely the truth. He was crying because he was in constant anguish and confusion about his identity!

That identity was, once and for all, memorialized in the role of Cal Trask in *East of Eden*, James Dean's finest performance, a naked portrait of himself, and the role that established forever the contours of his fame.

He is first glimpsed in the film's opening sequence, sitting on a curbstone, a boy in white trousers and sweater, waiting and watching as his mother, all in black, passes by. He follows her, watches her make a bank deposit, then pursues her from a distance as she returns to her home—the brothel that has made her rich and notorious. "Would she talk to me?" he asks her house guard. "I just want to talk to her!" But he is dismissed, and calls angrily over his shoulder, "You— you tell her I hate her," which of course is not at all true. The desire to talk to her, to his father, to the girl he loves—this amalgam of suppressed desires and thwarted exchanges defines the character of Cal/Jimmy.

Audiences then and later needed little more than the image of James Dean in that first scene to find an irresistible combination of sadness, need and alienation. Here was a young man who cried out for help; from this point, no viewer of the film can doubt that *East of*

Eden is a picture about a young man's emotional turmoil.

At the barn, where Cal's father, Adam, hopes to perfect a method of refrigeration for transporting fresh vegetables, Jimmy added to his portrait the tentative gestures, the pauses with hands outstretched, the halting diction that were his trademark: the edges of anything like a Brando imitation were softened, the arched eyebrows stressing confusion as well as the pain of rejection—never an amalgam of feelings associated with the Brando persona. Indeed, all the markers of Dean's identity were clarified in this picture: the quiet allure, the sudden eruptions of fury, the diffuse rage, the hunching lope, and the face full of fearful entreaty. With Massey, Davalos and Harris, Jimmy conveyed the torment of a neglected teenager with few words but subtle expressions, registering jealousy of his brother and pain because of his alienation from his harsh father.

Dean invested in Cal a series of chain reactions, a Richter scale of his father's disciplinary tremors. Rejected by Adam, Cal retreats into the barn stocked with ice blocks; he is a temperamental animal in a chilly, rigid north sea. When he spies on Harris and Davalos planning their future, we see what he sees: Abra as mother, cradling Aron's head in her lap, stroking his brow, humming to him—everything, in other words, that Cal (and Dean) longed for.

To atone for bad conduct, Cal is required by his father to read from the Bible—which he does, but muddies the text and enrages his father by mumbling the words and emphasizing verse numbers. (Massey's patience ran out at this point, when Jimmy interjected into the verses a stream of four-letter words later covered by re-recording. As it happened, he had been encouraged to do this by Kazan, who wanted a close-up on Massey's enraged features.) "Talk to me, Father," Cal pleads when scolded for his obstinacy. "I got to know who I am, what I'm like." He must, he concludes, learn about his mother, who he knows is not dead, as his father insists.

Cal's first confrontation with his mother, Kate, also provides the film's first scene of almost unbearable emotion. Self-conscious and shy when he enters the saloon of the brothel, Cal attracts the attention of the barmaid (Lois Smith): "You're just a kid," she says as he plies her with questions about his mother. Wide-eyed and knowing, he is also shrewd and insistent. Entering his mother's room, he and we see her asleep in a chair—and then there is a cut to a huge close-up of her fine, smooth fingers (moments before praised by Adam as the most beautiful hands in the world). Jimmy kneels before Jo Van Fleet as if in prayerful supplication before some dreadful Madonna. "Will you let me talk to you?" he begs—the motif now thrice established. "Please! I got to talk to you!" Her protectors then drag him from her room by his feet, and he grasps door frames, pipes—anything to stay with her: "I want to talk to you! I have to talk to you! Talk to me—please, Mother, talk to me!"

His second encounter with his mother is the business scene, when he receives $5,000 from her to help his father's commercial venture. Kazan constructed cunningly the Dean–Van Fleet sequence, balancing a wary mutual longing between mother and son with a gritty dual independence. Van Fleet rightly played the scene with a harsh edge, as one who may have been a young Cal, denied the love of a once adored husband; Dean, on the other hand, played Cal as one who might yet grow to be a hardened replica of Kate. "Maybe you are like me," Van Fleet whispers—and then surprises him: "You're a likable kid."

The Abra-Cal meeting at the fairgrounds, culminating in the great Ferris wheel sequence, is the structural midpoint of the film, a delicate delineation of love and longing. At first a randy, slick, overconfident teen, Jimmy/Cal slowly modifies his conduct in the presence of Harris/Abra's loving tenderness; promised to Davalos, she instead begins to love the one who most needs to be loved. Each reference to Aron is like a knife to Cal's heart—until Harris says quietly, "You've been awful nice, taking care of me [while Aron is busy]"—and then they move together in a kiss so tentative that Dean (in an inspired moment unguided by Kazan) slightly lifts his left hand during the kiss, as if both to embrace and to retreat. When Harris aborts the kiss and cries that she must be faithful to her love for Davalos, Cal turns away and rests his chin on his hands, his gentlest hopes apparently dashed forever.

But it is the birthday sequence that, decades later, continues to astonish and move audiences.

The episode begins with the anticipation of a surprise birthday party for the boys' father. Dean, nervous and playful, has decorated the home and prepared dinner. When Massey enters, he is momentarily delighted and accepts a wrapped packet from Dean—until Davalos, now the jealous outsider, announces his engagement to Harris (who seems not at all pleased with this sudden development). Massey embraces the pair, turning his back on Dean. "But you haven't opened Cal's present yet," says Abra/Harris. "No," replies Massey, "but I can't imagine having anything better than this."

Finally, he unwraps the gift—the money Cal has earned from his bean farm (for whose purchase he borrowed from his mother), which will repay his father's business loss.

MASSEY: What's this? What is this?

DEAN: Well—uh—I made it, and it's for you. It's all the money you lost on the lettuce.

MASSEY: You made it? But how?

DEAN: Beans.

MASSEY: Beans?

DEAN: We bought futures at five cents, and war came along, and the price went sky high. So—that's for you and it's all the money you lost on the lettuce business. That's for you. And I made it for you.

MASSEY: Cal, you will have to give it back.

DEAN (beginning to panic): No, I made it—I made it for you, Dad. I want you to have it.

MASSEY: You'll have to give it back.

DEAN: Who—I can't give—to who—?

MASSEY: To the people you got it from.

DEAN: No. The British Purchasing Agency? I can't give it back to them, Dad.

MASSEY: Then give it to the farmers you robbed.

DEAN (pleading): We didn't rob anybody, Dad! We paid two cents a pound over market for that stuff.

MASSEY: Cal, I sign my name [as head of the local draft board for the war] and boys go out and some die and some live helpless without arms and legs. Not one will come back untorn. Do you think I could take a profit from that? I don't want the money, Cal. I couldn't take it. I thank you for the thought, but—

DEAN (almost weeping): I'll keep it for you. I'll wrap it up and we'll just keep it in here and we'll never even—

MASSEY: I'll never take it. Son, I'd be happy if you'd given me something like—well, like your brother's given me—something honest and human and good. Don't be angry, son. If you want to give me a present, give me a good life. That's something I could value.

Dean, torn apart in this great final rejection, has begun to break down. He turns away, clutching the money and bending over, sobbing on the table. He then turns back toward Massey, the weeping now a low, almost silent plea—and as Massey moves away from this display of emotion, James Dean acted the conclusion of the scene in a manner entirely unrehearsed, and for which Massey was completely unprepared. Jimmy held the money forward in his hands, offering, grief-stricken—and then slowly wrapped his arms around his father's neck, as if he would crawl into his arms for loving acceptance. The bills flutter in front of and around the outraged Massey, who does not return the embrace and could only shout, "Cal! Stop it!! Cal!" And then a terrible cry bursts from Dean's throat. Tears streaming down his face, he turns, crying like a hideously wounded animal or a beaten child. He stumbles from the room, a dreadful wail resounding behind him.

Repudiated one final, fatal time, Cal now takes Aron to see their reprobate mother—an act of vengeance (Steinbeck's murder of Abel by Cain) so appalling that it leads Aron to a drunken departure for war. Seeing his beloved son leaving the train station and mocking him, Adam/Massey collapses, with a massive stroke, into Cal's arms—an action choreographed to repeat Cal's earlier collapse into Adam's arms.

The film's final sequence—at the bedside of the stricken Adam—provided James Dean and Julie Harris with their finest moments. Distraught and comforting, Harris as Abra begs Massey to ask his son for something—a request Massey fulfills when he whispers to Cal his hatred of an unsympathetic nurse and adds, "You, Cal—I want you to take care of me." With the encouragement of the "good mother" Abra (the script has simply forgotten poor old Kate), the new "bad mother" in the person of the cold, ornery nurse is displaced. Cal nods in agreement, his eyes glazed with tears of love and remorse; his love for his father begins in earnest when Dean, with slow deliberation, places a chair at Massey's side and, with a loving and knowing gaze at the faithful Abra, promises to care for him. Bathing the scene in a tenebrous, haunting green glow, Kazan concludes *East of Eden* with an unsentimental promise of redemptive love, which springs from the grace of mutual forgiveness. Never mind that Cal has done a dreadful thing to Aron: he has displaced him, and is accepted by a father, dare it be said, who has no other choice for support than to hope in Cal.

Thanks to Elia Kazan—and to the brilliantly moving and evocative score composed by Leonard Rosenman, whose complex harmonies moved forward the

psychological wholeness of Cal Trask especially—
James Dean offered American audiences a new image
of the rebel as poetic antihero, as the misunderstood
but vulnerable herald of a new generation—the boy in
anguish as a disturbed animal, so needy of love that
nothing else has any reality: not school, or career, or
friendship. For most of the picture, he was dressed in
white, like an angel manqué in a world on the brink of
war and a family disconnected. Osborn and Kazan created, with James Dean's anguish as the principal focus,
the ultimately irresistible young man, one who has not
been loved enough—a lack probably felt, at some time,
by everyone under the sun.

When *East of Eden* opened in the spring of 1955, the
critics were virtually unanimous. Although some
wrongly judged Jimmy's performance as stenciled on
the pattern of Marlon Brando, most saw the emergence
of a major, attractive new talent:

- "The picture is brilliant entertainment, and more
  than that it announces a new star: James Dean,
  whose prospects look as bright as any young
  actor's since Marlon Brando."*
- "Dean is an exceptionally sensitive young actor
  whose fault is a slight sibling resemblance to
  Marlon Brando. Like Marlon Brando, Jimmy
  Dean approached Hollywood with a profound
  indifference to dress and manners. He wore

---

* To which Jimmy replied: "People were telling me I behaved like Brando before I
knew who Brando was. I am not disturbed by the comparison, nor am I flattered. I
have my own personal rebellion and don't have to rely on Brando's."

shabby sport shirts, faded blue jeans, a leather jacket. He rode a motorcycle . . . loved to play bongo drums and recorder."

- "Everything about him suggests the lonely, misunderstood nineteen-year-old. He has the wounded look of an orphan trying to piece together the shabby facts of his heritage. He smiles as if at some dark joke known only to himself. You sense badness in him, but you also like him."

- "Young James Dean is the screen's most sensational male find of the year. His talents are extraordinary."

- "Looking again at this film [six years later], I am astounded by his performance. It is even better than I had thought: more truly anguished, more delicately poised between the awkward, sulky scapegoat and the young creature exploding with love. It gives heart and centre to the film."

- "When the last scene faded from the Astor Theatre screen last night, a new star appeared— James Dean."

- "The box-office asset that is most important is the debut of a handsome and dynamic young actor named James Dean. He is that rare thing, a young actor who is a great actor, and the troubled eloquence with which he puts over the problems of misunderstood youth may lead to his being accepted by young audiences as a sort of symbol of their generation. It is inevitable that he will be compared to Marlon Brando, though he is no carbon copy of that capable player. He

has a completely individual screen personality.
No time should be lost in giving him a big fan
magazine buildup—not because he is trivial, but
because it's the quickest way to rally young people to his support. He's the only performer I've
ever seen who'd be completely right for
Romeo."

In fact, by the time *East of Eden* completed production that August of 1954, James Dean had found his
Juliet.

chapter nine

> A celebrity is one who is
> known to many persons he is
> glad he doesn't know.
>   H. L. MENCKEN

During the half-year he spent in Hollywood in 1954, James Dean had one great obsession when he was not appearing in *East of Eden*, and that was racing his sports car or motorcycle.

"He loved the damned motorcycle," recalled his agent, Dick Clayton, "and he tried to get just about everyone he knew to ride with him on it. I think he loved to frighten people, actually. I finally quit going on those wild spins up on Mulholland Drive, because he just drove so damned fast."

In this regard, Jimmy was not, after all, so very different from countless young American males before and after him. From the days of the "one-hoss shay" to the first "flivvers," from the collegian's jalopy to the socialite's roadster, from the preppie's convertible to the playboy's Porsche, from the first stock car to the

Formula Super Vee, from quiet scooters to the roar of a Harley-Davidson, vehicles command attention, bestow a facile sense of power, challenge pride and give to the driver and his onlookers a sense of drama and of risk. From *Scarface* and *Little Caesar* to *The Wild One*, *American Graffiti*, *Trains, Planes and Automobiles* and *Speed* (not to say the virtually obligatory car chase in almost every American action thriller), popular culture has known how to exploit the fact that guys just love the thrills and risks of speed. In Western movies, it was the chase on horseback; in contemporary stories, in a car.

And the sudden explosion of the suburban middle class in postwar America brought cars and bikes into the homes of more American teenagers than ever; like television sets and portable radios, these luxury items became standard necessities. Indiana-born James Dean always studied the details of the Indianapolis 500 race every May. That event was first held in 1911 and had been directly inspired by the French daredevil tour at Le Mans, inaugurated in 1906.

At age twenty-three, it was logical, therefore, for Jimmy to spend his money on racers and motorbikes. "He was absolutely suicidal with a car," recalled Leonard Rosenman, "and people shied away from him when he invited them for a spin because they didn't want to get killed! He was a good driver, no doubt about that, but that wasn't enough. He had to be the fastest, the best, the most impressive." By late September, Jimmy had added a used but precious Alfa Romeo to his growing collection. "He was a reckless driver, but utterly without fear," recalled his former Santa Monica College drama teacher, Gene Nielson

Owen. "He came to the house to take me and my ten-year-old daughter for a ride, and he immediately demonstrated the capacity of the car to turn square corners. The quiet streets of Pacific Palisades have never heard such squealing of tires!" To the objections of his passengers, he replied, "I've got to go places in a hurry. There just isn't enough time."

Quickness and confusion defined the second passion that year, too—or more accurately, the passion that was directed at him by the young actress Pier Angeli, then one of the loveliest and strangest creatures ever to emigrate to Hollywood. Their brief, aborted relationship provided movie lore with one of the most fantastic and most misrepresented love stories in the history of a business known for fabricating intense fantasies both on- and offscreen.

Anna Maria Pierangeli was born on the island of Sardinia on June 19, 1932. In her childhood, she moved with her parents and twin sister Maria Luisa to Rome. There, the family lived comfortably in a penthouse with a wide view over the city. Luigi Pierangeli worked successfully as a civil engineer, while his wife, Enrica—a frustrated actress—encouraged their daughters to attend art and drama school. This refined and ordered life, however, was overshadowed by the deprivations and anxieties of daily life during World War II.

By the age of eighteen, Anna Maria had been cast in an Italian movie by no less than the great actor-director Vittorio De Sica—a performance that inspired the screenwriter Stewart Stern to recommend her for the title role in his picture *Teresa*, directed by Fred Zinnemann; the film was nominated for best screenplay. Now known as Pier Angeli, she rose to stardom in this touching story of a young Italian bride and her American husband. Metro-Goldwyn-Mayer placed her under contract, and in late 1950 (just after her father's sudden death), Pier, Enrica, Maria Luisa and a baby sister named Patrizia came to America. There, Pier Angeli's elegant Italian-accented diction and her wistful, petite charm augured well for stardom, and Metro—eager to cash in on her international appeal— shipped her back and forth between Europe and Hollywood for her first several films. At five feet, two inches and 110 pounds, with green eyes, bronze hair, a dash of freckles and a lyrical laugh, she was a romantic addition to the studio roster. At the same time, her twin sister, Maria Luisa—rechristened Marisa Pavan— also went into the movies.

From June to August 1954, while Jimmy was appearing before the cameras in Burbank, Pier was on a neighboring soundstage in *The Silver Chalice*, on loan from Metro to Jack Warner. Jimmy met her quite by chance when he went to watch Paul Newman film a scene in the same picture.

Jimmy and Pier, it was soon reported, were instantly in love, and the affair between the two young stars (he was twenty-three, she twenty-two) blazed that summer—only to end abruptly, the story continued, when Pier's mother objected that non-Catholic Jimmy was unacceptable to her devout, virginal daughter. According to the traditional tale that subsequently circulated for decades, Pier obeyed Mama and then fell precipitously into the arms of singer Vic Damone, whom she married that autumn. The spurned Jimmy Dean, the story concluded, carried a torch to his dying day.

This is a nicely poignant legend that could have come straight from a nineteenth-century opera or even from the files of any B-movie studio, but it bears only the vaguest resemblance to facts. By all accounts, Pier Angeli was indeed a sweet, somewhat shy young rose in public and at work. But in private she was no convent schoolgirl, and little in her life was either prim or serene. After the horrors of war-torn Rome—where, at fifteen, she was raped by an American soldier—she was thrust into the limelight as a starlet and, soon after arriving in Hollywood, leaped into a series of torrid but ultimately disappointing affairs with, among many others, Kirk Douglas, John Drew Barrymore and Eddie Fisher. Pier also had quite tender feelings for Vic Damone long before they wed: they had met in New York at the Rainbow Room in 1950, and then later in Europe in 1951, when he was in military service and she was making a film called *The Devil Makes Three*. Their fondness for each other was renewed, and they dated frequently thereafter. Vic Damone was never, from 1951 to 1954, far from the thoughts and attention of Pier Angeli.

Of the other various affairs, Pier's mother did not prudishly disapprove, as some have claimed. Enrica Pierangeli had no objection to romance; she hoped only that her daughter would eventually choose a decent, well-born man who would be a loyal husband and a good father. La Signora was also savvy enough to realize that Pier was, after all, supporting herself (as well as Enrica and Patrizia) in the freewheeling atmosphere of Hollywood, where parental censure of a desirable, exotic starlet is not very effective. "For Mrs. Pierangeli, religion was not the determinative factor," according to Stewart Stern; manners and common courtesy were.

When she met Dean, Pier described herself as "greedy for life, romance and emotion—I am eager to experience everything." So far, given her amours and her love of fast cars and a faster nightlife, she was doing fairly well in the area of experience, if not in the arena of maturing. "When Pier takes the keys to the car, I hold my breath until she gets back," said Enrica Pierangeli. "She's so quick and impulsive. But Marisa—ah, that is different. I never worry." While her twin sister turned into a sensible, serious and stable professional actress, Pier was easily tossed into emotional turmoil and tended to retreat into a fantasy world, bringing home stray dogs and cats by the dozens and insisting that her vast doll and stuffed-animal collection comprised her closest array of friends. At twenty-two, she was a curious mixture of child, waif and minx. "I don't like to grow up," she told a reporter. "I just want to be young and have fun." And with that, she resumed sucking her lollipop and humming a nursery tune to the dolly in her arms. "She is," said a friend, "too much concerned with childish things." Indeed.

By the end of June, Pier and Jimmy were riding horses in Griffith Park, strolling on the beach at Malibu, snuggling into movie seats and munching hamburgers at roadside drive-ins. But their time together was severely limited: each was required at work six days a week, often as much as ten hours daily. There was no doubt that Jimmy found Pier exotic, attractive and amusing—and, perhaps most of all, he loved the attention she lavished on him, whom she considered much like one of her stray puppies.

Arthur Loew, Jr., who had produced *Teresa* and became friendly with both Dean and Pier, did not attach much importance to the Angeli affair. He recalled the couple at the girl's home where, when Pier was cuing Jimmy on some lines in a script, the atmosphere became solemn to the point of funereal. "He's a little shy and diffident," said actor Rod Steiger to Loew one evening. Loew broke the ice and earned Jimmy's respect by an inspired bit of mimicry of the earnest Dean, rehearsing a scene with exaggerated gravity.

Loew also recalled the tricks with which Jimmy loved to entertain a gathering. With a panache and skill no one could fathom, for example, he would excuse himself and go to the bathroom, lock the door behind him and a moment later appear at the front door affecting the attitude of a newly arrived guest. When friends went to the bathroom door, it was still locked from the inside, and the window lock, too, was intact. The secret, worthy of Houdini, was never revealed.

Other bits of legerdemain were equally memorable, as when Jimmy poked both cigarette and lighted match into his mouth and put his lips together; when he reopened his mouth, the cigarette and the match were both lighted. "Despite taking himself and his work very seriously," according to Loew, "he could be a lot of fun, and I saw that he could have a sense of humor even about himself. The last time I was with Jimmy, he had a terrible cold. 'Show business is in deep trouble,' he told me gravely. 'Barrymore is dead and I'm not feeling well.' And with that, he threw my coat over his shoulders with a theatrical gesture." Jimmy's statement to Loew has often been reported by fans with great awe and wrenched out of context toward the end of his life, as if it were a mystic prophecy of premature death. Quite the contrary, Loew has insisted. "He could be very funny, and those of us who were present took it the way he intended. He joined us in the laughter."

As for the attraction between Jimmy and Pier, it may not have been the hot Hollywood romance then broadcast, but in its own way it was very strong, as Loew's cousin, Stewart Stern, believed. "I thought it had to do with the child inside each of them. Their affair was like a game, their relationship like a Hollywood fantasy." And in this fantasy, Jimmy was Peter Pan, Pier was Wendy Darling—and their small retinue of fans and contract players were the Lost Boys. "We were like kids together and that's the way we both liked it," said Pier after Jimmy's death. And to Elia Kazan, Jimmy never appeared so much an unformed kid as when he was dating Pier Angeli.

Stern and Kazan were both on the mark. However much Warner Bros. and Metro encouraged the rumors of passionate young love, the fact is that the relationship was strained from day one. Jimmy infuriated Pier with his rude manners—coming to a formal luncheon party in dirty jeans, barefoot and without shirt or socks; or, when he visited her home, deliberately offending Mrs. Pierangeli by resting his boots on an antique coffee table. Nor did the accounts of Jimmy urinating in public (against a wall at the Burbank studio, among other places) endear him to Pier's mother. "She cared a great deal about form and manners," as Stewart Stern said, "and in this regard Jimmy offended her. I don't think her dislike had anything at all to do with religion."

Jimmy's rudeness might seem incongruous in light

of his stated love for Pier (which the studio successfully got into the fan magazines). But in fact he was again playing the bad boy, this time perhaps to demote or even to sabotage the affair with Pier. As before with other women (and with some men), Jimmy shunned intimacy when it became serious, when commitment appeared on the horizon. Like many people who believe they have been so wounded they can never give or receive love, he created a situation in which it was possible and then, before he could be disappointed, he ended it.

"He was intensely determined not to be loved or to love," said Nicholas Ray, who met him that autumn and was preparing to direct Jimmy's next picture, Stewart Stern's script for *Rebel Without a Cause*. "He could be absorbed, fascinated, attracted by things new or beautiful, but he would never surrender himself. There were girls convinced they were the only ones in his life when they were no more than occasions." As long as a man or woman made no emotional demands, all was acceptable; but if feelings were generated, Jimmy could be callously, coldly rejecting.

Pier was the prettiest occasion of all, and somehow she suited his personal and public relations needs that season. But very quickly, she became serious about him; drawn to his cool toughness and evident need of nurturing, she was confident that only she could break through his diffidence and teach him to love. But it was a lost cause. Elia Kazan thought he heard Jimmy and Pier making love in the trailer adjacent to his at the studio, but all he could be sure of was that they usually argued. "He always had uncertain relations with girlfriends," Kazan reflected years later, adding that he "did not think Jimmy was a very effective lover with women."

Dick Clayton, who often helped Jimmy and Pier to meet without her mother's knowledge, agreed: "On his part, I never really thought it was that serious." The fact is that no one but studio publicists spoke much about a consummated love affair. The image of an attractive young couple together at the studio was the public relations currency of the day—never mind that Jimmy and Pier never told anyone that they were lovers. "It was all so innocent," she said wistfully years later.

So it seemed to studio personnel at Metro, too, where Jud Kinberg, then associate producer to John Houseman, was preparing *The Cobweb* with director Vincente Minnelli. Kinberg recalled the day Jimmy zoomed over to the Thalberg Building in Culver City to talk about playing the role of a young psychopath in that film. "Jimmy wanted the role for three reasons," according to Kinberg. "For one thing, he liked it and saw its possibilities. Second, he had the idea that if he could land the role, he could use it as leverage either to break his contract with Jack Warner or to improve its terms. And the desire to go over to MGM was related to the third reason—to be near Pier Angeli." (In addition, Leonard Rosenman had been signed to compose the score for this picture, and Jimmy was eager to renew their friendship.) Kinberg also recalled that Jimmy's ardor for Pier Angeli was complicated by his painful sexual conflict. "I recall escorting him down to the set where she was working, and his very awkwardness and shyness around us and around her made him somehow very endearing. In fact, we would have been delighted to have him in *The Cobweb*." But for the time being, Metro's executives would not agree to help James Dean out of a deal at Warner Bros. John Kerr, who had gotten the role Jimmy had wanted in Robert Anderson's *Tea and Sympathy*, on Broadway, again supplanted Jimmy in *The Cobweb*.

These visits occurred in 1954, before the release of *East of Eden*. The following year, MGM's studio head Dore Schary and producer Charles Schnee were only too happy to have Jimmy agree to portray middleweight champ Rocky Graziano in Ernest Lehman's dramatic, deeply emotional and at times hilarious biographical screenplay *Somebody Up There Likes Me*, to be directed by Robert Wise. This was enthusiastically agreed to by Dean, and the deal was set. This had easily been arranged, for Metro's loan of Elizabeth Taylor to Warner for *Giant* guaranteed them the ability to sign James Dean for a picture. But even after Jimmy was officially signed and announced (in April 1955), Lehman had serious misgivings about the actor's slight, unmuscular build—and hence his possible unsuitability in the role of a prizefighter.*

The uneasy friendship between Jimmy and Pier—an amorous fantasy on her part, a mere fancy on his—

---

* Dean's sudden death then caused hasty recasting of the Graziano role. Both producer Schnee and screenwriter Lehman happened to see the relatively unknown Paul Newman a few nights later, in a Hemingway-based television drama, "The Battler." Immediately, they chose Newman—to play opposite Pier Angeli—and Newman turned out to be spectacularly right for the role of Rocky Graziano. *Somebody Up There Likes Me* won two Academy Awards, vaulting to immediate stardom thirty-two-year-old Newman in a role in which, perhaps for the only time in his long career, he played someone other than himself.

endured for only three months, from late June to September 29, when the couple attended the Hollywood premiere of Judy Garland's new film, *A Star Is Born*. (A week earlier, he had blithely escorted movie actress Terry Moore to the opening of *Sabrina*.) On October 1, Pier was surprised to learn from Dick Clayton that Jimmy had fled to New York on the thirtieth, for the second time in a month. The first trip was for a role in a television drama ("Run Like a Thief"); this journey, she learned when she tracked Jimmy down at his apartment on Sixty-eighth Street, was simply to visit friends. And with that, Pier realized that Jimmy was not to be hers, that his career and his whims ruled his life. Exactly three days later, she announced her engagement to Vic Damone, who had always been in the wings, who loved her dearly and was a far more reliable character. They were married on November 24, and for years an unveri-fiable legend circulated that Jimmy, astride his motorcy-cle, awaited the exit of the bride and groom from St. Timothy's Church at Beverly Glen and Pico—and then leaped on his motorcycle and zoomed away in angry disgust. In any event, Jimmy and Pier never met again.

From that time, Pier Angeli's life was a descent from one sad episode to another. She and Damone had a son in August 1955, and shortly thereafter the marriage went sour; they separated in 1958 and divorced in 1959, after highly dramatic scenes in which she was alternately a hysteric and a fantasist not above threatening suicide. In 1962, she married bandleader Armando Trovajoli, who was fourteen years her senior, and the following year she had a second son. By this time, her film career, which had begun with such charm and promise, was over; her second marriage was terminated in 1966.

In her mid-thirties, Pier Angeli became a tragic figure, wandering to and fro in Europe and Hollywood, accepting the rare bit role in this or that cheap foreign movie. Finally, she crept into the dangerous comfort of the twilight world of drugs. The actress Susan Strasberg befriended Pier in Rome but found her mired in addiction—"still beautiful even with the heavy makeup she wore, although it couldn't cover the strain in her features."

That strain, Pier confided to close friends like Stewart Stern, derived from a passion for James Dean that haunted her for the rest of her life. "It was heartbreaking to hear her speak about her love for him," Stern recalled. "I had the impression that she wished she'd had something of him to be close to"—by which she implied a child. For years she was, as she said in March 1971, "emotionally crushed" by the loss of the one she believed she loved "more than either of my husbands—I could think only of Jimmy when I was in bed with them. I could only wish it was Jimmy and not my husband who was next to me."

The fantasy finally destroyed her. Lost, lonely, beset by financial difficulties in Italy and with her career only a dim memory in Hollywood, she visited America during the summer of 1971. In Los Angeles, on the night of September 9, she swallowed a massive dose of phenobarbital. A friend found her lithe, lifeless body next morning. Pier Angeli was thirty-nine.

That same season, Jimmy formed a very different relationship with a colorful Hollywood eccentric named Maila

Nurmi, an actress who—usually billed as "Vampira," a character straight from a Charles Addams cartoon—appeared in five low-budget films and was known around Hollywood as a hostess of the macabre. Announcing horror films on television and presenting herself as a ghoulish neurotic, always all in black, she became something of a fixture among the denizens of Googie's, a popular all-night coffee shop on Sunset Boulevard. There, the insomniac James Dean often held court in the small hours, surrounded by a band of admirers that included Nurmi, with whom his relationship was strictly platonic. (She was eight years older than Dean and, at the time, happily married.) Never mind how much more money he had than others at the table, Nurmi recalled, he paid only for his single cup of coffee—"no tip and no treating: he was a miser and he hung onto the money he earned."

At first, he was merely fascinated by her and went along with her deadpan comic routine; then, over the course of their several meetings, a kind of odd friendship developed, and often they talked about the ultimate reality, death. Why was he so obsessed? she asked one evening. "That's the only way I'll have any peace," he replied—a melodramatic response apt for a young actor who takes himself very seriously.

The connection between the two led to a misunderstood joke. For a publicity photo, Nurmi posed at a local cemetery, as if attending her own funeral. Just as she received the contact prints, she heard that Jimmy, in a typically odd moment of prankishness, had visited a funeral home in Indiana and crawled inside a coffin to have his photo taken. Taking one of her own contacts, she scrawled on the back, "Having a wonderful time—wish you were here"—meaning in California, not in the realm of the dead. Unsure of his address, Nurmi sent it to the Villa Capri, a favorite Italian restaurant in Hollywood—where a friendly waiter misinterpreted Nurmi's card as in bad taste. Told about the photo and message (which he had not seen), Jimmy feigned hurt feelings when Nurmi rang to explain. "But I didn't tell him the joke, because I'd ruin the punch line. 'You'll understand when you see it,'" she said, promising to send another. That was September 29, 1955, the day before James Dean died. He never received her card.

But by this time, as so often, Jimmy had wearied of his new friend. "I was interested in finding out if this girl was possessed by a satanic force," he said. "But she knew absolutely nothing. I found her devoid of any true interest except her Vampira makeup."

Jimmy made several trips to New York for the autumn and winter of 1954–55—for television appearances and to renew old acquaintances. Photographer Roy Schatt, who took many photos of Jimmy that season and taught him the rudiments of the craft, recalled him as a young man with "a great emergent talent, a screwball sense of humor, a flair for daredevilry—perpetually both at ease and on guard. But he could never be a real person himself—he was always hiding behind someone else's persona." At impromptu gatherings in Schatt's studio, Jimmy entertained with stunts—including his favorite, in which he removed his two false front teeth and offered them to guests ("Wanna buy thum gold, man? I need thum thoup."). He also banged his bongo drums rather too loudly, and if someone complained or he felt ignored, he pouted or stormed out, like a spoiled, petulant child. "I'm playing the damn bongo and the world can go to hell," he announced, and that was that.

"He could be sullen and childish," recalled Schatt, "but he could also use his feelings of outrage to create outlandish situations that often bordered on the dangerous." One such moment occurred when Jimmy left a gathering at Schatt's home carrying a chair and, moments later, was seen in the middle of a busy street, sitting in the chair, smoking, delaying traffic and daring cars or trucks to smash into him. "Don't you sons of bitches ever get bored?" he asked his friends when they came to his rescue. "I just wanted to spark things, man—that's all!" He had, concluded Schatt, "a mania for taking chances," a desire to be noticed that was sometimes nearly pathological.

Another new friend was the singer Eartha Kitt, whom Jimmy had met briefly in Los Angeles and whom he now recontacted. She taught an informal dance class he attended a few times, as he did those led by the choreographer Katherine Dunham. Jimmy liked Kitt's sense of humor, her exotic trademark feline purr and her refusal to be surprised when he telephoned at four in the morning to suggest a motorcycle ride. The relationship was, as Kitt confirmed in her published memoirs, not sexual.

As the Warner Bros. publicity machine shifted into high gear before the premiere of *East of Eden*, Jimmy was permitted—in fact encouraged—to accept television roles during the autumn of 1954. Among six shows in which he performed in either New York or Los Angeles between September and January, two have survived. In "I'm a Fool," based on a story by

Sherwood Anderson and broadcast from an old Los Angeles warehouse-turned-studio, he was an imprudent, poor farm boy who leaves home and takes refuge in role-playing at a racetrack. There, in an immature desire to impress a young girl, he fabricates an elaborate history, a fancy name, an elegant address and phony details about family wealth. But he forever loses the girl when they are suddenly parted, she promises to write, and he realizes that she will be writing to a nonexistent person. Forever after, he regrets this youthful, foolish indiscretion.

Jimmy's attack on the role was properly callow, his protestations of self-importance more sad than pompous, his affection for the girl rightly pathetic in its doomed, precipitous misjudgment. "Most of us at that time [in television] were from Broadway, acting as if we were on a stage," recalled Eddie Albert, his co-star. "But Jimmy brought a whole different 'inside' thing that was like the Actors Studio, but with a sense of humor in it, too." *Variety* singled out Jimmy's "excellent work, [his] sensitive and moving performance." On the set, however, producer Mort Abrahams recalled Jimmy as a loner who did not socialize with the cast and wanted to be left alone.

But the program was not easily realized. Don Medford, who directed "I'm a Fool" and three other of Jimmy's television roles, found him "virtually impossible. One day in rehearsal he would do something brilliant, the next day he was all over the place. He had no discipline at all." And then Medford decided on a novel approach. "Sit there and try to keep in mind how you got there," he told Jimmy after a particularly good scene. "He looked at me as if I were crazy." And then Jimmy gave a first-rate performance.

The girl in "I'm a Fool" was played by sixteen-year-old Natalie Wood, who had appeared in twenty films and was both thrilled and anxious about acting with the most discussed rising star of the year. The first day of rehearsal that November, Jimmy kept the entire cast and crew awaiting his good pleasure. Finally, he arrived, wearing filthy clothes, his trousers held together with a safety pin, barely acknowledging Natalie's presence. During the week of rehearsals, he was amusing, he was flattering and funny—and just as quickly, he was distant and brooding. But the day before the broadcast, he invited her to lunch and a fast friendship was established that lasted through the production of *Rebel Without a Cause* months later.

The second extant teleplay may well be ranked as James Dean's finest performance in the medium. "The Thief" was adapted by Arthur Arent from an old play by Henri Bernstein; produced by the prestigious Theatre Guild, it was directed by Vincent J. Donehue. Jimmy's co-stars formed an impressive list: Diana Lynn, Mary Astor, Paul Lukas and Patric Knowles. Lynn liked him and Astor tolerated him, but the rest of the cast and crew had unhappy memories of working with James Dean. Director Donehue began a rehearsal with a polite invitation to Dean: "How would it feel, Jimmy, to try the scene this way?" And with that, Jimmy performed his typical shock tactic: in front of everyone, he unbuttoned his trousers and urinated on the stage floor.

In his most affecting and poignant television role—and perhaps his best performance after *East of Eden*—Jimmy played a lovesick nineteen-year-old, the stepson of Lukas and the son of Astor. Secretly in love with

Lynn, who is married to a much older man, he knows no way out of his dilemma. At the same time, there has been a series of burglaries in the vast Paris mansion, and according to a detective, the signs point to Jimmy, who is accused of stealing from his stepfather. But as it happens, Lynn's husband discovers that she is the thief, who has stolen the cash to buy beautiful clothes to please her husband—whom, she thinks, she disappoints with her youthful frivolity. (The story, gravid with French ironies, could have come from the pen of de Maupassant.) Jimmy, to protect his beloved, takes the blame for her and is banished to work in the colonies by his stepfather, who believes him guilty.

"You're sending me away?" Jimmy asks Lukas, his words choked back with pain as if he were remembering himself as a nine-year-old, sent on the lonely funeral train and dismissed from his father's life. "You're turning me out? But Father, I've never been away from you!" Wisely, Donehue kept the camera focused on the great mist of pain that washed across Jimmy's features; only rarely was television acting so immediately credible.

Finally, Lynn admits the truth to Lukas—but remains with the husband she truly loves, and Jimmy, noble to the end, suffers the greatest loss of all. "Now you're going away from me forever," he says to her, his heart and voice breaking. "Do you know what my love for you is like?" And she departs, the drama concluding with a close-up of his tearstained face.

"The Thief" remains a small miracle of early television, one of the few dramas justifying something like the trite epithet "golden." But once again, the program was only realized after considerable difficulties with the youngest star. For public relations, some actors gave parties, others gifts: James Dean gave offense. "Did you hear what he did today?" had become almost a studio motto at Warners during his tenure there.

In addition, the veteran actor Paul Lukas reacted to Jimmy's unpredictability much the same way as Massey, Lockhart and others: he never knew what Jimmy would do in rehearsals, where he would stand, how he might alter a line. At one point, Lukas had the line, "Excuse me, but my son is a little peculiar." At the final technical rehearsal, Lukas repeatedly stumbled on the line. When Donehue asked the reason, Lukas was blunt: "I can't say my boy is peculiar. He is not peculiar." And pointing at James Dean, Lukas explained, "This young man is crazy."

The same consternation was felt, although less frankly and more politically expressed, by none other than Ronald Reagan, who appeared opposite Jimmy in December 1954. *The Dark, Dark Hour* reunited Jimmy with Constance Ford (his co-star in *See the Jaguar*) in a drama about a crook (Dean) who terrorizes a doctor and his wife (Reagan and Ford). "I think in a way he was experimenting with his part," recalled Reagan years later, "because in an all-day rehearsal he would vary the performance, [but] by showtime he had arrived at the performance he wanted." At every moment, in other words, his partners could expect anything. He was, concluded Reagan, "not easy to know."

The buzz of publicity was becoming a roar of Hollywood news: there was a new talent, an unpredictable one. Columnist Sidney Skolsky, who for decades kept a sensitive finger on the pulse of Hollywood, admired Dean but put the matter succinctly: "He is undisciplined and irresponsible."

Among the New York holiday parties at year's end was a singularly unmerry one for his old flame Dizzy Sheridan, who had not seen Jimmy in two years. She had just returned from a long and successful stage of her career that had taken her to the Virgin Islands, where she had become a popular singer and dancer. She found the reunion

> a little strange. He wanted to hear all about my life, which was totally different from his. At the time I had a long braid, and he just hung on to it as we went from room to room at the party. And then I was kind of surprised, because he spent the entire evening insulting people, and that cleared the room. One moment he seemed happy, then he was just miserable. His rudeness seemed to me a kind of disturbance. Maybe he didn't want all those other people around.

Jimmy insisted that Dizzy leave the party with him and Leonard Rosenman, and the trio shared a taxi. She was en route to Grand Central Station, and then to visit her family in Larchmont, so she could not be persuaded to join them at another party. Just before they parted, Jimmy took her hand and, with not very great enthusiasm, offered to help further her career in Hollywood. But she knew the score by this time, and she was looking forward to returning to her work in the Caribbean. They hugged, and then he leaped back into the cab. They never met again.

Decades later, Dizzy could not shake off the memory of that evening. "There seemed something very unhappy about him, something desperate and disturbed. I knew that as an actor he felt things very deeply. But I sensed that as a young man he was—how shall I put it?—'unformed' is the word that comes to mind."

chapter ten

> The young always have the
> same problem—how to rebel
> and conform at the same
> time. They have now solved
> this by defying their
> parents and copying one
> another.
>
> QUENTIN CRISP

In early 1955, technicians were working overtime at Warner Bros. to refine the sound and perfect the color of the wide-screen prints of *East of Eden* in time for the March premiere in New York and the national release in April. At precisely the same time, experts over at Metro-Goldwyn-Mayer were supervising the final details of *Blackboard Jungle*, a grainy, powerful black and white picture that made America sit up and take notice, and not only because it was the first Hollywood product with rock and roll music. It was readily booked everywhere in the country, for it sensed the fearful temper of the times about a problem everyone wanted to ignore—the growing epidemic of juvenile delinquency. In 1953, Brando as *The Wild One* had suggested the threat of morose motorcycle gangs vexing an anonymous small town somewhere in middle America. "What are you rebelling against?" asks a girl he meets. "What have you got?" is his quick reply. Director Nicholas Ray and his colleagues at Warners picked up on this.

Hence, when a March release date was announced for *Blackboard Jungle*, Warner Bros. put forth its own news. Since 1946, the studio had owned the rights to a book by Dr. Robert Lindner called *Rebel Without a Cause: The Hypnoanalysis of a Criminal Psychopath*, a clinical account of an institutionalized young madman. That same year, this was to have been a project for Marlon Brando, but no satisfactory script could be obtained, and the enterprise was shelved. Now, after numerous delays and several attempts by other writers (among them Clifford Odets and Leon Uris) and a draft and adaptation by Irving Shulman, Stewart Stern was finishing a compelling screenplay for director Nicholas Ray. Ray had outlined his own seventeen-page story ("The Blind Run") and wanted to unite the themes of generational strife, adolescent alienation and social dysfunction in a story of juvenile delinquency and its effect on polite, middle-class families. Borrowing the original title, Warner announced a forthcoming picture called *Rebel Without a Cause*, about a sensitive, confused high-school senior, a boy of goodwill oppressed by family divisions and peer violence. As late as March 1, some executives held out for Robert Wagner, Tab Hunter or John Kerr to play the boy. They were resoundingly overruled by Ray, Stern and the producer, David Weisbart. James Dean would have star billing above the title. Still, *Rebel* was planned as a black-and-white picture, and there was no established star—hence, Jack Warner did not yet see it as a major motion picture.

Meantime, the subject of all the talk about *Eden* and the still inchoate *Rebel* spent the first two months of 1955 in a small, rented bungalow at 1541 Sunset Plaza Drive, just off the busy Sunset Strip. From there he zoomed around town on his new 500 Triumph Trophy motorcycle or in his white Porsche 356 Super Speedster. Descending down Laurel Canyon on the Triumph at a ferocious speed early one morning, he was very nearly killed when he ran the light at Sunset Boulevard. "We were on a collision course," recalled photographer Phil Stern. "We both braked and careered through the intersection. I came close to killing him—just a few inches saved his life. I stuck my head out the window, screaming profanities, as he got up off the bike with a dopey grin on his face."

Stern then recognized him, they shared breakfast at Schwab's, and Jimmy accompanied the photographer to the set of *Guys and Dolls* at Metro, where Stern was scheduled to take publicity stills of Marlon Brando and Frank Sinatra. Dean stood sheepishly on the sidelines, content to worship from afar. Again, Brando had the distinct impression of a highly disturbed young man and again he recommended to Leonard Rosenman that Jimmy seek psychiatric help.

Irving Shulman, who also worked on the screenplay preparation for *Rebel Without a Cause*, also recalled a hair-raising moment when Jimmy careened down Barham Boulevard. "I was in the gas station," said Shulman, who was a witness, "and his way of stopping was to cut across the street, run through the gas station and drive into a wall. That he didn't kill himself or crush a leg was a miracle."

There was no doubt about it. The shock of imminent fame was not good for Jimmy Dean, who, according to the journalist George Scullin (who actually liked him), "collected a small crew of sycophants, and what gaucheries he couldn't think of, they did." These actions included party-crashing, becoming rudely drunk at gatherings and, with rather too much calculation, offending for the apparent sake of offense, as if controversy and ill manners were themselves guarantees of publicity. Which of course they were.

Jimmy spent late hours at Googie's (the all-night coffee shop adjacent to Schwab's), taking care to be seen in the right places at the right times but never altering for anyone's sake his casual, unkempt appearance, his nearly incoherent speech or frequently rude manner. This, as usual, was all part of a careful strategy, as if he would patent the image of the disaffected loner. "I came to Hollywood to act, not to charm society," he said more than once when challenged for his disorderliness or incivility. The public relations staff at Warners had to tap every bit of ingenuity to deal with reports about his unsociability, although to their great relief he renounced public urination. Stewart Stern recalled the afternoon Jimmy was introduced to a major Warner Bros. stockholder: "I'd like you to meet the man with the money," said an executive genially. With that, Jimmy reached into his pocket, withdrew all the change, flung it at the man's feet and loped away.

It must also be stressed that Jimmy's other side—the shy, mild and genial boy—could emerge and touch

people, especially when he recontacted his old friend
Leonard Rosenman (who was supervising the final
scoring of *Eden*) and his protective agent Dick Clayton
(who was revising his client's contract with Warners).*

But there were other odd developments even the
savviest publicist found it difficult to finesse. For one
thing, Jimmy formed an intimate attachment to a
young apprentice actor named Jack Simmons, who
could usually be found at the apartment on Sunset
Plaza Drive. "He was absolutely devoted and committed to Jimmy," said John Gilmore, who had returned to
Hollywood and knew them at the time, "and made
himself very important. But he was compartmentalized
in Jimmy's life, and then finally he was dropped."
Sidney Skolsky, among others, recalled that wherever
Jimmy went, Jack was sure to go: "He gets Jimmy coffee or a sandwich or whatever Jimmy wants. Jack also
runs interference when there are people Jimmy doesn't
want to see." Eventually, thanks to the star of the picture, Jack appeared fleetingly in *Rebel Without a Cause*.

For years, the Dean-Simmons friendship was the
subject of wild speculation and considerable pornographic imagination. But both men died without utter-
ing a word about the specifics of their relationship, and
as the old maxim runs, no one held the lamp. Most
people in their social circle saw the devotion as
painfully one-sided, however: it was a case of the adoring Jack, an acolyte to the diffident Jimmy who made

---

* Although Dean was under exclusive contract to Warners, he did not have a so-called
term deal: his agents, therefore, were able to negotiate the price of each film for him.
Had he refused the offer of a particular script, the studio had the right to suspend him
without pay; it would, of course, have been suicidal for them to do so.

of him a kind of hip valet. Faye Nuell Mayo, for one, noticed that Jack Simmons adored Jimmy, "but how seriously Jimmy took him was really unclear to everybody."

But this attachment, which stayed quietly in the background, whatever it was, did not bother Warners nearly as much as the one Jimmy formed with a doe-eyed, desperate woman who had lost a leg in a motorcycle accident; her name has evaporated into the mists of Hollywood antiquity. They met one evening at a bar on Sunset Strip, where the young girl was tippling rather too much. Jimmy apparently tried to amuse her with imitations and jokes, gained her confidence and then extracted the details of her accident, the reasons she often neglected to wear her prosthesis, and the feelings she had about being (so she thought) an outcast. With clinical, dark intensity, he courted her, and for weeks that winter it was widely believed that she shared his bed.

On at least one occasion, Jimmy took the girl along to a professional meeting. He had very much admired a sculptured head of Marlon Brando by the artist Kenneth Kendall and, just a few weeks before the premiere of *Eden*, went to Kendall in the hope of being similarly immortalized. "I had the feeling he brought her along to play off her," recalled the artist. "He wanted to make an impression on her as well as on me." At first, Kendall thought Dean had come to the studio simply to admire the artist's work, and initially he was unimpressed with Dean, whose unshaven, almost chalky features suggested a homeless waif rather than a budding star.

"Dean was obsessed with Brando," Kendall added,

"and he went over to my Brando sculpture and was fascinated by it and by a likeness of Steve Reeves I was working on. He sat down and went through my complete file of Brando pictures, and then he took me by surprise. 'would—would—you be,' he said almost stuttering, 'Would you be interested in sculpting me?' I remember thinking to myself, 'Do you really think you're in the world class of people I'm doing?'"

The lame girl, meantime, chain-smoked and chattered ceaselessly, hence allowing Jimmy the chance to convey for Kendall's benefit a rogue's gallery of portraits: exasperated boyfriend, patient lover, devoted aide. About a possible bust of James Dean, Kendall temporized, offering the excuse of time to complete the head of Reeves. But when Jimmy departed Kendall's studio he turned on a thousand-watt smile of charm. "He almost bowed as he extended his hand to me, and, looking up into my eyes, he projected that entire personality that was about to become so famous. He smiled, his dimples appeared, and he suddenly transformed himself into the most beautiful person I had ever seen. My feet seemed to burn into the pavement!" Two weeks later, Kendall saw a preview of *Eden* and decided to do a sculpture. The artist's magnificent work of Dean, finally installed at Griffith Park and in Fairmount, was completed only after Dean's death. As for the unfortunate girl, she seemed to have fallen in love with Jimmy. And then one day that spring of 1955, she left town: he tired of her, or she wearied of his moods—no one was ever certain.

There was, at the same time, a brief romance with a nineteen-year-old aspiring actress named Lili Kardell, who had yet to appear in a picture. She was a Swedish immigrant, then under contract to Universal-International, who could have passed for a reverse image of Jimmy himself: they wore their hair similarly, they wore matched bathing suits, they favored black leisure outfits. As with Pier Angeli, Jimmy (like his idol Brando) favored exotic foreign ladies to escort in public.

"He was very moody, secretive one minute and up and dancing the next," Kardell recalled years later. "Often at dinner he went over to his buddies to talk about racing. It didn't do any good to complain. That's just the way he was. No excuse, no reason for the half-hour he was gone. He was deep in thought one minute, joking the next." And, she might have sensed, forever awkward with girlfriends. Leonard Rosenman, for one, felt this brief tryst was very like that with Pier Angeli: "Jimmy knew that in order to make it big, he had to hang out with these attractive people: he had to date this one, he had to go there with that one. It had to do with the columnists, who he was seen with."

As with all his attachments, Jimmy could not sustain the interest of either young woman. Taking his curiosity as a sign that he would be her lover, guardian and protector, the injured girl was doomed to disappointment. Evident devotion—any devotion, in fact—still frightened him, and he had to subvert it. "He hadn't been the kind of friend one could count on or whose actions you could predict," as Roy Schatt recalled. The girl with one leg, as she was always called, was the latest casualty. Lili Kardell's role, too, was soon reduced.

Otherwise, that warm winter in Los Angeles, Jimmy was astonishingly uncooperative with Warner's publicity department, whose staff was working overtime to build up his image prior to the release of *Eden*. He

came to interviews messily dressed, his hair
uncombed, wearing a torn purple sweater out at the
elbows and (forty years before it was terribly chic)
jeans torn at the knees. He was, according to one colleague, "really filthy, with heavy dandruff and a really
bad appearance"—and so Jimmy alienated the very
people assigned to help him.

"He has been absolutely impossible," reported publicist Herman Golob to his chief, Mort Blumenstock.

> Has been extremely uncooperative and [has]
> refused to see fine lineup of newspaper inter-
> views we had set for him. Finally convinced
> him to sit for interviews, whereupon he fouled
> himself up and got one magazine writer sore as
> blazes. Have asked Kazan [to] give us assist
> and confidentially Gadge says he doesn't want
> to be Father Confessor to this kid. [We] Could
> have used Dean to great advantage for *Eden*
> publicity, but the way he is acting, he can do us
> more harm than good. He needs a good scrub-
> bing behind the ears.

With one bit of publicity, however, Jimmy cooperated
fully. One Sunday afternoon in January, Nicholas Ray
was entertaining some of those signed for *Rebel* in his
rooms at the Chateau Marmont Hotel, the apartment-
hotel built in the delirious Hollywood-Norman style,
complete with turrets, spires, arched windows and but-
tresses. Cheap red wine flowed like cheap red wine, and
as guests arrived and departed, Jimmy was introduced

to a young photographer named Dennis Stock, who was invited to a preview of *Eden*. Stock, already known and much in demand as a celebrity documentarist, was so impressed with Jimmy's performance that he was able to sell to *Life* the idea of a photo story.

The magazine was delighted with the idea, but not nearly as much as the men at Warner Bros.—especially since Stock's idea was to photograph Jimmy in Fairmount and New York. "I wanted to show where he had come from," Stock recalled, "[but] I didn't feel it was truly a case of wanting to go home. I think Fairmount was a place he had been happy to get away from."

At first, Jimmy stipulated that *Life* put him on the cover, and that he have the right to edit the accompanying text. "It was an unusual and highly egocentric gesture," recalled Stock, who refused to make such requests to *Life* on Jimmy's behalf. "I told Jimmy the editor's answer was no. For days he acted like a spoiled kid." Finally, in early February, they left the warmth of Southern California for the frigid Midwest and then the damp chill of New York.

The Indiana ground was hard as iron, and everywhere there was a thin layer of icy snow. Jimmy strolled down Fairmount's Main Street like a figure out of a Beat Generation novel—hands stuffed in his pockets, cap at a rakish angle, cigarette stub clenched tightly between his lips. He loved being photographed, recalled Stock, and was fully aware of projecting the image of an alien outsider—"but I don't think he knew who he was." That, of course, was the opinion of everyone who knew James Dean. It was, in the final analysis, a consensus precisely because there was still no formed character in this boyish twenty-four year old.

For other photos, Jimmy sat dining in the Winslow house with his relatives, nuzzled animals in the barn, stood casually at streetcorners and visited the family gravesites. The Winslows and Deans were thrilled to have him home, for he was to them still the simple Indiana farm boy they remembered—and yet he was now a famous movie star, too, and perhaps no family can be indifferent to or unaffected by that startling status. Aunt Ortense fretted over his pale, somewhat neurasthenic manner, but she knew not to flutter nervously about. Hearty meals were the stuff of love.

Jimmy also attended Fairmount High's "Sweethearts Ball" on Valentine's Day, playing his bongo drums with the band and basking in the limelight of the students' admiration. The photo sessions with Stock went remarkably well, especially since often enough the subject looked (in Stock's words) "like utter hell—[with] a two- or three-day growth of beard, and enormous bags under his eyes. His insomnia posed a special problem [and although] he was only twenty-four, the effects of his life-style were already beginning to show." A few months earlier, Jimmy had asked Roy Schatt, "Don't you think I look like Michelangelo's *David*?" Schatt had smiled indulgently. But by midwinter, the image was closer to that of a consumptive Romantic poet, worn out by insomnia, cigarettes and a deep inner misery. "When Jimmy posed in the driveway of his aunt and uncle's house, he'd already written the caption for the picture: 'You can't go home again.'" *Life* used neither the photo nor the Wolfe-inspired caption.

Then, during a tour of the town's stores, another odd moment occurred. Jimmy led Dennis Stock to Hunt's Funeral Home, and there, without prompting, he climbed into a coffin. At once fascinated and appalled, the photographer clicked away as Jimmy struck a variety of poses, sitting up and lying down like a corpse alternately still and revived, all the while affecting funny, sad and quizzical expressions. "It was a surprise to me," recalled Stock. "I let him fool around, and when he had finally cooled down, I found a moment that showed the truth—that James Dean was a lost person." The photo—of a tousled, tired, suddenly childlike young man, sitting up in a casket, his hands folded on satin quilting—remains one of the most haunting of this haunted person.

The moment should perhaps not be easily interpreted as many have—namely, that in this singular moment James Dean showed himself to be longing for death or (a still more cheaply academic Freudian explanation) that Fairmount had brought Jimmy more intense thoughts of his mother, whom he longed to rejoin in eternity. Everyone who knew James Dean dismisses as undiluted rubbish this reading of the apparently morbid moment at Hunt's.

On the one hand, the ghoulish mannerism is typical of a boy's macabre sense of humor—a tasteless Halloween stunt madly wrenched back to Valentine's Day. Movie stars pop up in coffins only in horror films, yet there was James Dean, in an inspired moment of public relations fancy, tweaking once again the collective nose of professional polite society. The more people discussed it, and the more horrified people would be, the better could he realize his goal of unpredictability. Just so Jimmy's public stunts. One evening in Fairmount, he and his old high-school friend, Bob Pulley, went to a bar in Marion, where Jimmy filled his mouth with lighter fluid, sprayed the fluid through a lighted match and sent a fireball leaping into the air.

But there is an element in Stock's comment about a "lost person" that cannot be dismissed, and that the photo itself discloses. This is not merely a canny actor conscious of his bad-boy image: as in his rendering of Cal Trask, James Dean is behind the persona of the character assumed. "Jimmy was a very pained young man," according to Stock. "He was subject to extreme mood shifts—up one minute and down the next. He was uncomfortable in his own skin." So says the photograph, which seemed to capture the haze of melancholy on the features of a lonely, abandoned child.

The photographs taken in Manhattan later that February show other aspects of the wanderer— huddled in a winter overcoat (loaned by Arthur Loew, Jr.), strolling along the wet streets of Times Square, attending a presentation at the Actors Studio, sitting in a barber's chair, practicing a dance step, playing bongo drums at an impromptu gathering. Not one of the photos, however, shows a carefree young man at ease, much less happy with himself and his prospects.

But there was, as it happens, very good reason for him to be pleased that season. His agents had negotiated improvements in his contract deals with Warner Bros. for his next two films, *Rebel Without a Cause* and *Giant*,* and there was now no doubt—even as the release date of *East of Eden* drew near—that precipitate fame and increased rewards were just around the corner. In

---

* *Giant* was to have preceded *Rebel Without a Cause* but was postponed because of Elizabeth Taylor's pregnancy. Her son Christopher was born on February 27, 1955, but she had a protracted recuperation.

addition, the studio was honoring Deacy's and Clayton's requests on Jimmy's behalf that he be permitted to do Broadway plays and television dramas, and that he have the right to refuse any uncongenial role. But as before, instead of welcoming the arrival of what he had worked for, he seemed more dissatisfied than ever. "I want to tell you what the word is out here," he said to Christine White in New York. "I'm a goddamned star out here!" But there was no joy in his voice.

He was, in fact, woefully depressed that winter, and according to Leonard Rosenman his ill temper was often manifest in a new tendency: "He started to boss people around badly." At the same time, Jimmy felt keenly his own father's lack of interest. "He was doing everything," Rosenman added, "for one person—his father. Not for a director, not for audiences, not even for himself. And his father never took the remotest interest." It is not difficult to see the connection between this disappointment, that of a still needy child, with the tendency to "boss people around," which is, after all, simply a way of establishing one's own importance when one is unsure of it.

Impetuous, manipulative, ever uncertain of himself, he worked hardest at appearing to resent the system that was honoring him. But at the same time he was fervent for all its advantages, especially the creative freedom that was not, at that time, routinely offered to someone so young, whose first film was still unreleased. As he told journalist Howard Thompson of the *New York Times*, "To me, acting is the most logical way for people's neuroses to manifest themselves." The neurosis was certainly firmly rooted: defiant and ungrateful as ever, Jimmy reneged on a promise to attend the benefit premiere of *East of Eden* in New York on March 9. "I can't make this scene," he told Jane Deacy in the idiom of the time. "I can't handle it. I'm going back to the Coast tonight." And so he did, on March 6.

But his friends sensed more than mere antisocial rudeness or lack of collegial teamwork. "He feels," ran the caption in *Life* beneath Dennis Stock's photo of Jimmy wandering in a rainy Times Square, "that his continuing attempt to find out just where he belongs is the source of his strength as an actor. [But] his top floor garret on Manhattan's West Side is no more home to him than the farm in Indiana." Thus the restless wanderer continued to drift.

And to try his friends' patience. "He was exceedingly testy with people that season," recalled Dennis Stock, "always asking people, 'Do you love me? Do you love me? Do you love me?' It was like a challenge to them, and I think it had to do with a sense of guilt he had"—namely, that he was so uncomfortable with himself that he had to reassure himself of others' devotion. "The only way he could be sure you really loved him," according to Stewart Stern, "was if you loved him when he was truly at his worst." But real affection can only be claimed when its expression is volunteered, not extracted. Such a gratuitous act of kindness he extended to Adeline Brookshire Nall on April 4, when he sent her a telegram of invitation to a private screening of the Kazan picture in Marion, Indiana.

With the publication of rave reviews for his performance in *East of Eden* that spring, the rumors about James Dean's importance to Hollywood were confirmed—as, alas, were many of the tales of the childishness and difficulties he caused. Aware of the image the film created for him and perhaps cognizant, too, how closely it suited his very self, he lived the rest of his life within an envelope of absolute self-consciousness. The adulation, the praise, the crowding, attention and adoration are intricate for anyone to finesse, and always tricky to fit within the context of a real life. But for one so inchoate in personal development, the fame was disastrous. People came up to him and asked not only for autographs but for dates. As interviews, gossip columns and magazine articles emphasized his childhood loneliness and his often shy behavior, an odd corollary occurred. Teenage boys wanted to be like him, or to have him for a buddy or big brother or lover, and girls wanted to mother or marry or protect him, depending on their instincts. A chance remark at a party or a dinner was quoted as a mystic revelation from a supernatural figure. And although he feared and hated the exploitation and the hype, he knew it was part of the territory.

Henceforth, he became more and more ornery with magazine photographers, disallowing this picture and insisting on that; he made all the demands (but had little of the expertise) of Marlene Dietrich, obsessed with the beauty of her own image after years of working with Josef von Sternberg. But it was not, in the final analysis, beauty that James Dean wished to project: it was something fearful and enigmatic, to inspire awe. He succeeded.

As it happened, Nicholas Ray came to New York, too—with the specific intention of studying James Dean outside Hollywood. They drank together, haunted the waterfront bars and recovered over cups of coffee at six in the morning. Jimmy learned much from Ray—about food and wine, about architecture and film direction, and about the hazards of casual sex. "I got crabs," he said one morning to Ray, who led him to a drugstore and a bottle of anti-lice lotion. All the while, even before he made a final deal with Jack Warner, Ray was extending and modernizing the character of Cal Trask in *Rebel Without a Cause*, and so even while Stewart Stern wrote the dialogue, the director drew Jimmy into the production preparations. At this point, the name "Jim Stark" was chosen for Jimmy's character in *Rebel*—a combination of his own name with an anagram of Trask.

"The drama of his life," Ray said of those days in Manhattan, "was the drama of desiring to belong and of fearing to belong—so was Jim Stark's. It was a conflict of violent eagerness and mistrust created very young. The intensity of his desires, his fears, could make the search at times arrogant, egocentric; but behind it was such a desperate vulnerability that one was moved, even frightened." The same reaction was noted by *Vogue* in a list called "The Next Successes" that highlighted eight notable Americans in the arts. "Dean is in," pronounced *Vogue*, and so he was, then and forever.

In fact, Warner Bros. was wasting no time. With the rights to Edna Ferber's sprawling 1952 novel *Giant* safely negotiated, a screenplay was already being prepared, to be directed by George Stevens and to feature, in a supporting role, James Dean. The stars were to be Elizabeth Taylor (at a salary of $175,000), who was borrowed from MGM, Rock Hudson (for $100,000), who came over from Universal, and Jimmy, who was cast as (what else?) a rebellious, crabby but at last financially successful maverick—at a salary of $1,500 a week, or about $21,000 if production went according to schedule late that spring and summer.

The weekend before *Rebel Without a Cause* began principal black-and-white photography, Jimmy drove his Porsche Speedster to the Palm Springs Road Race, where to his dismay he came in third. Nicholas Ray, who seemed not to share the anxiety of his old friend Kazan about the possibility of disaster, cheered on his new protégé, who (as if in self-defense before his father) promised that next time he would win first prize. But he did not: on May 1, at a race in Bakersfield, he again placed third, and slipped to fourth in Santa Barbara on May 29.

Kazan had advised Ray to keep a tight rein on Jimmy's wild tendencies, but Ray (who had acted onstage with Kazan and had been his assistant director on *A Tree Grows in Brooklyn*) was unperturbed. His own personality, after all, urged him to project precisely the querulous, risk-taking attitude of the rebel in his next film, just as his first nine films scrutinized the fates of those not integrated into society's mainstream. Trained as an architect, Ray made pictures (among them *They Live by Night*, *Knock on Any Door*, *On Dangerous Ground* and *Johnny Guitar*) that feature characters marginalized and disillusioned in a hostile society—which is just how he perceived himself and his young star.

On Wednesday, March 30, Ray directed the first scenes of *Rebel Without a Cause*, which were exterior shots outside the planetarium at Griffith Park in Los Angeles. Jimmy worked nine hours that day, as well as most days and many nights over the next nine weeks.

Principal photography concluded on May 26, just before the long Memorial Day weekend, eleven days behind schedule and well over budget—the financial factor caused by Jack Warner's decision, after a week of production, to make the film in color. The upgrading of *Rebel* to major status was directly due to Dean's sudden fame. "He will be the most dynamic discovery since Marlon Brando," gushed *Look* magazine, which featured him along with two other newcomers—Julie Andrews ("an unknown English stage ingenue") and Shirley MacLaine ("a chorus-girl understudy signed for the movies").

"We started out making a routine program picture in black-and-white," recalled Jim Backus, who played his father. "It was going to be a picture about teenage kids that I thought was going to be a sort of *Ozzie and Harriet* with venom. Then the reports started coming in on *East of Eden*, and they knew they had a star on their hands."

A memorandum from Jack Warner to producer Weisbart confirmed the major changes, as the budget was increased, costumes were redesigned and interiors more lavishly decorated. "THIS IS A VERY IMPORTANT PICTURE," Warner insisted, "and Nick Ray should lose no time in picking up in color the scenes he has already shot [in black-and-white]." One element in the decision to turn *Rebel* into a color film entered the American iconography associated with James Dean: a red windbreaker replaced a black leather jacket.

Set in Los Angeles, *Rebel Without a Cause*, still a classic more than four decades later, explores the lives of three teenagers, each of whom is deprived of paternal counsel—Jim (Dean), Judy (Wood) and John, nicknamed

Plato (Sal Mineo, then also sixteen, in his film debut). Jim, alienated from his weak father (Jim Backus) and domineering mother (Ann Doran), drinks heavily and runs afoul of the police, while Judy's father (William Hopper) refuses to offer any normal affection and Plato is abandoned to the care of a housekeeper by his absentee, divorced parents.

Jim is attracted to Judy. As a newcomer, he is taunted by a gang of high-school kids and, at a field trip to the planetarium of the Griffith Observatory, is forced into a knife fight with a rival named Buzz (Corey Allen). He reluctantly accepts a challenge from Buzz, who dies in a daredevil auto race. Threatened by the dead boy's cronies, Jim, Judy and Plato (a sort of new teenage "family") hide in a deserted mansion. The gang members find them, and Plato shoots one of them and a policeman.

The action then moves back to the planetarium, where earlier the students had been deeply moved by a program about the eventual explosion that will herald the end of time. The earth, a lecturer said, "will be destroyed as we began, in a burst of gas and fire . . . The heavens are still and cold once more. In all the immensity of our universe and the galaxies beyond, the earth will not be missed. Through the infinite reaches of space, the problems of man seem trivial and naive indeed, and man, existing alone, seems himself an episode of little consequence." The story, localizing the cosmic apocalypse in family dysfunction, concludes with the killing of Plato by the police and the possibility of a new understanding by Jim's troubled parents. Man alone is of little consequence indeed.

Underneath a rather straightforward story about a

clash between juvenile delinquents and sensitive teens—and their mutual alienation from parents—*Rebel* locates the factors contributing to confusion: an excess of material comfort, inadequate fathers and an alarming desire for death. In this regard alone, the film was tragically prophetic for the next two generations of American teens, many of whom slipped from mild rebellion in the 1950s to utopian optimism in the 1960s to a frightful and frightening pessimism by the 1990s, when suicide could be ranked as the third most frequent cause of adolescent deaths.

"Don't we give you everything you want?" Jim's parents ask, but he does not reply. Materially, he lacks for nothing, but emotionally he is a pauper, with no family inheritance of value or love. This can lead to dangerous conduct, as Jim realizes when he confides to a social worker, "Please lock me up. I'm gonna do something. I'm gonna hit somebody!" Later, he does indeed nearly strangle his father. "I want answers now!" screams James Dean, and millions in the new generation of affluent teens agreed. The broken homes, suggests the picture, are microcosms of a fragmented universe racing toward extinction. Perhaps the film's most famous line—"You're tearing me apart!" Jim shouts at his arguing parents—became a kind of verbal talisman, describing the unsticking of things in the polite America of the 1950s. "Things fall apart; the centre cannot hold," wrote the poet Yeats.

Mere anarchy is loosed upon the world,
The blood-dimmed tide is loosed, and everywhere

The ceremony of innocence is drowned;
The best lack all conviction, while the worst
Are full of passionate intensity.

That, in the final analysis, sets forth the themes underlying Stewart Stern's script, and of the forlorn spirit that everywhere infused James Dean's performance.

Compared to Wood, Mineo, Nick Adams and the other youngsters in the story, James Dean (at twenty-four credible as a seventeen-year-old) brilliantly conveys the adolescent's dissatisfaction with empty excuses from parents. Here he combines the world-weariness of Humphrey Bogart with the aloof, repressed anger of Brando. "You know something?" he drawls when Buzz slashes his auto tires. "You read too many comic books!" Grandly bored by everything he sees, he resembles the persona patented by Bogart—as if that actor's portrait of Duke Mantee in *The Petrified Forest* has sprung to new life. Henceforth, James Dean would be (in words describing Bogart's character in that film) "the last great apostle of rugged individualism in a world of outmoded ideas—in the graveyard of civilization."

Rebel Without a Cause is finally a film about the need to belong and the general impossibility of belonging—hence the picture's popularity for every succeeding group of teens. The ultimate pathos of his character is that his elders have unwittingly pushed him far away. Jimmy's performance—in the role by which he entered American mythology—was composed by him and Ray from bits and pieces of carefully concocted business, and the whole blends an explosive energy with a calm, sad rationality. Just as Kazan had done in *East of Eden*, so Ray and Dean constructed a film that drew on Jimmy's own history, his longing for parental support, his anger and longing for his father, for the film's major emotional impact. The star insisted that his name be the character's, just as Jim Stark's nicknames— "Toreador" and "Toro," he is called—reflect Jimmy's fascination with bullfighting.

Patronized by his parents in an early scene, Jimmy made an odd choice: to giggle inaptly, and to hum a few measures of Wagner's "Ride of the Valkyries." That bellicose tune reaches its term later, when he resorts to violence to shake sense into his father. Gone are the conventions of respect for elders who seem not to deserve it. Dean's Jim Stark yearns for righteousness at any price: hence, at the film's conclusion, he becomes the father he always desired—protective of Plato, loving toward Judy, old before his time. In *East of Eden*, Jimmy had found the empathetic center of the film in himself when he wept and longed for his father to embrace him. Just so here, in the film's poignant final moments, when Jim—weeping over the dead body of his friend—crawls sobbing and wraps himself around his father's legs.

His performance forever established the new image of the young middle-class loner; his defiant stoop and despondent gaze, his hesitant mumble and tentative plea for love canonized a new characteristic of saintliness— simply being misunderstood. More to the point, his vulnerability, his desperate need "to belong, to have one day without confusion and shame," struck resonant chords all over America. A strong, attractive young man wept for love and death, and longed for companionship, guidance and just a touch of clarity amid all the muddle. Here was a living counterstatement to John Wayne and company; here was the symbol of a generation—the boy who did not know who he was or what was right or where he was headed. Susceptible to adulation and fearful of rejection, he rebelled not against parents or the law, but against a kind of universal situation in life—hence the planetarium sequence.

James Dean, even more than Cal Trask/Jim Stark, was the rebel without a cause—and just as in *East of Eden*, he was playing himself. The inarticulate manner, the halting phrases that comprised an essentially nonverbal communication, the furtive glances, the awkward gestures, the sudden smile and equally surprising frown, the puzzling blend of sweetness with violence—these described both actor and role. Stewart Stern, by instinct if not by design, seems to have had Jimmy in mind when he wrote on the final draft of his script, three days before filming began, that the character of Jim Stark was "filled with confusion about his role in life. Because of his 'nowhere' father, he does not know how to be a man. Because of his wounding mother, he anticipates destruction in all women."

Nicholas Ray's partisans have rated him among the great filmmakers. He may be. But he was also a man of dark, convoluted passions, a man who at the age of forty-four saw himself as an innocent adolescent whose passions deserved free rein—a kind of rebel Jim

Stark, in fact, or an older Jim Dean. "He seemed to me to be high on something all the time," recalled Warner Bros. executive William Orr, who had his hands full with the dramas swirling in and around the production of *Rebel Without a Cause*. Early during preparations, ex-architect Ray (still married to his second wife) easily seduced sixteen-year-old Natalie Wood, and throughout production kept her in the thrall of a fierce sexual passion. Wood, an affecting and attractive presence, was appearing in her twenty-first film. She had already endured an unhappy home life with her mother (a former ballet dancer) and father (an architect and designer). Nicholas Ray—intelligent, urbane, unctuous—tapped readily into the deep needs of this lovely, trusting girl.

"Nick Ray was a self-dramatizing man," recalled Stewart Stern, "and everyone had a mercurial relationship with him. He was the maypole around whom everyone needy and dependent swirled and danced, and he enthroned himself as guru at the Chateau Marmont, where he seemed to possess the souls of both James Dean and Natalie Wood." Jimmy was (according to Stern and Wood, among others) anxious about acting under the tutelage of anyone but Kazan and required constant attention and assurance.

Faye Nuell Mayo, a dancer and actress who was Natalie Wood's stand-in and double for the long shots on *Rebel*, was one of the few cast members with whom Dean felt comfortable during production; they quickly became sincere but unromantic friends. Years later, she recalled that Ray's Sunday afternoon gatherings at the hotel were "sometimes a bit wild, because everyone was avidly competing for the director's attention and approval." Mayo agreed that Ray himself was "very dour, very serious and seemed emotionally scarred." As for Jimmy, she remembered his insecurity. "He couldn't get a handle on what was happening to him—it was as if there was something unreal about the sudden lurch to fame—and he hated the machinery of studio politics."

For decades, rumors circulated of an erotic relationship between Dean and Ray (especially during their time in New York earlier in the year, when Ray often stayed the night in Jimmy's tiny garret). The suggestion, however unverifiable, is not outlandish: it is easy, for example, to imagine Ray making love to the image of himself (whom he saw in Jimmy Dean as in Jim Stark)—an image that was then taking concrete shape. It is equally understandable if Jimmy had tried to please another respected mentor-father (like Rogers Brackett, for example). What might have happened between them sexually is less important than the fact that the bond between Dean and Ray was, according to Stewart Stern, "an odd version of acolyte and master, because Jimmy was torn between fear of Nick and a desperate need to trust him."

The symbiosis led Ray to treat Dean as his closest colleague on the picture—"practically the co-director," according to Jim Backus. "He [Dean] swerved easily from morbidity to elation," Nicholas Ray wrote in 1968. "He needed a special kind of climate [and] reassurance, tolerance, understanding. An important way of creating this climate was to involve him at every stage in the development of the picture."

Steffi Sidney, who played teenager Mil in the picture, noticed at once "the real collaboration between

Nick and Jimmy, and it's my guess that, as a result of their working relationship, Jimmy felt he might want to direct in the future." Sidney was on the mark, for from the time of *Rebel*, Jimmy spoke often of directing—specifically, he wanted to make a film of Saint-Exupéry's *Little Prince*, and another about Billy the Kid. "I've got to know everything about everything to be a good director—and that's the goal," he told the press. "Acting is wonderful and immediately satisfying, but it is not the end-all, be-all of my existence. My talents lie in directing even more than acting. And beyond direction, my great fear is writing. I can't apply the seat of my pants right now to write—I'm too youthful and silly. But someday."

But for all the intensely private discussions between Ray and Dean, they took contributions from the cast and allowed them considerable latitude in developing their own characters. The villainous, doomed Buzz, for example—played by a very different type of man, the amiable and intelligent Corey Allen—recalled Nick Ray gathering the youngsters. "I want to tell you something," the director said. "Each one of us has his own way of working, and that individuality is necessary to the success of the film. Everyone has to be restrained and uncritical of the other." Similarly, Steffi Sidney devised a wonderful moment when a gang member snatches the cap from the head of a scolding guard at Griffith Park—a comic-defiant touch that would have been even better from her own character Mil, but which Ray gave to the character of Moose (played by Nick Adams).

Nineteen-year-old Dennis Hopper, who appeared in both *Rebel* and *Giant* and was in awe of Dean and in love with Natalie Wood, paid tribute forever after to Jimmy as to a genius mentor. Just so was Sal Mineo, who worshipped Jimmy even more offscreen than he did in the story. Years later, just before he was murdered at the age of thirty-seven, Mineo spoke plainly. "I realized later that I was homosexually attracted to him. When he showed love to me, when he said it, that did it. He was really overwhelming." But there was no sexual activity. "We could have—like that," said Mineo, snapping his fingers. But it is doubtful that James Dean—as insecure as Sal Mineo, and just as terrified that his homosexual inclination would be known among working colleagues—would ever have risked the kind of emotional involvement the adoring (not to say underage) Mineo attached to his hero; besides, Mineo could do nothing for him. Even Jack Simmons had a purpose.

In addition, the quality Stewart Stern called a "metal-hard core prevented Jimmy from ever being a victim," and this, too, would have forestalled any invitation to intimacy with a younger devotee at work. "People sensed Jimmy," according to Stern, but never really knew him—and that phrase indeed neatly summarizes the reactions of very many people who knew James Dean. And sex with a male co-star was a chancy invitation to parity. And so Mineo was content to stand by, feelings suppressed and erotic energy denied, while he watched Jimmy rehearse a love scene with Natalie or a fight scene with pugilist and stunt coordinator "Mushy" Callahan, who had taught him to fight for scenes in *East of Eden*.

Nor was Natalie Wood dismayed by the private bond between Dean and Ray. Jimmy was "incredibly encouraging and very sweet to me" as she struggled to balance her affair with her director and her work with other players in her first non-juvenile role. For a scene in which she was to act agitated and tense, for example, Wood affected just that—but the result was over the top. Relax, Jimmy told her: tension could only be conveyed if the actor was internally calm and the anxiety appeared repressed. It was, she later said, precisely this sort of thoughtful, carefully considered technique that was responsible for his best scenes in the small legacy of his work.

Years after the deaths of Dean and Wood, her consistently warm remarks about him are endearing—especially because he was often frankly cruel to her at the time. Carroll Baker recalls meeting them that season, and after an appreciative glance at Baker, Jimmy turned to Natalie, who was wearing a peasant blouse, gypsy skirt and several pieces of jewelry. Complaining that she looked "corny," he compared her to Carroll: "Look at Carroll. Do you see what she is wearing? A plain, simple dress and it's lovely . . . Carroll, why don't you teach Natalie how to dress?" And poor Natalie Wood remained transfixed and hurt, tears streaming down her face while (according to Baker) "Jimmy lifted his head with a wicked little grin. He was being deliberately callous and cruel, and he was obviously enjoying his domination of her." The rank unkindness is not difficult to understand in light of her intimacy with Nicholas Ray, which throughout production exasperated Jimmy and made him all the more jealous—not, perhaps, from his desire for either Natalie or Ray, but from a wish to have his director's devotion entirely to himself.

Because of the excitement over *Eden*, released nationwide just a week after *Rebel* began filming, it is easy to understand the shyness of several younger players around the new star. Beverly Long, in the role of teenager Helen, recalled that Jimmy tried to coax her to go for a spin in his Porsche during a break in filming. Aware of his reputation for speed, she declined, saying, "You drive too fast!" She never forgot his reply: "I gotta drive fast. I'm not going to be around too long." Jimmy was also known for his unexpected double entendres, whispered to embarrass the girls. Beverly Long was also a bit uneasy when, another afternoon, Jimmy asked if she wanted to see some pictures he carried in an envelope.

> He whipped out these pictures—I didn't know what to expect—and they were of him in the Palm Springs race! It was the most important thing in his life, and if he had a good listener, he could be very funny and very sweet. But at other times, he just walked by without a word, as if you were a total stranger, and refuse to answer a greeting. He was completely unpredictable.

Steffi Sidney, on the other hand, had an unexpected first day's work with Jimmy.

"How are you?" she said, extending her hand.

"He looked at me and punched me playfully in the stomach," Sidney recalled. "My first thought was to punch him right back, but then he smiled and at last replied, 'Oh, pretty good,' and walked away," leaving her nonplussed. Later, Steffi accepted his friendly offer of a drive in his Porsche during one lunch hour of location shooting at the planetarium. "We got in the car and I turned on the radio. But he flicked my hand away from the dial, saying, 'I don't like any distractions when I'm driving.' Then he really gunned the car around the hills of Griffith Park, and when we got back to the shooting, I said, 'I don't think I'm going to do that again.' He never said a word during the drive, and he was very safe, but it was like a wild ride at Disneyland!" Nicholas Ray tried to explain Jimmy's silence even when he reached out to other actors: "He was the child who goes to a secret corner and refuses to speak."

Older cast members, too, sensed the confusion as well as the raw talent in the young star. "He was a lost kid in real life, just as he was on the screen," recalled Jim Backus, who was equally impressed by Jimmy's enormous power of concentration as he prepared himself for every scene. "Before the take of any scene, he went off by himself for five or ten minutes to think about what he had to do, to the exclusion of everything else." Nor did Backus ever forget April 22, when they had to film the scene in which the enraged Jim Stark drags his father from a stairway landing, across a room and over a chair and then nearly strangles him. Jimmy was

so carried away that he grabbed the railing and broke part of it. He seized me by the lapels of my bathrobe. He forced me down the stairs and across the living room. We went over a

couch and knocked over a table. I thought I
was a goner. I might have been, but this boy is
as strong as a bull. Even while he was flinging
me around, he held on to me so that I wouldn't
fall.

Jimmy's realism in this sequence surprised Ann
Doran, too, who was playing his unsympathetic mother.
"He knows what he's doing all the time," she told the
press. "He pounces on lines and devours them as if they
were the substance of life!" But privately she was concerned about the degree to which Jimmy Dean was
becoming Jim Stark. In the middle of one night she was
awakened by him shouting "Mom! Mom!" at her door,
and Doran looked out to see a drunk Jimmy pleading,
"It's your son!" She brewed coffee while he poured out
his heart to her. "He was not the self-assured person
everybody believed he was," she recalled. "He had great
doubts about himself and where he was going—he
was that lost." The "lost" James Dean for a new "lost"
generation—it was the single adjective most often used
(most recently that year by Stock and Backus, among so
many others) to describe the boy who both touched and
troubled them.

Jimmy's natural conjunction of wounded despair
and aching desolation was seen in his last television
appearance, as a drifter in an indifferent story called
"The Unlighted Road," filmed on April 14 and 15 and
broadcast on May 6. The actor is again indistinguish-
able from the character, who lands a job in a roadside
café and is drawn into what he thinks is complicity
in a crime because of a crooked boss. Saved from

self-hatred (and prison) by a girlfriend, he has a chance—
one of the few times the actor indulged himself—to
smile.

According to William Self, the show's producer,
Jimmy was indifferent, shrugged when given direction
and did exactly what he wanted. Very likely he recognized the abyss separating the good film dialogue of
Paul Osborn and Stewart Stern from the turgid melodramatics of television, for which this was his last role.

After that annoying interruption, Jimmy returned to
the set of *Rebel*, where he was the undisputed star, and
strove for a kind of hyperrealism. "He suffered a badly
bruised right hand today," reported the unit manager
to the executive offices on April 22. "Dean slammed his
right fist into the side of a desk a little harder than the
script called for. He was taken to Riverside Drive
Emergency Hospital where X-rays revealed no broken
bones. Dean will have to keep his hand wrapped in an
elastic bandage for at least a week, but the injured hand
will not prevent him from working." Thus the explanation for one of the film's most powerful moments—
when an anguished Jim Stark erupts furiously at the
police station. With reason Dennis Hopper called
Jimmy "the first guerilla artist ever to work in movies."

Although *Rebel* is the film for which Dean is most
remembered and most identified, it is perhaps less successful than *East of Eden*—a fact acknowledged by the
author, Stewart Stern. "Much of the writing and direction of the parents was exaggerated and heavily biased,
and brought a cartoon aspect to the film, so it never
seemed to be all of a piece. The poetic truth of the relationships among the young people was constantly
being undermined by the way the parents were made

to behave." This flaw, however, has not affected the cult status of the picture, to which very many young people still respond decades later, their nerve endings raw after the tragic finale.

The emotional impact of the last half-hour, as Dean, Wood and Mineo form a private domestic circle before finally returning to the dark world of violence, has at its center a remarkably controlled performance from Jimmy, who had clearly learned a great deal from Kazan about focus and concentration, and who was, at last, comfortable with Ray and confident with his new status. "I don't know that he could have articulated where, from deep inside him, that performance originated," said Corey Allen, "but he had an innate appreciation of Jim Stark's condition. There was a new maturity in his work on *Rebel*."

In his portrait of pain and confusion, James Dean pushed to the limits, for a new generation, the notion that it was all right to feel insecure, to be uneasy about the present and fearful of the future. And so he was—a powerful yet tender man without the sullen withdrawal projected by Marlon Brando or the highly neurotic anguish communicated by Montgomery Clift. In *Rebel Without a Cause*, James Dean's Jim Stark gave a warning, but he also invited the sympathy of adults even as he evoked the empathy of adolescents.

"The picture itself is excellent," cheered Jack Warner in a studio memorandum. "Dean is beyond comprehension." As testimony to his enthusiasm, he gave Jimmy billing above the title; doubtless he had been informed that the studio mailroom was now flooded with over a thousand fan letters a week addressed to James Dean.

Had the star lived to see the completed film, he might well have understood the remark of Dennis Stock, who worked on the production team: "When you saw *Rebel Without a Cause*, that was Jimmy you were seeing up there on the screen." This sentiment was shared by many who knew Dean. And in this regard, it is often said that the best performers never appear to be performing at all, and that in their greatest roles, something true of themselves is found in the characters they portray. If that is a tenable criterion for assessing the results of such arduous work, young James Dean may be called a great actor.

chapter eleven

Honor has not to be won; it
must only not be lost.
                    ARTHUR SCHOPENHAUER

Elia Kazan, recognizing the sensitivity, the needs and the unskilled but undeniable talent of James Dean, had nurtured him from first day to last for his debut in *East of Eden*. Treating him like a precious porcelain, Kazan extracted a rich and complex performance. Nicholas Ray raised him even higher, making the sole star of *Rebel Without a Cause* virtually the co-producer and associate director.

It was perhaps inevitable that James Dean would be miserable during the production of *Giant*, on which he had third billing after Elizabeth Taylor and Rock Hudson. More to the point, he had what amounted to a small role in a big picture, and the undisputed star was the director, George Stevens, who was not much interested in the moods of his players and had no inclination to yield an inch to them when it came to his films.

Why, then, did James Dean campaign for the role

after reading the script? First of all, he knew what an Elizabeth Taylor/George Stevens picture could do for his career. Second, he believed the description of Jett Rink attached to his script would be realized in production—and even that his scenes would remain intact as written. In these assumptions he could not have been more wrong.

"Jett Rink had many reasons to be angry," ran the character note that attracted James Dean.

> First, he was a drifter in a world where he found himself one of the few underprivileged and yet non-Mexican employees of a young man of vast wealth [Jordan Benedict, played by Rock Hudson]. He seemed to occupy a small place in the dim conscience of man . . . Also, he was angry because he was smart enough to appraise the world in terms of his opportunities. At twenty-one, he was a man of restless anger without profession or property. He believes in a legend and is in the rare position of making it seem to come true. Discontented, cheated out of his birthright, feeling deeply the inequality and unfairness of his position, it must have been hard for Jett Rink.

Dean might indeed have been reading a précis of his autobiography.*

---

* Among others Stevens briefly considered for the role of Jett Rink: Marlon Brando, Robert Mitchum, Charlton Heston, Anthony Quinn, Montgomery Clift, Jack Palance and Gordon MacRae.

In 1955, Stevens was a fifty-year-old Army veteran with a wide variety of credits—Katharine Hepburn in *Alice Adams*, Astaire and Rogers in *Swing Time*, Elizabeth Taylor and Montgomery Clift in *A Place in the Sun*, and Alan Ladd in *Shane*—and two Oscars on his shelf. He had a strong sense of his value to Hollywood, had become producer of his own films, and did not suffer fools gladly. The wise, too, were often reduced to stammering subservience: Stevens was fearless, for example, when directing a force of nature like Katharine Hepburn, who always had a clear viewpoint on things, and Elizabeth Taylor, who was so beautiful that other directors were sometimes content merely to photograph her.

When the final script for *Giant* was submitted that spring and Stevens outlined his plans to Jack Warner, the chief accurately predicted that Stevens would earn a third statuette for his collection. *Giant* was to be produced as a three-hour-and-twenty-one-minute epic spanning almost thirty years in the life of a Texas family. Like many Hollywood films of the 1950s (*The Greatest Show on Earth*, *The Ten Commandments*, *The Big Country*, *War and Peace* and *Around the World in 80 Days*), *Giant* was an extravagant, sprawling, overlong jumble with mild insinuations of such daring topics as sex and racism—everything, in other words, that audiences could not find on their little black-and-white television screens. It was "George Stevens's *Giant*" at the beginning of the screen credits, too; the name of Edna Ferber, the little lady who wrote the big novel, appeared only much later. Decades later, it seems too long and without focus, too pretty, too bloodless, without a sure sense of whether it aimed to be a family saga or a film about civil rights. There is, in the final analysis, entirely too much of its muchness.*

Giant tells a rambling tale of Leslie and Jordan Benedict (Taylor and Hudson); their children (Carroll Baker, Dennis Hopper and Fran Bennett); Jordan's spinster sister Luz (Mercedes McCambridge) and the ranch hand Jett Rink (Dean), to whom Luz wills a parcel of land that eventually yields fabulous wealth in oil. Dean's character, underwritten and unattractive, was that of a somewhat sinister, poor outsider who is jealous of Hudson, lusts after Taylor and, once he has his millions, becomes an alcoholic degenerate and years later tries to seduce their daughter.

From the start, no one had any doubt that this was George Stevens's production of *Giant*, and that the actors were present to take orders. This he made clear straightaway to James Dean, who was forced by the demands of *Rebel* to arrive two weeks after *Giant* had begun production and so was from the start something of an outsider. After only a day for himself, he rushed to join the cast and crew for location shooting in Texas on June 3. During the next month, daytime temperatures routinely hit 120 degrees in the shade.

Marfa, a town of just over two thousand, is sixty miles from Mexico and three hours by car from El Paso; from there, the *Giant* company went into the scorching Texas desert to film impressive but finally lifeless

---

*Edna Ferber very likely based her novel, at least in part, on the lives of the Kleberg family, owners of the King Ranch in Texas. Jett Rink was almost certainly inspired by the Texas oil millionaire Glenn McCarthy, the poor boy who made a killing through wildcat operations. See the Warner Bros. studio memorandum to producer Henry Ginsberg dated December 14, 1954, in the Warner/USC archives; *Fortune*, May 1949; and *Time*, Feb. 13, 1950.

sequences. Jimmy was installed, with Rock Hudson and Chill Wills, in a rented house and at once prepared to work. But Stevens kept him waiting three days before even acknowledging his presence, much less putting him in a scene. That finally occurred on June 6, but in defiance Jimmy failed to report. Next day, Stevens loudly reprimanded him in the presence of the entire company. This Jimmy endured stoically, but from that day to the end of production he made no attempt to make himself agreeable.

Carroll Baker, cast in the role of daughter to Taylor and Hudson, recalled that, during the torrid month's work in Texas, many in the cast (including Taylor, Hudson, Hopper and Mineo) "carried on like absolute fools—laughing and crying and partying and drinking, and hardly ever sleeping." Jimmy rarely joined in these distractions and was, at first, shunned by his colleagues for his moody manners. But then he hit on an inspired tactic. Rightly sensing that Elizabeth Taylor was drawn to the lost and ostracized, and that she had an immediate affinity for the outcast, he won her over with his wounded, sad and confused demeanor. "He stole Elizabeth away from us," according to Baker. "She went off mysteriously each evening with Jimmy, and none of us could figure out where they went." At the time, many thought the pair were off to bed; as it happened, they went off to talk.

Taylor had already befriended Rock Hudson, whose personality greatly differed from Jimmy's. Both men shared a common terror: that disclosure of their unconventional sexual lives would jeopardize their careers, for in 1955, being gay was considered far worse than being Communist, and death was, for some, preferable to either. In addition, there was considerable sexual tension between Hudson and Dean—a wary, mutual attraction paradoxically (as so often) fueled by taboo, fear, resentment and perhaps the desire to dominate. Hudson was very tall, very conventionally handsome, very eager to please (even to the point of submitting to the studio's demand that he marry). Jimmy was short, rude, sloppy, often antisocial and rarely cared about gratifying anyone except himself.

For his part, Hudson was an easygoing, affable soul, accustomed (like Taylor) to being judged merely an attractive presence, with no fair assessment of his desire and ability to be a good actor. Dean was a tangle of conflicts, equally committed to his craft but caught in a vise of anxiety and insecurity. To both, Elizabeth Taylor was a comforting friend (as she was to Montgomery Clift and other gay actors), completely accepting of their homosexuality, which she regarded as unremarkable. To her, life was a chain of mysteries and nothing was more enigmatic than sex, for which rules and norms of conduct seemed to her absurd. Shy, she identified with homosexuals' fear of disclosure; compassionate, she condoled what she saw as the needless suffering caused by the smug moralism of the time.

And so Elizabeth Taylor (seven years younger than Hudson and a year younger than James Dean), nurturing and maternal, won the confidence of both her leading men, and in so doing aggravated their dislike of each other. "Sometimes Jimmy and I would sit up until three in the morning talking," she recalled,

> and he would tell me about his past life, his conflicts and some of his loves and tragedies.

And the next day it was almost as if he didn't want to recognize me, or to remember that he had revealed so much of himself the night before. And so he would pass me and ignore me, or just give me a cursory nod of the head. And then it took him a day or two to become my friend again. I found all that hard to understand.

She was, of course, not the first to be treated this way. At the time, she felt he was a boy she had to care for. "But even that was probably his joke," she said later. "I don't think he needed anybody or anything—except his acting." This was an accurate and not unkind assessment.

Hudson was blunter.

Dean was always late and really very unprofessional, [behaving like] the Broadway actor who comes to California and deigns to make a motion picture—that attitude . . .

I didn't like him. Dean was hard to be around. He hated George Stevens, didn't think he was a good director, and was always angry and full of contempt. He never smiled, was sulky and had no manners.

Whatever the core of his resentment, Hudson was certainly on the mark on the last point: all during production, Jimmy Dean regularly urinated in public—against a set, in a gutter, in the town square. "Because nothing else was happening"—that was the reason he gave Mercedes McCambridge for this behavior. As usual, however, it was a way to assure notoriety. "He loved being a star," according to Carroll Baker, who recalled that he would do anything for attention. "He wanted [attention] desperately, but it mattered so much that he almost had to treat it with contempt"—hence the public rudeness. "He couldn't admit how much it meant to him."

McCambridge, among a few, liked him, although she believed that "nobody had more problems with Jimmy than Jimmy. You could feel the loneliness beating out of him, and it hit you like a wave." Jane Withers (who played Vashti in *Giant*) agreed: she was saddened that he was "so insecure, so afraid to get near anyone or attached to anyone." Edna Ferber, who was present for much of the filming, thought he "suffered from success poisoning . . ." He was "utterly winning one moment, obnoxious the next." And composer Dimitri Tiomkin reported, in his thick Russian accent, to colleague Leonard Rosenman: "I met your friend in Texas. Was very sensitive young actor, interesting person and big schmuck. Most of people in picture he bossed terribly. Insecure, I say." Cinematographer William Mellor, who admired Jimmy's calm control before the camera during *Giant*, remembered him as "a small-town boy rocketed to success without warning, without preparation—an average young American still confused by a new life, not yet adjusted to fame, fortune and fan mania."

Forty years later, Rosenman elaborated:

> I really think Jimmy had no idea in the world
> who or what he was. Obviously he identified
> with the three movie roles he had, but I think
> they were given to him because he was those
> roles, or in some ways they were created for
> him—and it all had to do with confusion!

This created an odd irony, for the twenty-four-year-old boy who had no identity, no clear idea about himself, was playing confused characters with no identity and, in the process, trying to find himself.

It was precisely that insecurity Stevens exploited and with which he had to cope during the filming of *Giant*. "Not always a benevolent dictator," in the words of Mercedes McCambridge, Stevens resented Jimmy's independence in creating the character of Jett Rink. The director saw *Giant* as an epic on an immense landscape; the actor saw it as a love triangle with epic associations with a larger society. And because Jimmy made no secret of his aspirations to direct, he told everyone how differently he would have handled *Giant*, and how he planned to direct a film based on the life of Billy the Kid. (The studio in fact issued a press release to that effect in August.)

"It was a hell of a headache to work with him," Stevens said when the picture opened. "He had developed this cultivated, designed irresponsibility. 'It's tough on you,' he implied, 'but I've just got to do it this way.'" Stevens did not appreciate Jimmy's need for concentration; much less did he approve of his rambling around a character in rehearsal until he found the tender spot where he could pin it down. But most of all, he loathed Jimmy's lust for publicity, his insistence on being included in as many photographs of the cast and crew as possible. According to Stevens,

> He worked hard to get publicity and always had a photographer with him. He had a fine concept of how Jimmy Dean could be made popular, and he and his personally attached cameraman roamed around looking for the right people to be photographed with. He did this with Elizabeth Taylor, Edna Ferber and many others.

Yet when there was no camera—and just a reporter—he was often indifferent. After several days, one lady tried to corner him for an interview: "Mr. Dean, I've come all the way from New York to see you!" To which he replied, "Madame, I've come all the way from New York to make a picture." And with that he was gone.

On his side, Jimmy loathed what he felt was the director's waste of time, and he had a point. Stevens was known for retake after retake, and in fact over 600,000 feet of film were shot and only 25,000 used. Jimmy also disliked Stevens's superior attitude, as he told Hedda Hopper when the company returned to Los Angeles:

> I don't take that bullshit from anybody. I realize I'm only a small cog in a big organization like Warners, but I'm an individual. I think I have talent, and with just a little bit of kindness I would have done anything in the world for

him. I'm insecure? I feel that George Stevens is insecure—and even that I could stand, but I'll be damned if I'll be his servant. Nobody's going to be allowed to step on me.

And no one did. Because he was required for so few exterior scenes that torrid July in Texas, Jimmy saw to his publicity, amused the locals with his imitation of Charlie Chaplin impersonating Marlon Brando, learned to ride at top speed, shot jackrabbits, practiced guitar and roped calves.

What remains is the filmed performance—not at all as impressive as his portraits of Cal Trask or Jim Stark, but that is due to the shallowness of the character. Although the script is unsatisfying and Jett Rink appears in only half a dozen sequences, Jimmy tried to inject some complex life into this unsympathetic, nearly one-dimensional spoiler. First seen alone in long shot, standing next to a jalopy, he is an isolated figure against the wide expanse of desert. Introduced to the newlyweds (Taylor and Hudson), he slouches and mumbles—a presage of his next sequence, when he is offered a pittance for land that may yield him oil. Here, Jimmy concluded brilliantly, sauntering from the room and, in a deft swipe of his arm, communicating both "Farewell" and "No deal" to the unctuous lawyers. He is then seen on his plot of land, taking inventory of the dimensions in a scene reminiscent of the beanfield sequence from *East of Eden*. James Dean, said the language of film, is one with the earth—solid, isolated, free.

Only in the sequence at his ranch with Taylor was

there an opportunity for him to humanize Jett Rink. Trying to please and impress the object of his suppressed desires, he does not fumble comically but plays the scene with simple earnestness—before snagging the wisdom in his reply to her statement, "Money isn't all, you know, Jett."

"Not when you got it."

The obvious choice for Jimmy's reading might have been for him to snarl the reply, indicating that all his life Jett has been at the mercy of her husband's whims. But instead Jimmy laughed self-deprecatingly, as if to say, "If only it were that simple, but it's kind of rough without money." After that tender, tentative moment, Jett declines as his fortunes rise—and James Dean, completely inarticulate in a drunk scene he loathed, was in fact so inaudible that his speech had to be looped. But because this was not evident until after his sudden death, Nick Adams (Moose in *Rebel Without a Cause*) was paid to dub the speech. In a curious way, James Dean's final performance was thus marred by the very quality that brought him notoriety—his naturalness. Just a year had passed since the creation of Cal Trask. In a way, Cal is James Dean before the sudden glow of his fame; Jett is James Dean in the final months of his life, willfully shut off from almost everyone, yet ever the center of attention and adulation because of his achievements.

Before his death, even the director had to admit that Jimmy had a better understanding of Jett Rink than the script conveyed. In the party scene near the finale, Stevens told him to approach Taylor and, as he passed the bar, pour himself a big drink or two. "Look," replied Jimmy on the set, "I have a flask in my pocket.

Why don't I just go over to the bar, get a glass and pour the stuff from my flask?" Stevens turned down that suggestion. "It's their booze. Pour yourself a big drink of their stuff."

But Stevens was wrong, as he later realized.

> What Jimmy wanted to do would have been the cutest bit in the movie. His point was that it had to do with pride—Jett was too proud to take a drink from their table. Usually I think I know a character better than anyone, but what I told Jimmy was damn wrong. His idea was too damn smart, and he didn't explain it to me, so I didn't get it then. But he really knew that character, and that's the best tribute I can pay to his talent as an actor.

By July 12, the cast and crew of *Giant* were back in Los Angeles for two months of filming interior sequences at the studio in Burbank. On the twenty-third, Jimmy (explaining later that he was "too tired to work") blithely ignored a scheduled work call to move his possessions from Sunset Plaza Drive to a rented bungalow in the San Fernando Valley, at 14611 Sutton Street, Sherman Oaks. The A-frame cottage resembled a Bavarian hunting lodge, with one vast room above which was suspended a sleeping alcove on a balcony. About the same time, he met the photographer Sanford Roth and his wife, Beulah. "He was the least self-revealing being I ever met," she recalled years later. Her husband described Jimmy as "intense, shy, dedicated to his career—an enigma or a trial to people." But they liked him, and their friendship was solid enough that they spent several evenings sharing suppers over the next month.

A nineteen-year-old starlet then awaiting an assignment at Paramount also found him intense and enigmatic. Like her predecessors Pier Angeli and Lili Kardell, Swedish-born Ursula Andress was an exotic, voluptuous beauty who had starred in two minor Italian movies and was rushed to Hollywood, where she languished, mostly because of her indifference to learning English. And like the previous affairs, more was presumed than occurred.

The "affair," such as it was, lasted for about a month that summer, when the couple was seen around town on Saturday or Sunday evenings—not more often, since Jimmy had early calls for long days. According to Andress, he was "like a wild animal and smelled of everything I don't like. We fought like cats and dogs—no, like two monsters. But then we made up and had fun." The arguments, often carried out in public, were duly documented by the press, which noted that Jimmy was learning German "so that he can fight with Ursula Andress in two languages."

Finally, she wearied of the melodramatics and began dating actor John Derek (whom she eventually married) while Jimmy withdrew to his cottage. "I tried to understand him," Ursula Andress said sadly. "But I just couldn't make it work." Now Jimmy's most frequent nighttime companions were the Roths and the Siamese kitten given to him by Elizabeth Taylor; he named the cat Markie, after his young cousin.

As the production of *Giant* drew to a conclusion in September, people glimpsed fewer and fewer fragments of James Dean, and later this withdrawal gave rise to wild speculation about some sort of suicidal depression after the breakup with Ursula Andress. Nothing could be farther from the truth. For one thing, his work on *Giant* continued until September 22; for another: "I'm just dog tired. Everybody hates me and thinks I'm a heel. They say I've gone Hollywood—but honest, I'm just the same as when I didn't have a dime. I'm just tired. Maybe I'd better go away."

Exhausted or not, he kept constantly occupied with plans and projects, even if he was absent from Googie's or his usual Sunset Strip haunts. Jane Deacy came to Los Angeles, met Dick Clayton and Jimmy, and was hammering out details of a new contract with Warners, according to which James Dean would receive $1 million for nine movies over the next six years. In addition, he was permitted to accept television offers and to do a Broadway play of his choice in 1956.

That summer, Jimmy was also in private training with boxer Mushy Callahan for his forthcoming portrayal as Rocky Graziano in *Somebody Up There Likes Me*, scheduled to begin shooting in January. In addition, he renewed one particular lifetime interest after seeing on television "The Death of Billy the Kid" (written by Gore Vidal and directed by Arthur Penn); at once he arranged a series of discussions with his agent Dick Clayton and executives at Warners for a film on Billy. As for playing this real, historic villain, Jimmy insisted he would "rather have people hiss than yawn." In 1958, *The Left-Handed Gun* would be released, with Paul Newman assuming a role once planned for Dean, just as Newman did in *Somebody Up There Likes Me*.

For the immediate future, there were discussions about a film with director James Sheldon, who had twice worked successfully with Jimmy on television. And on the schedule was a fall television presentation of Emlyn Williams's *The Corn Is Green*, to co-star Judith Anderson. John Kerr eventually played the Williams role, just as he won the roles Jimmy wanted in *Tea and Sympathy* and *The Cobweb*.

Waiting for shots to be lined up on the set of *Giant* that summer, Jimmy read and studied the text of *Hamlet*, which he hoped to perform on Broadway in 1956—a concession his agents won from Warner Bros. "Only a young man can play him as he was," Jimmy told Hedda Hopper—and then added rather ungraciously (and inaccurately), "Laurence Olivier played it safe. Something is lost when the older men play him." Besides, he missed New York: "It's a wonderful, generous city, if you accept its violence. It offers so many things to do. I go to dancing school, take percussion lessons, acting lessons, attend concerts, operas." As he had told Howard Thompson of the *New York Times* that March, "In Hollywood, there are human beings just as sensitive to fertility, but they're a little harder to find."

As for the rumored depression, those who really knew him (friends like Leonard Rosenman, Dick Clayton and the Roths) recalled nothing of the kind that summer of 1955. Quite the contrary: the Roths recalled his excitement when they invited him to travel to Europe with them the following summer and they made distant but firm plans. "He wanted to walk down the Boulevard Montparnasse in Paris," according to

Sanford Roth, "to study sculpture there, to buy crazy sweaters in Capri and to meet Cocteau and Miró."

Rosenman and others did recall, however, that Jimmy tended to drink rather too much that summer. Steffi Sidney remembered meeting him in August at the Villa Capri restaurant, for a party honoring Frank Sinatra.

> He arrived with Ursula Andress and came over to me, saying, "You know, Steffi, we've never really had a picture taken of the two of us together. Why not do it now?" I was delighted, of course. He put his arm around me very gently and summoned the photographer. Within ten minutes he was asked to leave because of his unruly behavior.

He was not much more cooperative with studio executive William Orr, who had known him since March 1954 and had supported and protected him in several contretemps with Jack Warner. "Everything to do with Jimmy was a kind of crisis," Orr recalled. "There was the crisis about him living on the lot, the crisis of trying to make a firm deal out of a term deal, the crisis of this or that act of public rudeness or lewdness. Finally there was the crisis of that public service announcement."

The National Safety Council often asked celebrities to donate a few minutes of their time to film a television spot urging safe driving. "The life you save may be your own" was a famous adage of the 1950s, when thousands of miles of resurfaced highways and new freeways and the massive proliferation of new cars—especially those owned by teenagers—contributed to dramatic increases in road accidents and deaths. The council had asked Orr if James Dean, much in the news that year with his Porsche 356 Speedster and his amateur racing, would be willing to donate a half-hour urging caution, especially on young drivers.

Orr telephoned Dick Clayton, who rang back with the news of Jimmy's refusal. "Look, he's not doing it for me, and he's not doing it for Warners," said Orr. "This is something for the public." When Clayton said Jimmy was adamant, Orr decided to speak with him directly. The reply was unchanged. "So I went down to his dressing room [on the set of *Giant*] and told him that the only people to benefit from this little effort were the general public."

"But I don't want to do it!" said Jimmy, standing up to Orr.

Angrily, Orr pushed Jimmy back onto a small sofa and stood above him. "Listen to me, you little son of a bitch! You've been nasty to a lot of people around here, but you're not going to be nasty to the whole country. You're going to go down and make this damned public service announcement, or I'll stand here until you do!"

And so he did: Jimmy recited the script with his usual casual indifference, in a brief spot with actor Gig Young on a set of *Giant*. "People say racing is dangerous," he replied to one question, "but I'd rather take my chance on the race track than on the highway." He was then asked if he had advice for young drivers. "Take it easy driving," Jimmy said, about to leave the scene. Then, puckishly altering the famous safety slogan, he smiled at the camera and added, "The life you save may be mine."

On Monday, September 19, while his Porsche Speedster was at Competition Motors on North Vine Street in Hollywood for regular maintenance, Jimmy chatted with mechanic Rolf Wütherich, a German immigrant who knew the Porsche family and their business. Wütherich told Jimmy that a powerful, snappy new car was available for sale—a silver Porsche 550 Spyder, an all-purpose racer that had gathered class wins at Avus, Le Mans, Sebring and the Mille Miglia. Only seventy-eight Spyders were shipped for private sale from Germany that year. Two days later, on Wednesday, September 21, Jimmy turned in the Speedster at Competition, added a check for $3,000, and less than an hour later he sped away in the new car. Producer Ray Stark, then an agent with Dick Clayton at Famous Artists, recalled years later that in fact the $3,000 was advanced by the agency against the income pending from a deal they were concluding for Jimmy to do a film, at an unspecified future date, for Italian producer Dino de Laurentiis.

A sleek convertible with only a token windscreen a few inches high, the Spyder was eggshell-thin and pitched low to the ground. Some might have described it as not much bigger than a tropical turtle, or as an outsize roller-skate. At the service of the wrong driver, it could be an accident waiting to happen. But in its favor it had widened front brakes for improved stopping. Jimmy bought it only after Wütherich agreed to prepare the Spyder for every race and to accompany him, as adviser and mechanic, to each event. Over the next week, he washed and rewashed it: it was his great new toy, and—a young man of his time and place—he cherished it as he had no previous possession.

In this regard, Jimmy was not exceptional. Thousands of young men who owned two-seaters routinely raced at unused airport landing strips with the Sports Car Club of America or the California Sports Car Club. There were practice circuits at places like Torrey Pines and Pebble Beach, and permanent courses were planned for Riverside and Laguna, among other sites. Most weekends, it was popular for folks to drive out to see champions like Johnny von Neumann, Bill Pollack, Ken Miles, Carroll Shelby and dozens of others competing for trophies.

That Wednesday afternoon—after leaving the detachable roof at Competition—Jimmy drove the car to George Barris's garage on South La Brea. There, Barris, known for providing custom-made auto designs for celebrities (among them Clark Gable, Bob Hope, Liberace and Frank Sinatra), followed Jimmy's instructions. On Thursday, the car was ready, with "Little Bastard" scripted prominently on the back—by which Jimmy meant himself—and his racing number (130) on the doors and hood. "Little Bastard" was not a term to be publicly displayed in 1955, but by this time Jimmy's knowledge of his illegitimate conception, and the haze of ambiguous memories about his parents' unhappy marriage, were used for another shock tactic. The distinction between himself and his car, once referred to as a lover and now the instrument of his ultimate competition, was at last forever blurred.

To the friends and colleagues to whom he showed the car over the next week, the matter of the car's suitability and safety for one inclined to take chances was of greater concern than the coarse advertisement painted for the world's reaction. "Thank you, but I'll walk home!" Beulah Roth told him after he drove her shopping, adding years later, "I couldn't be in that car!" For the first time in weeks, he drove to the home of Ursula Andress, who declined a ride and warned him about his driving habits. Racing champion Phil Hill, who had seen him race, was equally concerned: "Dean had a scary, unpredictable element, as if he had too much to prove to the world."

That evening, Jimmy dined at the Villa Capri, where he happened to meet the actor Alec Guinness, who considered the car sinister. "She'll do a hundred and fifty [miles an hour]," Jimmy said—to which Guinness prophesied that if Jimmy risked himself in that car, he would be dead in a week. "Don't be so mean!" countered the driver, laughing. During the week he owned the car, Jimmy drove 250 miles.

On Friday, September 23, Jimmy zoomed through the front gate of Warner Bros., where he insisted on taking George Stevens for a spin—partly as a friendly gesture (although he wanted to assure himself that Stevens would not edit his scenes too heavily) but also to show off on his last day of work on *Giant*. When he deposited Stevens back at the soundstage, he was approached by guards, who told him that henceforth he could not bring the Spyder onto the property. Jimmy then shook his director's hand, smiled agreeably and said, "Now that it's all over, we don't have to bug each other anymore."

Jane Deacy, who was in town for meetings with Dick Clayton and the legal department at Warners, hosted a party for Jimmy on Sunday evening at the Chateau Marmont Hotel, where they told friends that in early October—about ten days or two weeks hence—they would travel together to New York, where Jimmy was scheduled to begin rehearsals for a television appearance in an adaptation of the Hemingway story "The Battler" (which co-starred Paul Newman and led to his playing the role originally assigned to Jimmy in *Somebody Up There Likes Me*). After she saw the Spyder, Jane asked if Jimmy had a good policy on the car; Pacific Indemnity, Jimmy replied, covered its full value—but no liability for him or his passengers. Jane sat him down for a stern lecture.

On Monday, September 26, Jimmy learned of a race to be held the following weekend in, of all places, Salinas—John Steinbeck's hometown and the setting for *East of Eden*. Ninety minutes south of San Francisco, the town was, before the completion of freeways and interstate highways, well over a day's drive from Los Angeles—even if one exceeded the speed limit. No longer required for any work on *Giant*, Jimmy at once decided to enter the race, although his name was submitted too late to be included on the printed program.

The next day, insurance agent Lew Bracker, whom he met through Leonard Rosenman, discussed a life insurance policy for Jimmy to sign. Jimmy named his beneficiaries: $85,000 to Marcus and Ortense Winslow, $10,000 for the education of young Marcus, and $5,000 to his grandparents, Charles and Emma Dean. These bequests should be stipulated in a will, said Bracker, especially because Jimmy refused to name his father. Jimmy promised to execute such a document the following week. But no Last Will and Testament was ever prepared, and months later the entire sum of $100,000 insurance money was ironically assigned by the court

to the next of kin, his father, Winton Dean.* Jimmy did
see to one obligation, however: because he would be
away the entire weekend, he left his Siamese cat
Markie with a neighbor, starlet Jeanette Mille. On
Thursday, he left the Spyder with Rolf Wütherich at
Competition Motors, where a final check would be
made before the race.

At home in Sherman Oaks, James Dean arose early on
Friday morning, September 30, 1955. After dressing
quickly in a pair of light blue trousers, a white T-shirt,
brown shoes and his trademark red windbreaker, he
slipped on his sunglasses and drove over the canyon in
a white 1953 Ford station wagon he had purchased late
in 1954 but rarely used. At Competition, he picked up
the new Porsche and Wütherich. A trailer was then
hitched to the Ford, and the Spyder was loaded into
that, so that it would not be used until Saturday.
Shortly after nine o'clock, Jimmy and Rolf drove to the
home of Sanford Roth, who had agreed to come along
and film the event at Salinas. At the Roths', Jimmy
made the sudden decision to drive the Spyder to
Salinas, the better (he said) to accustom himself to handling the car at higher speed than town driving had
allowed. At the same time, it was agreed that Roth

---

* Winton Dean died on February 21, 1995, at the age of eighty-seven. He had suffered
the ravages of Alzheimer's disease for many years. His parents, Charles and Emma
Dean, had predeceased him in 1961. Marcus Winslow died in 1976 and his wife,
Ortense, in 1991. As of 1996, Marcus Winslow, Jr., and his family continue to reside at
the Winslow homestead in Jonesboro.

would follow in the Ford with Jimmy's buddy Bill
Hickman, a fellow racer he had known since the days
they both played bit roles in *Fixed Bayonets*.

As it happened, Winton Dean's family had been visiting in Los Angeles, and a few days earlier Jimmy had
welcomed them all for a brief visit to the bungalow in
Sherman Oaks. It was an awkward hour, since Jimmy
and his father had met only very rarely in the last two
years, and never warmly. By September 30, Ortense
and Marcus Winslow had departed for Indiana but
Charles Dean remained, and he said he wanted to see
the new car. Winton and Uncle Charlie met Jimmy at
Patsy's Pizza in Hollywood, and after a quick lunch
they separated. Jimmy leaped into the Spyder,
Wütherich at his side, and Roth and Hickman piled
into the Ford. They stopped for fuel and a few photographs and then began the trip north. It was just after
one o'clock on a cloudless, hot afternoon.

The journey took them along Route 99 (later
replaced by Interstate 5), where at about three-thirty,
Officer O. V. Hunter pulled over the Porsche and the
Ford, citing both drivers for exceeding the speed limit
by ten miles. Then the cars resumed the road, and
Jimmy, according to Wütherich, continued to discuss
only one thing—winning the race in Salinas. Of this he
was very confident, he said: he felt one with the car. In
Wasco, Jimmy turned west onto State Road 466 (later
Route 46), heading toward Paso Robles. The road was
smooth, the passengers in a fine mood; behind them,
Roth pressed the pedal of the Ford to keep up.

A few minutes after five, the two cars pulled into
Blackwell's Corner, a general store and diner at the
junction of Route 466 and Highway 33. There they

spotted Lance Reventlow, son of the heiress Barbara Hutton, who was also heading for the race at Salinas; they agreed to meet for dinner that evening in Paso Robles. After munching an apple and gulping a glass of Coca-Cola, Jimmy motioned to Wütherich, Roth and Hickman, snapped his sunshades over his prescription eyeglasses, and the four set off again. The road ahead was clear, the sun a brilliant gold disk hanging over the rural knolls. Jimmy drove as fast as the law allowed—sixty-five miles an hour—but no faster, as Wütherich insisted for years after.

Just before six, Donald Turnupseed, a student from the Polytechnic Institute at San Luis Obispo, was driving his black-and-white sedan for a weekend visit to his parents' home in Tulare. Just beyond a tiny backwater called Cholame, Turnupseed headed northeast along Route 41, which crossed Route 466 at a Y-shaped junction. At the same time, Jimmy came from the opposite direction. His Porsche, low and gray, hugged the road and, for just a moment, was not clearly visible in the shadow of an incline. At the crossing, Turnupseed slowed, as if he saw the Porsche, and Jimmy, with the right of way, continued.

Then, inexplicably, Turnupseed's car began to cross 466.

"That guy's gotta see us—he'll stop," Jimmy shouted to Rolf against the wind. And with that, Jimmy accelerated—but so did the other vehicle.

The Porsche smashed into the large, heavy sedan and was completely demolished in an instant. Twenty-three-year-old Donald Turnupseed stepped from his car, dazed but with only a slight bruise. Rolf Wütherich, twenty-seven, was thrown clear of the

Spyder and landed in a ditch; he suffered numerous fractures and contusions and required several operations. But he lived until 1981, until he was killed at the age of fifty-three in his native Germany—in another road accident.

James Dean had multiple fractures of his jaw and arms and numerous internal injuries. But pinned behind the wheel, he had no chance. His head snapped back grotesquely, and his chest was smashed beneath the pressure of the steering column. For just a few seconds, as he was lifted into an ambulance, Wütherich heard "a soft cry escaping from Jimmy—the little whimpering cry of a boy wanting his mother or of a man facing God."

And then there was silence. James Dean, his neck twisted and broken, was dead at twenty-four. The landscape, shattered only for a moment by the gruesome crash, became still again as dusk gathered over the California hills.

chapter twelve

> In my end is my beginning.
> MARY STUART'S MOTTO,
> WHICH SHE EMBROIDERED ON
> HER CHAIR OF STATE

Miss Taylor, grief-stricken, was unable to work." This production note was added to the Warner Bros. files for *Giant* on Saturday, October 1, 1955—and every day thereafter until October 11. Jimmy's death at twenty-four pitched her into a depression from which it took weeks to emerge.

"In sixteen months of acting, he left a more lasting impression on the public than many stars do in thirty years," said producer Henry Ginsberg. "I can understand why the impact of his personality was so great. Though he was not an easy person to know, he was an exciting and stimulating person to be with." Privately, Ginsberg remained a canny observer:

> The consensus of opinion—and I share this view—is that this boy was a rather unique personality and may develop into something of a

legend. Considering that he was a character actor, the feeling is that his appearance in films will not be affected at all—if anything, there may be greater anxiety on the part of the public to see him . . . He reached stardom overnight.

Ginsberg was on the mark. Nine months after Dean's death, there were more than four hundred fan clubs in America, Canada, Europe and South America; it took another year for them to organize in Africa, Australia and Japan.

By 1957, James Dean had been posthumously nominated twice as Best Actor by the members of the Academy of Motion Picture Arts and Sciences, for *East of Eden* and for *Giant*. (Rock Hudson was nominated for Best Actor for *Giant*, too.) Oddly, Dean was not cited by the Academy for *Rebel Without a Cause*, for which he gave a fuller and more significant performance than in *Giant*.* Abroad, he won the Best Actor award in Britain for *East of Eden*, and the highest citation from the French Film Academy. Similar top honors were announced in Belgium, Finland, Japan and Germany.

From late 1955 through 1957, movie magazines around the world—which at the time had enormous influence on studio marketing decisions—bestowed more than twenty awards on the late James Dean as "the Best" in some category or other. Two years after his death, the Hollywood Foreign Press Association proclaimed Jimmy "the World's Favorite Actor." Poet

---

* The Best Actor Oscar for 1955 went to Ernest Borgnine for *Marty*; for 1956, it was awarded to Yul Brynner for *The King and I*.

Frank O'Hara (who was twenty-nine the year Jimmy died) was at the center of the New York School of Poets. He wrote in *Poetry* magazine:

> *Men cry from the grave while they still live*
> *and now I am this dead man's voice,*
> *stammering, a little in the earth.*
> *I take up*
> *the nourishment of his pale green eyes,*
> *out of which I shall prevent*
> *flowers from growing, your flowers.*

No other screen actor, alive or dead, ever received so many distinctions in so short a time.

For a year, George Stevens was constantly distracted by threats to his life from Dean fans who warned that any editing or cutting of Jimmy's scenes in *Giant* would result in terrible harm to the director. But Stevens was not easily intimidated. "Anyone who subscribes to this phony morbidity cult is doing an injustice to the memory of a great actor," he told the press. "I'm sure Jimmy would want to be judged solely on his talent and nothing else." As to the emergence of rumors about a death-wish, Stevens was contemptuous, as were those closer to Dean, like Leonard Rosenman, Dick Clayton and Natalie Wood. "Morbid nonsense!" cried Stevens (whose direction of *Giant* won him an Oscar). "Jimmy had no will to die. He was very much planning for the future. He was a boy with a wonderful sense of theater, a boy on the rise. A few more films and the fans wouldn't have felt so bereft.

The first bright phrase would have become an ordinary light and not produced this kind of thing"—by which, of course, he meant the rise of the legend of James Dean.

It all started somewhat more quietly.

On Saturday, October 8, a funeral was held at the Friends Church, Fairmount, and State Police estimated the crowd outside at over three thousand, almost twice the population of the town. The six pallbearers were high-school classmates of the deceased. Flowers from Elizabeth Taylor in Hollywood and Geraldine Page in New York were added to more than a hundred wreaths sent from people who never knew James Dean but had seen him in *East of Eden*. A month later, after the release of *Rebel Without a Cause*, florists were weary from a dozen deliveries a day to the cemetery.

That crisp autumn day in 1955, Ethel and Winton Dean, who had brought the remains back from California, led the bereaved, among whom were the Winslows; John Wilson, Jimmy's maternal grandfather; and the Dean grandparents. The burial followed that afternoon in Park Cemetery; it was wrongly reported then (and repeated by biographers over the next forty years) that Jimmy was laid to rest next to his mother's grave. But she had been buried eleven miles away, in Marion.

"The career of James Dean has not ended," said Reverend Xen Harvey in his eulogy that afternoon. "It has just begun. And remember, God himself is directing the production."

And the postmortem production had a wide press. The reviews of *Rebel Without a Cause* (which opened in

New York on October 26, 1955) helped the cause of canonization.

- "The most moving job of all is turned in by James Dean."
- "He stands out as a remarkable talent."
- "His rare talent and appealing personality even shine through this turgid melodrama."
- "Dean is very effective as a boy groping for adjustment to people. Here was a talent that might have touched the heights. His ability to get inside the skin of youthful pain, torment and bewilderment is not often encountered."
- "The best thing about the film is James Dean, a player of unusual sensibility and charm."

Shortly after, the foreign reviews were equally enthusiastic. Typical reactions were summarized by no less a critic than François Truffaut, who wrote that Dean

contradicts fifty years of film acting. Each gesture, each pose, each reaction is a slap in the face of the psychological tradition of acting. He does not exploit his dialogue with insinuating force (like Edwige Feuillère), he does not "poetize" (like Gérard Philipe), he does not try to outsmart anybody (like Pierre Fresnay). He isn't concerned to show that he understands everything better than you . . . He carries

within himself our own ambiguities, our dual-
ity and every human weakness.

A year later, when *Giant* premiered on October 10,
1956, word was even more ecstatic, and for a performance far less demanding. Elizabeth Taylor and Rock
Hudson, who were required to do much more with
their roles, acted with remarkable subtlety and to far
more emotional effect. They could not have been
happy to read that critics wrote almost exclusively of
the supporting player:

- "James Dean gives the most striking performance, creates the most memorable character
  [and] makes the most sedate onlooker understand why a James Dean cult came into existence."
- "The film only proves what a promising talent
  has been lost."
- "It's Dean, Dean, Dean the audience will be
  watching—and there are many who will be
  watching with fascination and love."
- "James Dean's talent glows like an oilfield
  flare."
- "This is the finest piece of atmospheric acting
  seen on screen since Marlon Brando . . . the blaz-
  ing up of a lost light.
- "James Dean clearly shows what his admirers
  always said he had: a streak of genius."
- "The picture belongs to the late James Dean . . .
  The young actor's death last year now emerges

as a much more significant theatrical loss to the
mature moviegoer than it is to the adolescent
cultists who have mourned so noisily."

- "This is a haunting capstone to a brief career
[and] the most tangy and corrosive performance
in the film."

Hence the Reverend Harvey's testimony that the true
career had just begun (which he doubtless meant as a
reference to the afterlife); very soon, that bore another
connotation. By early November 1955, the mailroom at
Warner Bros. was deluged with three thousand letters a
week from fans, and that number doubled over the next
two years. Executives were obliged to employ a special
fan mail agency, for most of the letters wanted a reply, a
photograph, an autograph, a lock of hair, a piece of
debris from the Porsche.

But at the same time, many of the correspondents
refused to believe Jimmy was dead. He was, they insisted,
so badly disfigured that he was confined to a sanatorium;
or he had suffered brain damage and was in a lunatic asylum. "Jimmy, darling," ran a typical letter, "I know you
are not dead. I know you are just in hiding. Don't hide,
Jimmy. Come back. It won't matter to us." Others were
bolder: starstruck maidens popped up everywhere, claiming they were each the true love of his life and some that
they were pregnant by him (by traditional or miraculous
means). But Jimmy did not come back. Observed
Humphrey Bogart, with his cool, sardonic imperturbabil-
ity: "Dean died at just the right time. Had he lived, he'd
never have been able to live up to his publicity."

Instead, savvy marketing people took up the cause,

sacramentally bringing back to life the icon who (conveniently for salesmen) remained quite dead. More than three hundred magazine articles were published in America alone between November 1955 and June 1957. James Dean posters flooded the world in growing profusion, as did T-shirts, linens, coffee mugs, masks, songs, calendars, pens, cigarette lighters.* By 1957, the craze was virulent not only in New York and Los Angeles, but as far away as Southeast Asia. On September 15 that year, the *New York Times* correspondent reported that one hundred miles from Jakarta, in the remote mountain village of Bandung, dozens of girls and boys roamed the streets in blue jeans and red jackets, mourning their idol.

So began the rise of the cult, and with it the mad, sad grappling for relics of the adored one. Five years later and forty years later, the worldwide fixation showed no signs of diminishing.

"Dear James," wrote a boy from Finland to Jimmy at Warner Bros. in September 1960,

> As one of your unknown admirers, I take
> the liberty of asking you for an autographed
> photo. You may be sure a photo will have a
> place of honor in my home, and at the same
> time I wish to thank you for the great pleasure
> your acting has given me.

---

* A sampling of recordings by singers from country, rock and blues singers: "A Boy Named Jimmy Dean," "Hymn for James Dean," "Jimmy Dean Is Not Dead," "The Ballad of James Dean," "Jimmy, Jimmy," "The Racer Lives Forever," "The Story of James Dean," "His Name Was Dean."

"I think you are wonderful," wrote a South African fan, "and I want to keep you as my friend. Please send photograph."

In 1977, a Tokyo businessman named Seita Ohnishi paid $15,000 to erect a memorial slab around a "Tree of Life," to mark the hallowed spot in Cholame.

"I identify with him," said a man named Tom Parker at a Dean memorial in 1980; he was born the year after Jimmy died. "I never had a good relationship with my father, like he didn't in his movies. And in real life too, I guess."

"Jimmy's my hero," said twenty-year-old Englishman Nick Taylor in 1981.

"He was a lot like me," added Californian Bob Carr that same year. "He was a realist and so am I." One wonders precisely how Carr knew what he knew.

"He had his own ways," said Tony Perez, explaining his own love of James Dean. The reporter from the *Los Angeles Times* did not ask whose ways Perez had.

Nor was the phenomenon limited to America. In London, too, God was still in charge of the production, and evidently He closed a lucrative deal in 1987, when the image of James Dean was used in full-page advertisements urging British students to open an account with the National Westminster Bank. Those who had "licensed" the image of James Dean might have been laughing all the way to their own banks.

The frenzy continued.

"I have 14 letters in my name," said sixty-year-old Arnold Siminoff in 1991. "Just like James Byron Dean." Siminoff added that Dean would have been sixty that year. "We would have been the best of friends."

Parts of the Spyder were sold at unimaginable prices

by the man who appropriated the wreck. Dr. William
Eschrich, a Burbank surgeon and racer who had competed against Jimmy in the May contest at Bakersfield,
paid $1,000 for the engine. The hull was sent around
the country on tour (ostensibly to discourage unsafe
driving), and awestruck fans paid fifty cents apiece to
see it. Gradually, so many fragments were filched that
the car literally vanished into thin air within four years;
the chassis survived until 1985, when it, too, disappeared. As for Jimmy's modest material possessions
(clothes, wristwatches, books, records, racing trophies),
they were appraised at about $1,500 and brought more
than $40,000 at auction. The proceeds, like the insur-
ance payout of $100,000 and Jimmy's $5,000 bank
account, went to Winton Dean.

For years, pious but impudent pilgrims chipped
away fragments from his tombstone and painted
indelible kisses on the marble. Amateur oil paintings
were in such demand that assembly lines were kept
busy around the clock. With mementos at a premium,
the distant disciples had to content themselves with
flickering images or photos, although some turned to
the original apostolic eyewitnesses for relics. Natalie
Wood received a mountain of mail asking what it felt
like to be kissed by James Dean. Sal Mineo and Dennis
Hopper pored through requests for anything Jimmy
had touched—a piece of wallpaper, a newspaper, a studio prop.

Pilgrimages are easily organized in the limited orbit
of James Dean's world, which comprised only Indiana,
New York and California. The Winslows and Deans
were awakened at all hours of the day and night by
unexpected visitors to Fairmount, as obsessed fans

began to trek in ever greater numbers to the places he lived. They frequented Jerry's Restaurant and Cromwell's drugstore in New York, and the Villa Capri in Hollywood, where they sat at his favorite tables and ordered his preferred foods. They sought out Louis Fontana, Jimmy's New York barber, and they asked the texture of Jimmy's hair. They pinned notes for Jimmy to the front door of the Manhattan apartment on West Sixty-eighth Street. They wanted to sleep in his room at the Iroquois Hotel, where the faithful try to contact Jimmy's spirit every year on his birthday and death day. "I don't think anyone has seen his ghost," said the manager of the Iroquois forty years later, "but they say there is definitely something up there."

Admiration went beyond reason. People built shrines in their homes to James Dean, imitated him in dress, stance and tone. Vampira, among others, claimed to summon up the ectoplasmic James Dean at séances ("although mostly he comes to me through the radio," she said with a straight face). Debi Bottigi, a twenty-five-year-old Virginian, was sleeping at James Dean's grave on the thirty-fifth anniversary of his death, when (she insisted) she heard footsteps. She looked up, but saw no one. "It was Jimmy in his boots," she concluded, "walking back to his grave." For months after that, the tombstone was a pillow to hundreds of Dean fans each week. Apparently those boots were made for walking.

Death turned the young man who was simultaneously suspicious and enamored of fame into one of the most celebrated stars in history, and not only in America but all over the world. Sometimes the morbid neurosis turned tragic. Several grieving young women

killed themselves straightaway in the autumn of 1955.
In 1958, the formation of the James Dean Death Club
resulted in the death by auto of two California honor
students, who tried to imitate the car race in *Rebel
Without a Cause*. In 1965, two teenage girls, members of
the thirty-five-hundred-member Frankfurt Dean Club,
committed suicide on the anniversary of Jimmy's
death: for them, life was too grim without him. In mid-
century, disturbed youth had chosen a disturbed youth
as hero, as a kind of collective personality to whom
they could affix their confusion and their fears.

Seven years after Dean's death, Marilyn Monroe's
dreadful end raised her to a similar doubtful throne,
although for decades she was misperceived. Fifteen
years after her death, Elvis Presley went down in a
haze of addictions, which is all right in America if one
has made a major impact on pop culture and made
many people rich and happy, which he certainly did.
Presley's original, stated goal was to be a movie star
like James Dean; the music, at first, was almost incidental. In fact, when he first came to Hollywood, Presley
begged for a meeting with Nicholas Ray, knelt down
before him and recited lengthy excerpts of the dialogue
from *Rebel Without a Cause*. Presley said he wanted to
be the next James Dean, but this was an aspiration of
which his handlers quickly disabused him.

James Dean lacked the sexual threat and the lightly
veiled contempt of Brando. In the 1950s, an era that
placed the highest value on conformity and the sup-
pression of individualism, Dean was the right one to
represent the safest kind of rebellion—the tender,
sweet-faced, strong-gentle boy who weeps easily. He
was, in other words, no threat at all. "I don't want any

trouble," he repeated several times in *Rebel Without a Cause*. He fought back only when forced.

As for Marilyn Monroe, she had to endure the fate of many attractive, successful women. After her death, a riot of lies circulated about her: she was a drug addict, an alcoholic, a woman of easy virtue; she slept her way to fame; she was stupid and inconsiderate; she committed suicide. All that was rubbish, but a deeply rooted American puritanism precludes accepting so luminous a creature as anything other than Eve the temptress. She was sexy and projected sex as classy fun, so she had to be considered no good. Often taken for granted during her life, she was in death vilified beyond all resemblance to the truth. Still, at the end of the century, it is not outrageous to say that Dean and Monroe— even to those who have a low estimation of them— remain the most royal of deified Americans, if only because of the brilliant marketing strategies of their celebrity. Nor was the academy immune. Scholarly monographs proliferated like autumn leaves on campuses. James Dean's death mask was placed beside those of Beethoven, Thackeray and Keats at Princeton University.

There was, to summarize the matter, something forever angry and sadly ungrownup about James Dean until he died at the tragically young age of twenty-four. After his death, he became a culture hero not because he had done something brave or great in his lifetime, but because in three films he presented something true about himself, a tortured, vulnerable, emotionally disabled soul. In his performances, his childlike distrust of adult society, an overwhelming confusion about the locus of real values, a lack of stability, discipline and commitment touched responsive chords in some young people who felt dislocated by the materialism of the 1950s. In subsequent decades, he became something of a marred stained-glass-window saint, on whom the frustrations of anyone could be attached; he became the patron of the disaffected, the excuse for many to hide behind a certain type of dark Peter Pan-ism. We will fly away, disappear forever, he seemed to say.

But the sad truth is that even in his lifetime the lad, like Peter Pan, remained forever mired in adolescence. Talented he certainly was, although genius he had no time to develop. "He just drifted from person to person," said Dizzy Sheridan sadly. "And I think he was confused about relationships because it had never been clear to him what his relationship was with the two primal people in his life, his mother and father. Nothing had ever been clear with them, nothing resolved. And I think that made him complex and troubled, as sweet as he could be." Photographer Dennis Stock, engaged later for a photo story on Dean, agreed: "He lived like a stray animal [in New York]; in fact, come to think of it, he was a stray animal."

Had he lived longer, Dean would have had to untangle some of this enormous conflict, or he would have courted any one of a wide variety of disasters that would eventually have short-circuited any kind of public adoration. As it was, he had the miserable and oddly good fortune to die young—and entirely enigmatic to his adorers, who really knew nothing at all about him and were thus free to transform him into their heart's desire, to believe that he was anything they wanted to believe. In reality, he was not wicked or shameful in his short life: he was simply unformed and terribly needy. Perhaps no one has ever been a better candidate for eternal stardom.

What was going on?

Very likely it had less to do with the real James Dean than with the really obsessive fans, who projected onto his image all their own confusions; in every generation, they are mostly young. Another factor was something James Dean shared with other great stars (Greta Garbo, Marlene Dietrich, Gary Cooper, Katharine Hepburn): there was something androgynous about him. Dean was a slightly raunchy man with the seductive smokiness of a nubile girl, playing a baffled teen and driven by the conflicted desires of a child: he was everything.

His three roles gave teens an icon of vulnerability and bewilderment—he validated, in other words, a rebellious discontent. "Jimmy is me" was a theme repeated endlessly in the fan letters sent to the studio, to the Indiana relatives, to the co-stars. As for the teenagers, who took Jimmy for a patron saint, they were the premier generation of Americans who had the money and the leisure time to consider themselves not merely "young adults," not just inheritors of their parents' values. For the first time, teens had the freedom to choose what was later called a "life-style," and so to reject parental influence and authority, often solely for the sake of rejecting it. It was, in the final analysis, a middle-class rebellion—teens rebelling not because of a war they decried or because of civil rights denied a minority group. They were, quite to the contrary, utterly without a cause except themselves. With the rarest exceptions, 1950s youth were not led to think there was more to this life than cars, television, rock and roll, "making out" and winning a passport (that is, a college degree) that would admit them to the commercial scramble.

The primacy of the teen factor cannot be underestimated. The word "teenager" did not occur in dictionaries until after World War II, perhaps because before that Americans did not consider this phase of life as anything other than childhood, youth or young adulthood—nothing, in other words, unto itself. Before the war, adolescent rebellion was a matter for young thugs and apprentice crooks, not mainstream boys and girls, and a major sociological study demonstrated that adolescents enjoyed going to school as their parents did not.

But after World War II, everything changed, and America had a word for those between the ages of twelve and twenty. "Teens" indicated a separate social entity whose needs, fads and fashions were worthy of consideration apart from the adult world. Wealth, self-consciousness and leisure time separated the new generation from nineteenth-century predecessors (who were forced to work to support themselves) and their forebears of the early twentieth century (who were forced to contribute to the support of their families). The buying potential of teenagers in the 1950s was thus arguably the biggest new market targeted by advertising: witness nineteen-year-young Jimmy (looking sixteen) and his friends in the television commercials for soft drinks.

At the same time, American teens suddenly seemed to nourish a typically American brand of paranoia: young people are dangerous! In November 1957, *Cosmopolitan* asked "Are Teenagers Taking Over?" in an article that conjured up an image of a vast throng of blue-jeaned storm troopers, forcing their elders to bow to their aggregate will. Meantime, teens got and spent, sometimes laid waste their powers, and the American economy benefited enormously from a new class of grumpy consumers.

Adolescents and their problems were not the stuff of serious films in Hollywood until the 1950s. *Our Dancing Daughters* (1928) and *The Wild Party* (1929) were mild American capers, while in England, Alfred Hitchcock's silent classic *Downhill* (a moral journey, not one on skis) starred Ivor Novello, a thirty-three-year-old adult matinee idol, as a spoiled schoolboy. The 1930s featured college "pigskin epics," that were unendurably spruce, and the Dead End Kids got their comeuppance or straightened out in the last reel. With the advent of World War II, movie young people were heroic abroad and terribly sweet at home—Andy Hardy and the gang, one and all. It was family time, as it was in the television situation comedies of the 1950s (*Trouble With Father*, *Father Knows Best*, *Life With Father* and others). And then along came Marlon Brando on his motorcycle in *The Wild One* (December 1953) and the urban punks of *Blackboard Jungle* (March 1955). But it was the red-jacketed *Rebel*, not the guy in leather, who touched the mainstream.

James Dean was a perfect patron for comfortable loners who after a certain point did not have to worry about the source of the next meal or month's rent. In this regard, it is interesting to see that James Dean was essentially a hero only to white, middle-class American boys and girls. After all, Dean was well compensated, he expected to advance in his career, he made plans and provisions. He wanted more and faster cars; he wanted to build a house in the Hollywood Hills with the same airplane view enjoyed by his agent Dick Clayton. But he never had to worry about money for all that. "He didn't have to," said Clayton. "Jane [Deacy] and I did."

Adolescents, who are predictably self-absorbed for a while, were lured by the marketing of James Dean, who was made to appeal to a new breed of young consumers. Girls wanted to be his, women wanted to protect and mother him, boys wanted to be his best buddy. "To us teenagers, Dean was a symbol of the fight to make a niche for ourselves in the world of adults," wrote Margaret Moran of Cleveland, Ohio, to *Life* magazine. Her letter was typical of tens of thousands of writers to the press, not all of them teens. "You have a sort of motherly feeling toward him," wrote a woman in her forties ten years after Dean's death. "But when you look into that beautiful, handsome face, you sometimes forget how old you are."

In this regard, it is important to remember a lady named Theresa Brandes, a fifty-two-year-old New York widow who founded the James Dean Memory Club in 1956; from that time until her death in 1972, she gave her life to Jimmy. Speaking around the world to massive audiences of fans, she reminded people how she missed James Dean and regretted, as they did, that there would be no more James Dean movies. "But I am happier now than when he was alive," she said with utter seriousness. "I have found contentment in helping to preserve his memory." People seemed not to appreciate the deranged irony of her passion. Theresa Brandes and her breed indicate something terrifically important: it is very safe to fall in love with a dead person, for there can be no responsibility, no threat of loss, no challenge, no change. Idealized beyond all resemblance to the truth, the beloved remains what he was, or what the lover wants him to have been. Harsh reality never intervenes.

This may help to explain why James Dean has become more popular than ever in an era of risky sex. He was never a lover onscreen; everything was suggested, and very obliquely. His only love scene in *East of Eden*, in a Ferris wheel, is interrupted when Abra (Julie Harris) breaks their kiss, feeling guilty for "betraying" Aron, from whom she is beginning to turn in any case. Similarly, Jimmy's kiss on the lips of Natalie Wood in *Rebel Without a Cause* is so tentative as to suggest that one of them has bad breath. In *Giant*, he gets fairly close to the noses of Elizabeth Taylor and Carroll Baker, but that is the extent of the intimacy. There was not a boy in the 1950s, and perhaps not a man since, who did not feel that once or sometimes or too often, that was the way it was.

Nineteen-fifty-six, the year James Dean was nominated for Best Actor for the preceding year (for *East of Eden*) and the year *Giant* secured his status, is regarded by social historians as the Year of the Teenager, the time when "teenage" defined and described a youth culture that had been forming since the end of World War II. Frankie Lymon and the Teenagers was the first pop group to identify itself with this new subculture, as music critic Stephen Holden has pointed out. Their hit song "Why Do Fools Fall in Love?" reached the top of the sales charts at almost the same time as Elvis Presley's "Heartbreak Hotel."

The proliferation of dirges and laments for James Dean began at precisely this time, and the attitude of romantic confusion was eventually summarized by another group, Dion and the Belmonts: "Each night I ask the stars up above/Why must I be a teenager in love?" Why, indeed.

But there is more to understanding the phenomenon of James Dean than the primacy of a youth culture.

James Dean died before he could fail, before he lost his hair or his boyish figure, before he grew up. He was something of a latter-day Peter Pan, telling his followers to hurry, to ride, to aim high, but never to grow up, as he never grew up. Marlon Brando, it may be noted, lost his iconic status before the 1950s were over, by simply living too long. He still commanded respect and occasionally deserved it, and he was a star—but not a heroic figure. James Dean, with the tales of his boyhood neatly tidied up and the accounts of his adolescence carefully sanitized, became the hero of a new generation.

For a century, Hollywood has of course been in the business of manufacturing legends. Tall, blond Francis X. Bushman captured hearts in hundreds of films from 1910, but his public luster dimmed somewhat when his secret marriage was revealed; the life of the flesh, after all, humanizes celestial beings. Wallace Reid was equally busy as a romantic lead, from 1910 to his death from drug addiction at the age of thirty-two. John Gilbert, Clark Gable, Tyrone Power, Ronald Colman, Cary Grant, Gary Cooper—each had a more or less strong but transient hold on the romantic affections of large numbers of the public. But they grew older than Dean, and the public saw enough of them that their status, in one way or another, diminished.

Rudolf Valentino's story most gripped the public in the days of silent film. He came from Italy in 1913, at the age of eighteen, and worked as a gardener, waiter and dancer before traveling to California. There he had bit parts until he was spotted by the influential writer and editor June Mathis, who got him the lead in *The Four Horsemen of the Apocalypse* in 1921. His striking sensuality was then daringly exploited in *The Sheik* and other films, until he died of a perforated ulcer in New York at the age of thirty-one in 1926. Thirty thousand people crowded outside the funeral parlor on the morning of August 25, and fifty thousand passed the open casket before midnight. Dozens of women fainted as they did so.

Valentino's death prompted a national outcry of grief unequaled for a mere celebrity, and after his death, a number of American women threw themselves from skyscrapers and bridges, claiming life was not worth living without Valentino to adore. Hearing the news, a boy in Paris and a girl in London (who did not know each other) covered themselves with photographs of Valentino, lay on their beds, and took poison. A New York mother of two, age twenty, drank iodine and shot herself twice in the head, but somehow her zest for life was stronger than her passion for Valentino: she survived. These grisly dramatics soon ceased, but not the adulation. In 1991, the sixty-fifth anniversary of Valentino's death was marked by the presence of 150 people at Hollywood Memorial Park Cemetery.

Adoration rarely goes as far as self-immolation, and Valentino's followers seem not to have gone in for

voodoo and demonic rituals, as was too often true of
Dean's mid-century maniacs.* Valentino attracted a
basic, atavistic sexual response; Dean drew the tor-
mented, the insecure, those who fancied themselves
misunderstood, when too often there was, alas, very little to understand.

Both Valentino and Dean came from humble backgrounds (which Americans like), both flashed briefly in
an astonishing burst of fame and both died young.
Untimely death has been a common motif in tragic tales,
from the Greek tale of Pyramus and Thisbe to Edgar
Allan Poe's "Annabel Lee" to the syrup of Love Story—
but it is especially irresistible in the twentieth century,
when people are expected to live to ripe old ages. That
changed by 1993, when twenty-three-year-old River
Phoenix succumbed to a drug overdose. In a few days,
the news died, too, for death was commonplace for the
young in the era of AIDS. In this regard, James Dean
was the first celebrity of talking pictures to die out of
time at the peak of his powers—thus he was the forerunner of all those young people who met an early death.
No subsequent passing has been quite so devastating.

He was also the forerunner of an entire generation
of actors. His influence can be seen in the styles

---

* Valentino's divorced second wife, Winifred Hudnut (who assumed the more colorful
name Natasha Rambova), claimed that after his death "Valentino is a citizen of the astral
plane. He has met Enrico Caruso and has heard the late tenor sing. He has visited the-
aters here and is pleased at the flattery. Everything, however, now seems strange to him
as he can see through all things." But from the great beyond Valentino made no mention of Pola Negri, who claimed they were engaged at the time of his death. (See the
Associated Press news release dated Nov. 25, 1926, and the New York Times, Nov. 26,
1926.)

(self-generated or studio-encouraged) of actors as differ-
ent from one another as Steve McQueen, Paul Newman,
Jack Nicholson, Robert De Niro, Warren Beatty, Dennis
Hopper, Clint Eastwood, Martin Sheen, Sean Penn,
Timothy Hutton, Matt Dillon, Jason Priestley, Johnny
Depp, Luke Perry, Emilio Estevez and the doomed River
Phoenix. Outside America, there were also Dean heirs:
Alain Delon, Gérard Philipe, Gérard Blain, Jean-Paul
Belmondo, Horst Buchholz, Hardy Kruger, Oskar
Werner and Zbigniew Cybulski. And the beat goes on.
The common denominator is an apathetic exterior that is
only apparently diffidence: underneath are banked fires,
and a caring too deep for full expression.

But it is not the image of a seemingly affectless teen
rebel that has guaranteed the endurance of the James
Dean legend. In the final analysis, he is the contemporary version of that hoariest of American heroes, the
cowboy.

The novels of James Fenimore Cooper, Owen Wister,
A. H. Lewis and E.Z.C. Judson ("Ned Buntline") never
determined the popular concept of the cowboy as much
as did Hollywood, from the days of Edwin S. Porter's
silent film *The Great Train Robbery* to Kevin Costner's
Wyatt Earp. The year James Byron Dean was born, the
western *Cimarron* won the Oscar for Best Picture, and
for years afterward, the sagebrush and the range were
the identifiable setting of the mythic American.

In childhood, Jimmy Dean and his buddies saw the
old one- and two-reel Westerns of rugged Bronco Billy
(G. M. Anderson) and of that dark-eyed, solemn statue
of a man, William S. Hart. The first clearly defined
characters in American movies were cowboys, and the
Western movie was a great baby-sitter, its adventure

story providing broad and sweeping gestures, a chase, and heroes and villains battling it out in vast spaces. Tom Mix, Buck Jones, Hoot Gibson, William Boyd ("Hopalong Cassidy"), Gene Autry and Roy Rogers all made fortunes in the genre. These men of the desert were the most popular, it should be noted, just when outlaws like Capone and Dillinger were tearing through the crowded cities of America.

The cowboy was presented as a totem of America itself to every generation of American boys until the late 1950s. Without credentials or identification, with no diploma and without a home base, the cowboy was a "natural man," at home in the wilderness, unfazed by wild animals, reptiles, rustlers or outlaws. In the Hollywood versions, the heroes were never lawless; in reality, of course, cowboys were for the most part violent and seditious crooks. No man's hat remained white very long.

For four decades, John Wayne typified the heroic cowboy, and more than any other he fused it with an unquestioning patriotism: hence his ten-gallon hat eventually became something else, the most eminent of the Green Berets (at the specific request of the Pentagon, when they needed him). Never mind that most authentic cowboys lived fast and loose and made up their own laws as they went along, pushing back the frontier and battling Indians and rejecting the allure of women.

From short silent movies to Clint Eastwood epics, the American cowboy was the guardian of rugged individualism. An isolated loner enticed by the schoolmarm and the saloon belle, he rides off alone into a stunning sunset. Nor was it much different in 1936, when little Jimmy Dean listened to *The Lone Ranger* on the radio or saw Tom Mix at the movies.

Giant was arguably the logical term of the American Western movie, and in a way its coda as well. It had been preceded, most recently, by *The Gunfighter*, *Winchester 73*, *High Noon*, *Shane* and *Johnny Guitar*. Two years after *Giant*, *The Big Country* virtually marked the end of the traditional Western; from the 1960s, Europe turned out more Westerns than Hollywood. American filmmakers turned to the issue of the Indian (*Little Big Man* and *Dances With Wolves*) and tried to deal with urban violence and an unpopular war in Southeast Asia (synthesized in, for example, *The Wild Bunch*). By the time of the disastrous *Heaven's Gate* in 1980, horses (in movies as in life) had been replaced by fast cars, although Clint Eastwood briefly revived the Western. He might even be regarded as the heir to a type introduced by James Dean in *Giant*.

Jimmy's fascination with Billy the Kid was at the center of his idea of common Americanism, for Billy was a cold-blooded little Method actor of a killer, a terrifying outlaw Dean did not want to glorify in his projected film. Yet (and here lay the ultimate confusion) although Jimmy believed part of himself was Billy the Kid, he also saw himself as the Little Prince, a mystic gentle boy—also a movie subject he hoped somehow to direct. Finally, the confusion of realms commingles in Jimmy's desire to play the ultimately bewildered little prince, Hamlet, who longs to set right a rotten family history.

And so we are left with the perpetually alluring image: James Dean, the modern cowboy, shunning the entrapments of civilization and the risks of commitment, riding off into the sunset—not on his horse, but in his Porsche. Then, in a blinding instant, he is apotheosized—a virgin martyr saint for the new faithful, who could make of him anything they wished. He had clearly suffered (onscreen and, it soon became clear, in real life); now he was a fit object for veneration. On September 30, 1955, the image of the enigmatic rider of the plains reached its zenith. From there, it was a long slow decline for the cowboy and a logical development to the heroic astronaut: once the frontier has been pushed to its limit, there is nowhere else to go but up in space. Riders of the purple sage became riders of rockets, the frontier tale became the space epic, and James Dean's death was perhaps the moment when the ground shifted.

The single most influential book for Jimmy as he prepared to play Billy during the last year of his life was *The Authentic Life of Billy the Kid*, an account published in 1882 (and republished in 1927) by Sheriff Pat Garrett, who cornered and killed Billy in 1881. Garrett describes a temperamental, moody young man who was shrewd, witty, loyal to his friends and devoted to his mother. At the age of twelve, he stabbed a man who had insulted her, and this precipitated his flight from home. Henceforth an outlaw, he rustled horses and cattle, cheated at gambling and killed anyone who threatened his freedom. Of the dozen murders he was said to have committed, five can be positively attributed to Billy. As for rumors that he randomly slew Mexicans, the reverse is true: he saw them as outcasts like himself. But Indians did not fare so well in his presence—he shot them for goods as well as in self-defense.

In Billy the Kid, James Dean saw almost a mirror image. Billy stood five feet, eight inches tall and weighed about 140 pounds, tended to stoop slightly, giggled disarmingly and had a surprisingly effeminate voice—the prototype of himself. In addition to being "light, active, and graceful as a panther," Billy's form, Garrett noted, was "well knit, compact, and wonderfully muscular." Billy also had a keen sense of humor. Once, when arrested, he gave his mare to one of the lawmen and said that "he expected his business would be so confining for the next few months that he would hardly find time for horseback exercise."

Billy was skilled at escaping from jail, and he killed two of his guards as he did so at the end. Sheriff Garrett was looking for the Kid in the bedroom of Billy's friend "Alias" when Billy entered the room and approached Garrett. The sheriff drew his gun and shot him dead. When asked later about Billy's motives, Garrett said, "The Kid's career of crime was not the outgrowth of an evil disposition, nor was it caused by unchecked youthful indiscretions. It was the result of untoward, in fact unfortunate circumstances, acting upon a bold, reckless, ungoverned and ungovernable spirit, which no physical restraint could check, no danger appall, and no power less potent than death could conquer." James Dean needed no more information than that to seal his decision to make a picture about Billy the Kid.

Since childhood, James Dean had cultivated an image similar to Billy's—a lone, self-determined individualist. But he was very much dependent on all the modern mechanisms necessary to succeed in Hollywood. A farm boy until 1949, Jimmy was experienced in the ways of nature, had gone to the urban wilderness of New York and had survived.

But there were differences between the cowboy and the farm boy. Jimmy knew he needed the press and the studio, and he courted both when necessary. Hence a more accurate representation of James Dean is not that of a rugged cowboy individualist alienated from a conformist society, but rather a contemporary cowboy capitalist who thrived on work at any cost. Bongos and rude manners do not an individualist make, and Jimmy earned his label as a cowboy capitalist by achieving a delicate balance of astonishingly antisocial behavior and earnest artistic collaboration. Ironically, this truer portrait of James Dean is closer to the early Western novels. In life and in books, in history and on screen, the cowboy needed a stage on which to play and an audience out front.

Just so, the use of violence in Jimmy's films (the fistfights in *Eden* and *Giant*, and the knife duel in *Rebel*) were important in establishing his image as a modern cowboy who had the wisdom to know when and against whom to be violent. His brutal actions, in other words, are provoked rather than devised. And then there were women, the ultimate threat to the cowboy's independence. Jimmy preferred cars: "My sex pours itself into fast curves, broadslides and broodings. I have been sleeping with my MG. We make it together," as he wrote to Barbara Glenn. In the end, he achieved immortality by being cut off in his prime, as a single, unattached boy—like his desperado predecessor, Billy the Kid.

At first, Jimmy seemed to everyone to be the American boy imagined by Norman Rockwell, William Saroyan and Frank Capra—until he went to UCLA, where he became a prototype of the postwar rebel severing family ties and embracing a new career. Always a stepchild, missing his mother and distant from his father, he longed for approval and attention in the most obvious place, Hollywood. That, it can be argued, was disastrous, for he sought himself in fiction and was not encouraged to the kind of hard inner work that leads to maturity. Nevertheless, he astutely combined the apparent innocence of a farm boy with the slow cool of a hipster, added a dash of world-weariness to street wisdom, and developed "attitude."

It was inevitable, then, that in death he would be exploited, and a part of him was evoked by every succeeding decade. From 1955 to the early 1960s, he was the idol of the high-school motorcycle set, who biked around and thumbed their noses, Jimmy-like, at the older generation. With the wilder confrontations of the 1960s, another aspect of Jimmy was handy: the sly and suspicious rebel who rejected the demands of polite society. Then, in the sexually freewheeling 1970s, Dean fulfilled yet another need, and on him were pinned the aspirations for acceptance by sadomasochists and exhibitionists. During all these years, James Dean was routinely altered, turned into a hieratic figure, adapted for every generation.

But the young man adored and idolized was neither angel nor demon; neither was he a sad saint, too good for the world. He was, like Fitzgerald's Gatsby, quite simply a boy whose desire for good work got confused with the lure of instant celebrity. Had he lived, he might indeed have developed the genius and the gravity to see mere fame for what it is, the most fickle of lovers. At the last, Dean belongs not with Marilyn

Monroe, who did grow and change and mature; nor
with Marlon Brando, who survived in some ways and
succumbed in others; nor with Elvis Presley, who triumphed and then collapsed. James Dean belongs
rather with the perpetually lost children. In important
ways, he knew this—hence his attraction to New York
and to the stage; hence, too, his edgy anxiety always to
be moving, always rushing.

A boy of his time, he simply wanted to be an actor,
which is neither a shameful nor an unworthy goal. The
crux of his problem, however, was that he developed
none of the necessary discipline. In the 1950s,
American culture (perhaps for the first time) communicated the seductive, vacuous message that things ought
to be easy, and he expected them to be so: he was the
first fatality in what might be called the era of entitle-
ment. To be sure, much in his achievement should be
admired. But in the final analysis he was an ordinary
boy, and to canonize him is to crush him. Three feature
films and a handful of television appearances remain
the testimony to an emerging talent, but Dean ought
not to be misshapen by a skewed vision of history, nor
deformed by the glow of misplaced votive lights.

And so, decades later, James Dean remains as powerful an image as ever: a boy at once rueful, querulous
and uncertain, an icon who validates confusion.
Perhaps there will always be conflicted young people
turning to him and finding that bewilderment has been
raised to the level of heroic stardom. There he is, in
jeans and T-shirt—focusing in himself the conflict
between a dangerous heartland and a frightening
metropolis. He is the modern cowboy, pushing back
the frontier for a new generation. Very many young

people have wanted to become James Dean, which is both terrifying and poignant, for the first person who did not want to be James Dean was himself.

Fierce and lovable, wild and gentle, obdurate and pliant, gauche and graceful, straight and gay, artless and calculating—he was and remains all things to everyone. For a culture short of any heroes except celebrities, James Dean is a new St. Sebastian, pierced (his faithful followers believe) by the arrows of society's misunderstanding.

Once recognizable and human, then recast and hallowed, he has become shrouded by the foggy mists of each generation's hunches and hopes. Revised and edited, canonized by new devotees everywhere, he remains comfortingly immutable for all time. For an age that relies on simple visuals for easy truth, James Dean is the perfect hip icon.

notes

CHAPTER ONE
Page
1   **This trip has been:** Associated Press news story dated Oct. 2, 1995.
1   **You could see:** Quoted in *New York Daily News*, Sept. 24, 1995; unless otherwise noted, the statements of visitors were made to DS in Fairmount on September 30, 1995.
2   **Jimmy died when:** *New York Daily News*, Sept. 24, 1995.
2   **He copied:** Ibid.
7   **The neck is designed:** "Fans of 'Rebel' Revel in Memorabilia," *Indianapolis Star*, Sept. 23, 1995.

CHAPTER TWO
Page
10 **an earthy, flamboyant:** Glen E. Harshbarger to Hedda Hopper, in a letter dated May 20, 1963; see the Hedda Hopper Collection at the Academy of Motion Picture Arts and Sciences, Beverly Hills (henceforth AMPAS).
10 **one of the best:** *Marion Leader Tribune*, Dec. 8, 1918.
11 **We're not rich:** Emma Woollen Dean, "James Dean—The Boy I Loved," *Photoplay*, March 1956.
16 **I never understood him:** Joseph Humphreys, consulting editor, *Jimmy Dean on Jimmy Dean* (London: Plexus, 1990), p. 8.
17 **He had a large anxiety:** Ibid.
17. For the history of crime in Indiana, see David J. Bodenhamer and

Robert G. Barrows, eds., *The Encyclopedia of Indianapolis*
(Indianapolis and Bloomington: University of Indiana Press,
1994); also, historical sources at the Indiana Historical Society in
Indianapolis.

21 **I thought so much:** *Indianapolis Star*, Sept. 22, 1985.

22 **When I was five:** From notes taken by Hedda Hopper for her
article, "Keep Your Eye on James Dean," syndicated article in,
e.g., *Chicago Tribune Magazine*, March 27, 1955; cf. the Hopper
Collection, AMPAS.

23 **You'd try to order him:** Venable Herndon, *James Dean: A Short
Life* (New York: Signet/NAL, 1975), p. 6.

23 **I tried to get it across:** John Howlett, *James Dean* (London:
Plexus, 1975), p. 11.

24 **Jim and I:** "Lone Wolf," *Modern Screen*, August 1955.

24 **she didn't want to die:** Quoted by Ortense Winslow in
Indianapolis Star, Sept. 22, 1985.

24 **I just knew:** Humphreys, p. 10.

25 **It seemed:** Ibid.

26 **Oh, Mother:** Quoted often by JD to friends and colleagues, and
through them to DS—e.g., Leonard Rosenman and Elizbeth
"Dizzy" Sheridan.

CHAPTER THREE
Page

27 **Of course he was:** *Indianapolis Star*, Sept. 22, 1985.

28 **He shut it all:** Humphreys, p. 12.

28 **Understandably, in light of:** Elizabeth "Dizzy" Sheridan to DS,
May 26, 1995.

29 **My uncle's place:** Humphreys, p. 12.

29 **I was never a farmer:** David Dalton, Ron Cayen and David
Loehr, *James Dean: American Icon* (New York: St. Martin's, 1984),
p. 16.

30 **Once he learned:** Lynne Brennan, "The Legend of Jimmy
Dean," *Indianapolis Star Magazine*, Dec. 10, 1967.

30 **Jimmy was never one:** Dalton, Cayen and Loehr, p. 21.

30 **He was sometimes:** David Dalton, *James Dean: The Mutant King*
(New York: St. Martin's, 1974), p. 32.

33 **They called him:** In the documentary film *The James Dean Story*,
produced by George W. George and Robert Altman (1957); see
also Herndon, pp. 17–19.

33 **If he'd fallen only once:** Dalton, p. 39.

33   **Jimmy didn't like anything:** Robert Middleton, on *The Steve Allen Show*, NBC-TV, Oct. 14, 1956.

33   **If Grandpa Dean:** Herndon, pp. 14–15.

33   **His gift for make-believe:** Evelyn Washburn Nielsen, "The Truth About James Dean," *Chicago Sunday Tribune Magazine*, Sept. 9, 1956.

33   **a real talent:** Brennan, "The Legend of Jimmy Dean."

34   **I felt a need:** This crucial admission was omitted by Hedda Hopper (or her editors) from the essay published under her name in her syndicated column dated March 27, 1955; in her own typed notes, however, the statement has been preserved; see the Hopper Collection, AMPAS.

34   **He broke fifteen pair:** In the documentary film *The James Dean Story*, George and Altman.

34   **You either wanted:** *Indianapolis News*, Jan. 19, 1966.

35   **He liked to perform:** Adeline Nall, in the documentary film *Forever James Dean*, written, produced and directed by Ara Chekmayan (1988).

35   **He just did things his own way:** Nelson Price, "James Dean in Fairmount," *Media Montage*, Spring 1977.

35   **Jimmy was very aggressive:** Brennan, "The Legend of Jimmy Dean."

36   **He was a little different:** Herndon, p. 25.

36   **He could be:** In the documentary video *Adeline Nall's Memories at Fairmount High*, Braunco Video, produced by Thomas R. Berghuis (1987).

36   **Frankly, he couldn't take criticism:** Nelson Price, "James Dean," *Indianapolis News*, Aug. 29, 1985.

37   **Jim knew how to play people:** Dalton, Cayen and Loehr, p. 16.

37   **He was often nothing more:** Paul Hendrickson, "Remembering James Dean Back Home in Indiana," *Los Angeles Times*, July 22, 1973.

38   **I was sure then:** Dalton, p. 34.

39   **Jimmy was usually happiest:** Nielsen, "The Truth About James Dean."

39   **He was not always as thoughtful:** *Indianapolis Star Magazine*, Feb. 22, 1959; see also the documentary film *James Dean Remembered*, Ramrus-Lyon-Haley (1974); and the documentary film *The James Dean Story*, George and Altman.

42   **The girls liked him:** Dalton, p. 44.

43   **"My Case Study"** is preserved in the Fairmount Historical

Museum and has been reprinted in Robert Headrick, Jr., *Deanmania* (Las Vegas: Pioneer, 1990), p. 13; and in Herndon, p. 1.

44 **brilliant guard:** *Black & Gold* yearbook for Fairmount High School, 1949.

49 **The effect was chilling:** Adeline Nall, as told to Val Holley, "Grant County's Own," *Traces*, Autumn 1989.

49 **I was deeply moved:** Ibid.

50 **The odd thing:** Larry Kart, "Giant Legacy: The Hero That James Dean Created Still Lives," *Chicago Tribune*, Sept. 15, 1985.

CHAPTER FOUR

Page

58 **People saw me:** Clifton Daniel, ed., *Chronicle of the 20th Century* (Mount Kisco, N.Y.: Chronicle Publications, 1987), p. 665.

60 **Dean was very conscious:** *Santa Monica College News*, 1971.

61 **his articulation was poor:** Gene Nielson Owen, "The Man Who Would Be 50: A Memory of James Dean," *Los Angeles Times Calendar*, Feb. 8, 1981.

63 **He was shy and awkward:** Quoted in Humphreys, p. 24.

64 **A boy I had dated:** Howlett, p. 22.

65 **Jimmy told none:** Terry Cunningham, *James Dean: The Way It Was* (London: Electric Reader, 1983); quoted in Riese, p. 170.

66 **One night shortly:** Stanley Kramer to DS, July 1977. For a fuller treatment of *The Men*, see Donald Spoto, *Stanley Kramer Film Maker* (Hollywood and New York: Samuel French, 1990), pp. 55–64.

67 **But the drunk:** Fred Zinnemann to DS, June 10, 1977.

68 **faggots and fairies:** Graham McCann, *Rebel Males* (New Brunswick, N.J.: Rutgers University Press, 1993), p. 84.

68 On Marlon Brando's sexual life, see Gerald Clarke, *Capote: A Biography* (New York: Simon & Schuster, 1988), p. 302; Peter Manso, *Brando* (New York: Hyperion, 1994); and Marlon Brando with Robert Lindsey, *Brando: Songs My Mother Taught Me* (New York: Random House, 1994).

70 **He needed glasses:** Dick Eschleman, in the documentary film *Bye Bye Jimmy*, produced and directed by Nick Taylor and Paul Watson (1989).

70 **void of exciting movement:** Harve Bennett Fischman, in *Spotlight*, the newspaper of the Theater Arts Department, UCLA, December 1950.

70   **made no impression:** William Bast, "There Was a Boy," *Photoplay*, September 1956.

71   **I wanted to be a professional:** Hedda Hopper with James Brough, *The Whole Truth & Nothing But* (New York: Doubleday, 1963), p. 173.

71   **So I busted a couple of guys:** Howard Thompson, "Another Dean Hits the Big League," *New York Times*, March 13, 1955.

71   **He was the kind of guy:** Ronald Martinetti, *The James Dean Story* (New York: Carol/Birch Lane, 1995), p. 23.

71   **He had a scary:** In the documentary film *Bye Bye Jimmy*, Taylor and Watson.

CHAPTER FIVE
Page

73   **Unpredictable in his moods:** These and other quotes from Isabelle Draesemer (Terry) are from Dave Delaney, "Woman Claims Dean's Discovery," *Anderson (Indiana) Sunday Herald*, Aug. 14, 1983.

74   **We rode on the carousel:** Beverly Long to DS, May 25, 1995.

74   **I didn't like Jim:** Donald von Wiedenman, "NBC to Air 'Portrait' of Dean," *Advocate*, Feb. 25, 1976.

76   **He was cocky and arrogant:** William Bast, in a series on Dean's appeal, thirty years after his death, presented on the syndicated television program *Entertainment Tonight*, September 1985.

79   **We did sense-memory:** James Whitmore to DS, March 21, 1995.

80   **the noticeable change that:** Bast, "There Was a Boy."

80   **I owe a lot:** Quoted in Howlett, p. 30.

81   **Jim was never honest:** von Wiedenman, "NBC to Air 'Portrait' of Dean."

81   **On JD as a homosexual hustler,** see, e.g., Joe Hyams, *James Dean: Little Boy Lost* (New York: Warner, 1992), pp. 58, 85, 89, 97–98; and Paul Alexander, *Boulevard of Broken Dreams: The Life, Times and Legend of James Dean*. (New York: Viking, 1994), pp. 83ff.

84   **He was almost constantly:** Beverly Wills, "I Almost Married Jimmy Dean," *Modern Screen*, March 1957.

85   **I'm so tense:** Sidney Skolsky, "Demon Dean," *Photoplay*, July 1955.

86   **Jimmy became subject:** Humphreys, p. 29.

87   **My primary interest:** Riese, p. 60; similarly, Martinetti, p. 37.

90   **He seemed very vulnerable:** Dick Clayton to DS, Feb. 23, 1995.

90   **There's always somebody in your life:** Original interview notes

by Hedda Hopper for her syndicated column dated March 27, 1955.

91 **New York overwhelmed me:** Often—e.g., Herndon, p. 67; and Gene Ringgold, "James Dean," *Screen Facts*, vol. 2, no. 2 (1964).

91 **a nice boy but moody:** Michael Reidel, "James Dean's Walk on the West Side," *New York Daily News*, Sept. 24, 1995.

91 **He seemed almost obsessed:** Roy Schatt, *James Dean: A Portrait* (New York: Delilah/Putnam, 1981), p. 36.

92 **a loner:** Schatt, in a seminar on James Dean at the Museum of Television & Radio (at the time called the Museum of Broadcasting), Feb. 18, 1986; recorded program in the museum archives.

92 **In one hand:** Often—e.g., in Hoskyns, p. 47.

CHAPTER SIX
Page

95 **We became friends quickly:** Elizabeth "Dizzy" Sheridan to DS: May 26, 1995; further interview, July 10, 1995.

98 **You talk just like grownups:** Antoine de Saint-Exupéry (trans. Katherine Woods), *The Little Prince* (New York: Harvest/Harcourt Brace [reprint of 1943 original], 1971), pp. 28, 89, 87.

98 **the writer's escapist attitude:** JD to Hedda Hopper, p. 170.

100 **He was a neurotic, mixed-up kid:** Alec Wilder, in Humphreys, p. 122.

104 **He did not hesitate:** Christine White to DS, April 5, 1995.

107 **I have made great strides:** JD to Marcus and Ortense Winslow, summer 1952. Cited in, e.g., Humphreys, p. 39.

109 **He just came in:** Elia Kazan to DS, March 15, 1995; see also Dick Williams, *Los Angeles Mirror-News*, April 25, 1957.

109 **a sad-faced:** Cindy Adams, *Lee Strasberg: The Imperfect Genius of the Actors Studio* (New York: Doubleday, 1980), p. 218.

109 **as a human being:** Ibid., p. 217.

109 **a gesture of defiance:** Ibid., p. 218.

117 **It's hard for Jimmy:** Sidney Skolsky, "That's Hollywood for You," *Photoplay*, November 1955.

117 **I'm a serious-minded:** Quoted in *Newsweek*, March 7, 1955.

118 **To Bill:** Cited often—e.g., Howlett, p. 52; Bast, third article . . .

119 **He was a dabbler:** Stock, p. 74.

119 **Being an actor:** Jeanne Balch Capen, "The Strange Revival of James Dean," *American Weekly*, July 29, 1956.

CHAPTER SEVEN
Page

122 **insecure, uptight:** Quoted in Riese, p. 212.

122 **wouldn't communicate:** Dalton, p. 114.

122 **mainly to listen:** Patricia Bosworth, *Montgomery Clift* (New York: Harcourt Brace Jovanovich, 1978), p. 260.

123 On Montgomery Clift's fear of being known as homosexual, see Bosworth.

123 **He arrived wearing:** Eric Bentley to DS, Aug. 22, 1995.

125 **He was wearing boots:** Andrew McCullough to DS, May 24, 1995.

126 **I'm here—pay attention:** Hume Cronyn, *A Terrible Liar: A Memoir* (New York: Morrow, 1991), pp. 277–299.

130 **Jimmy was wonderful:** James Sheldon to DS, Sept. 2, 1995.

131 **a piece of shit:** *Emmy*, October 1990; see also the Franklin Heller oral history of television, preserved in an interview at the Museum of Television & Radio, New York.

132ff. On the Communist witch-hunt infecting radio and television, see Erik Barnouw, *The Golden Web: A History of Broadcasting in the United States, 1933–1953* (New York: Oxford University Press, 1968) and the same author's *The Image Empire: A History of Broadcasting in the United States From 1953* (New York: Oxford University Press, 1970).

133 **There was something:** John (Jonathan) Gilmore to DS, Aug. 19, 1995.

136 **Got a new pair of shoes:** Cited in Dalton, p. 102.

139 **a kind of liberalism:** Eric Bentley, in *New Republic*, March 22, 1954.

140 **the quality of sweetness:** Ruth Goetz, in the Italian television documentary *Hollywood: The Rebel James Dean*, produced by Donatella Baglivo and directed by Claudio Masenza (19??).

140 **Herman was intrigued:** Vivian Matalon to DS, July 10, 1995.

140 **a remarkable and unusual:** Quoted in Martinetti, p. 84.

141 **I had this strange young man:** Quoted in Dalton, p. 145.

141 **The little son of a bitch:** Herndon, p. 89.

142 **I thought:** Dalton, p. 146.

142 **Okay, Dean:** Incident quoted to DS by Vivian Matalon, July 10, 1995.

143 **Jimmy was the last:** William Orr to DS, March 29, 1995.

143 **James Dean is a young man:** William T. Orr to Steve Trilling at Warner Bros., Burbank; letter dated December 16, 1953; in

Warner Bros. archives, University of Southern California, Los Angeles.

CHAPTER EIGHT
Page

145 **insidious charm:** Brooks Atkinson, in *New York Times*, Feb. 14, 1954.

146 **realistically unpleasant:** Richard Watts, Jr., "A Grave Drama About Abnormality," *New York Post*, Feb. 9, 1954.

146 **colorfully insinuating scapegrace:** Walter Kerr, "The Immoralist," *New York Herald Tribune*, Feb. 9, 1954.

146 **clearly and originally underlines:** William Hawkins, "'Immoralist' Marked by Tender Tragedy," *New York World-Telegram and Sun*, Feb. 9, 1954.

146 **especially good:** Unsigned review, "The Immoralist," *Theatre Arts*, April 1954.

147 **James Dean came:** Elia Kazan to DS, March 15, 1995; additional quotations from Kazan are drawn from Michel Ciment, *Kazan on Kazan* (New York: Viking, 1974); Kazan's autobiography, *A Life* (New York: Knopf, 1988), pp. 534–539; Derek Marlowe, "Soliloquy on James Dean's Forty-fifth Birthday," *New York*, Nov. 8, 1976; the television documentary *Elia Kazan–A Director's Journey*, Lorac Film for Castle Hill Productions, produced by Julian Schlossberg (1994); Herndon, pp. 96–98; Kazan in the *Los Angeles Times*, Sept. 30, 1985; in *Picturegoer*, Dec. 14, 1957 and *Photoplay*, June 1972; Howlett, pp. 86–87; Dalton, Cayen and Loehr, p. 53.

149 **You're going to need:** Cronyn, p. 279.

152 **I think Dean is o.k.:** Elia Kazan to Jack L. Warner, March 2, 1954; correspondence in Warner Bros. archives, *East of Eden* files, USC.

152 **Inasmuch as your impression:** Jack L. Warner to Elia Kazan, March 10, 1954; Warner Bros. archives, *East of Eden* files, USC.

154 **When I finally met:** Leonard Rosenman to DS, June 1, 1995; a second interview was conducted on July 3, 1995.

157 **Obviously there was a strong:** Kazan, p. 535.

157 **His funny little laugh:** Quoted in Dalton, Cayen and Loehr, p. 44.

158 **I don't think I ever:** Dick Clayton to DS, March 1995.

164 **Jimmy wasn't easy:** Kazan, p. 535; see also Jim Koch, "Relishing the Role of Outsider," *New York Times*, Aug. 24, 1995, p. C4.

164 **impossible:** Elia Kazan, in the television documentary *Elia Kazan*, Schlossberg.

164 **a rebel at heart:** Raymond Massey, *A Hundred Different Lives: An Autobiography* (Boston: Little, Brown, 1979), p. 376.

166 **Just being in:** Richard Davalos, in Dalton, Cayen and Loehr, p. 57.

166 **Why do you put your hands up:** Julie Harris to DS, Aug. 7, 1995.

167 **Can't you have a child:** Susan Ray, ed., *I Was Interrupted: Nicholas Ray on Making Movies* (Berkeley: University of California Press, 1993), p. 110.

168 **When I first came to Hollywood:** Quoted in Ray, pp. 107–108.

169 **objective artist:** Quoted by Carl Combs, publicity agent for Warner Bros., March 9, 1955; see Leith Adams and Keith Burns, eds., *James Dean Behind the Scene* (London: Smith Gryphon, 1990), p. 56, 62.

169 **In this business:** Lloyd Shearer, "Dizzy? Not This Dean," *Parade*, May 15, 1955.

170 **Have been very dejected:** Humphreys, p. 76.

171 **was so adoring:** Kazan, p. 538.

171 **I could see:** Brando with Lindsey, pp. 223–224.

171 **How about coming out:** Leonard Rosenman to DS, June 1, 1995.

178 **The picture is brilliant:** *Time*, March 21, 1955.

178 **Dean is an exceptionally:** *Newsweek*, March 7, 1955.

179 **Everything about him suggests:** William K. Zinsser, in *New York Herald-Tribune*, March 10, 1955.

179 **Young James Dean:** *Cue*, March 12, 1955.

179 **Looking again:** Dilys Powell, in *New York Times*, Aug. 6, 1961.

179 **When the last scene faded:** Kate Cameron, in *New York Daily News*, April 10, 1955.

179 **The box-office asset:** Jack Moffitt, in *Hollywood Reporter*, Feb. 16, 1955.

CHAPTER NINE
Page

181 **He loved the damned motorcycle:** Dick Clayton to DS, Feb. 23, 1995.

182 **He was absolutely suicidal:** Leonard Rosenman to DS, July 3, 1995.

182 **He came to the house:** Owen, "The Man Who Would Be 50"; see also Thom Dilts, "James Dean," *Santa Monica College* (bulletin), Winter 1974.

182 **I've got to:** *Los Angeles Citizen-News*, Oct. 1, 1955.

185 **greedy for life:** *Los Angeles Examiner*, May 16, 1954.

185 **When Pier takes the keys:** *Life*, July 29, 1952.

185 **I don't like to grow up:** Theodore Strauss, "Hollywood Natural," *Collier's*, April 26, 1952.

185 **She is too much concerned:** Ibid.

186 **He's a little shy and diffident:** Arthur Loew, Jr., to DS, Sept. 27, 1995.

187 **I thought it had:** Stewart Stern to DS, Aug. 30, 1995.

187 **We were like kids together:** Dalton, p. 196; see the interview Pier Angeli gave to the *National Enquirer* in 1968, when she was short of cash.

187 **He was intensely determined:** Ray, p. 112.

188 **He always had uncertain relations:** Elia Kazan to DS, March 15, 1995.

188 **Jimmy wanted the role:** Jud Kinberg to DS, Oct. 4, 1995; on Ernest Lehman's evaluation of Jimmy's unsuitability for the role: Ernest Lehman to DS, Oct. 3, 1995.

191 **still beautiful:** Susan Strasberg, *Bittersweet* (New York: Putnam's, 1980), p. 52.

191 **emotionally crushed:** Dorothy Manners, "Pier Angeli—Not So Serene," *Los Angeles Herald-Examiner*, March 7, 1971.

192 **no tip and no treating:** Robert R. Rees, "Vampira and James Dean: Cult Vs. Occult," *Screem*, no. 5 (1994).

193 **a great emergent talent:** Schatt, pp. 27–29.

193 **I'm playing the damn bongo:** Ibid., p. 108.

193 **a mania for taking chances:** Ibid., p. 43.

194 **Most of us at that time:** Susan Bluttman, "Rediscovering James Dean: The TV Legacy," *Emmy*, vol. 12, no. 5 (October 1990).

194 **excellent work:** *Daily Variety*, Nov. 11, 1954.

194 **virtually impossible:** Bluttman, "Rediscovering James Dean."

195 **How would it feel:** The anecdote was reported to DS (May 24, 1995) by director Andrew McCullough, who knew Donehue.

196 **Excuse me:** Quoted in Humphreys, p. 53.

197 **I think in a way:** Ronald Reagan, in a letter to Ronald Martinetti dated March 14, 1973, on display at the Fairmount Historical Museum, Fairmount, Indiana.

197 **He is undisciplined:** Skolsky, "Demon Dean."

197 **a little strange:** Elizabeth "Dizzy" Sheridan to DS, May 26, 1995.

CHAPTER TEN
Page

201 **We were on a collision course:** Phil Stern, *Phil Stern's Hollywood: Photographs, 1940–1979* (New York: Knopf, 1993).

201 **I was in the gas station:** Humphreys, p. 92.

201 **collected a small crew:** George Scullin, "James Dean: The Legend and the Facts," *Look,* Oct. 16, 1956.

202 **I came to Hollywood:** Skolsky, "Demon Dean."

202 **I'd like you to meet:** Mike Steen, *Hollywood Speaks!—An Oral History* (New York: Putnam's, 1974), p. 138.

202 **He was absolutely devoted:** John (Jonathan) Gilmore to DS, Aug. 19, 1995.

202 **He gets Jimmy coffee:** Skolsky, "Demon Dean."

203 **I had the feeling:** Kenneth Kendall to DS, June 12, 1995.

205 **He was very moody:** Lili Kardell, in the documentary film *The James Dean Story*, George and Altman.

205 **Jimmy knew:** Leonard Rosenman to DS, June 1, 1995.

205 **He hadn't been:** Schatt, p. 43.

205 **really filthy:** Herndon, p. 158.

205 **He has been absolutely impossible:** Golob to Blumenstock, telegram dated Feb. 11, 1955; Warner Bros. archives, *East of Eden* publicity files, USC.

206 **I wanted to show:** "Legend," *London Telegraph Magazine*, Sept. 23, 1995.

206 **It was an unusual:** Dennis Stock, *James Dean Revisited* (New York: Penguin, 1978), p. 21.

208 **When Jimmy posed:** Dalton, Cayen and Loehr, pp. 15–16.

209 **Jimmy was a very:** *Telegraph Magazine*, Sept. 23, 1995.

210 **I want to tell you:** Quoted by Christine White to DS, April 4, 1995.

210 **He started to boss:** Leonard Rosenman to DS, June 1, 1995.

210 **I can't make this scene:** Herndon, p. 119.

210 **He feels:** "Moody New Star," *Life*, March 7, 1955.

211 **He was exceedingly testy:** Dennis Stock in the documentary film *Hollywood Close-Up: James Dean, An American Original*, produced by Arthur Drooker and directed by Craig Haffner, (ABC-TV, 1983).

211 **The only way:** Quoted in Martinetti, p. 40.

212 **I got crabs:** Ray, p. 113.

212 **The drama of his life:** Ibid., p. 112; see also Dalton, Cayen and Loehr, p. 87.

212 **Dean is in:** *Vogue*, Feb. 1, 1955.

214 **He will be the most dynamic:** "These Will Be the Bright New Stars of 1955," *Look*, Jan. 11, 1955.

214 **We started out:** Jim Backus on CNN, cited in Riese, p. 434.

214 **THIS IS A VERY IMPORTANT PICTURE:** Jack L. Warner to David Weisbart, memorandum dated April 2, 1955; Warner Bros. archives, USC.

218 **He seemed to be high:** William Orr to DS, March 29, 1995.

219 **Nick Ray was a self-dramatizing:** Stewart Stern to DS, Aug. 30, 1995.

219 **sometimes a bit wild:** Faye Nuell Mayo to DS, Nov. 1, 1995.

220 **practically the co-director:** Jim Backus, *Rocks on the Roof* (New York: Putnam's, 1958), p. 153.

220 **He swerved easily:** Nicholas Ray in Ray, p. 111.

220 **the real collaboration:** Steffi Sidney to DS, June 3, 1995.

220 **I've got to know everything:** *Motion Picture*, May 1955.

220 **Acting is wonderful:** From the original unedited version (preserved in the Hopper Collection, AMPAS) of a story on Dean by Hedda Hopper that ran in her syndicated column on March 27, 1955.

220 **I want to tell you something:** Corey Allen to DS, June 28, 1995.

221 **I realized later:** Derek Marlowe, "Soliloquy on James Dean's Forty-fifth Birthday," *New York Magazine*, Nov. 8, 1976.

222 **incredibly encouraging:** Ibid.

222 **corny:** Carroll Baker, *Baby Doll: An Autobiography* (New York: Arbor House, 1983), pp. 118–119.

224 **He was the child who goes:** Humphreys, p. 101.

224 **He was a lost kid:** Jim Backus, in the documentary film *Hollywood Close-Up*, Drooker and Haffner.

224 **Before the take:** Backus, p. 154.

224 **so carried away:** Jim Backus to Harrison Carroll in *Los Angeles Herald-Examiner*, May 21, 1955.

224 **He knows what he's doing:** Warner Bros. publicity release dated May 23, 1955; Warner Bros. archives, *Rebel Without a Cause* production files, USC.

224 **Mom! Mom!:** Ann Doran's recollection is included in Paul F. Boller, Jr., *Hollywood Anecdotes* (New York: Morrow, 1987), pp. 79–80.

225 **He suffered a badly bruised:** Warner Bros. archives, *Rebel Without a Cause* files, USC.

225 **the first guerilla artist:** Quoted in Humphreys, p. 95.

226 **Much of the writing:** Steen, p. 140.

226 **I don't know that he could:** Corey Allen to DS, June 28, 1995.

227 **When you saw *Rebel*:** Humphreys, p. 105.

CHAPTER ELEVEN
Page

230 **Jett Rink had many reasons:** Description of Jett Rink in the pro-
     duction files on *Giant* from the Jack L. Warner Collection at the
     University of Southern California. All materials relative to this
     picture are located in Box 24.

232 **carried on like:** Baker, p. 126.

234 **Sometimes Jimmy and I:** Elizabeth Taylor, in an interview with
     Susan Winslow for the documentary film *George Stevens: A
     Filmmaker's Journey* (pr./dir. George Stevens Jr., 1985); also, see
     notes in the George Stevens Collection, AMPAS.

234 **But even that:** Humphreys, pp. 126–127.

234 **Dean was always late:** Rock Hudson folder in the Stevens
     Collection, AMPAS.

234 **I didn't like him:** Ray Loynd, "Some Unsentimental Memories
     of James Dean by Rock Hudson," *Hollywood Reporter*, Aug. 9,
     1968.

234 **Because nothing else:** Mercedes McCambridge, *Mercedes
     McCambridge: The Quality of Mercy* (New York: Times Books,
     1981), pp. 204–205.

235 **nobody had more:** Humphreys, p. 107.

235 **so insecure:** In the documentary film *Hollywood Close-Up*,
     Drooker and Haffner.

235 **suffered from:** Humphreys, p. 122.

235 **utterly winning:** Stock, p. 119.

235 **I met your friend:** Quoted by Rosenman to DS, June 1, 1995.

235 **a small-town boy:** William C. Mellor, "The James Dean I
     Knew," *Picturegoer*, Dec. 29, 1956.

236 **It was a hell of a headache:** Hollis Alpert, "It's Dean, Dean,
     Dean," *Saturday Review*, Oct. 13, 1956.

236 **He worked hard:** Alfred C. Roller, "The James Dean Myth Blows
     Up," *World-Telegram and Sun Saturday Magazine*, Nov. 3, 1956.

236 **Mr. Dean, I've come:** Jon Whitcomb, "Liz Taylor as Edna
     Ferber's Heroine," *Cosmopolitan*, Aug. 1956.

237 **I don't take:** JD to Hopper, Aug. 8, 1955: "A conversation with
     Jimmy which I didn't print" was her annotation on this page, in
     Hopper Collection, AMPAS.

238 **Look, I have a flask:** Humphreys, p. 120–122. See also the files on *Giant* in the Stevens Collection, AMPAS, and the Warner Collection, USC.

239 **too tired to work:** Memo from Eric Stacey to Tom Andre dated July 25, 1955: Warner Bros. archives, USC.

239 **He was the least self-revealing:** Beulah Roth, *James Dean* (Corte Madera, Calif.: Pomegranate Artbooks, 1983), p. 52.

239 **intense, shy:** Sanford H. Roth, "The Late James Dean," *Collier's*, Nov. 25, 1955.

240 **like a wild animal:** Humphreys, p. 126.

240 **so that he can fight:** *Hollywood Reporter*, Aug. 12, 1955.

240 **I tried to understand:** *Los Angeles Herald-Express*, Oct. 1, 1955.

240 **I'm just dog tired:** *New York Journal-American*, Aug. 4, 1955.

241 **rather have people hiss:** Quoted by Stock, p. 124.

241 **Only a young man:** Hopper, p. 171.

241 **It's a wonderful, generous city:** Hedda Hopper, syndicated column dated March 27, 1955.

241 **In Hollywood, there are:** *New York Times*, March 13, 1955.

242 **Everything to do:** William Orr to DS, March 29, 1995.

242 The information from Ray Stark was provided to DS in an interview on March 30, 1995.

243 For data on the Porsche 550 Spyder, see Jack R. Nerad, "On the Trail of James Dean," *Motor Trend*, September 1985.

245 **Thank you, but I'll:** Roth; see also Riese, p. 397.

245 **Dean had a scary:** Phil Hill, in the documentary film *Bye Bye Jimmy*, Taylor and Watson.

245 **She'll do a hundred and fifty:** Alec Guinness, *Blessings in Disguise* (New York: Knopf, 1986), pp. 34–35.

249 **That guy's gotta:** Rolf Wütherich, "James Dean's Last Passenger Recovers—Tells Complete Story of Fateful Death Drive," *Modern Screen*, October 1957.

249 **a soft cry:** Ibid.

CHAPTER TWELVE
Page

251 **In sixteen months:** Henry Ginsberg to his son John, in a letter dated Oct. 6, 1955, Warner Bros. archives, USC.

251 **The consensus of opinion:** Quoted in Gene Ringgold, "James Dean," *Screen Facts*, vol. 2, no. 2 (1964).

253 **Anyone who subscribes:** George Stevens, in Associated Press news features dated Aug. 29, 1956.

253 **Morbid nonsense:** Ezra Goodman, *The Fifty-Year Decline and Fall of Hollywood* (New York: Simon & Schuster, 1961), p. 291; see also Goodman, "Delirium Over Dead Star," *Life*, Sept. 24, 1956.

254 **The career of James Dean:** Goodman, p. 289.

254 **The most moving job:** *Newsweek*, Nov. 7, 1955.

254 **He stands out:** Arthur Knight, in *Saturday Review*, October 1955.

254 **His rare talent:** William Zinsser, *New York Herald-Tribune*, Oct. 28, 1955.

254 **Dean is very effective:** *Variety*, Oct. 19, 1955.

254 **The best thing about the film:** *Time*, Nov. 28, 1955.

254 **contradicts fifty years:** "*contredit cinquante ans de cinéma . . . chaque geste, chaque attitude, chaque mimique est une gifle à la tradition psychologique. James Dean ne met pas [en valeur] son texte avec force sous-entendus comme Edwige Feuillère, il ne le poétise pas comme Gérard Philipe, il ne joue pas au plus malin avec lui comme Pierre Fresnay . . . Il n'est pas soucieux . . . de montrer qu'il comprend parfaitement ce qu'il dit et mieux que vous . . . [James Dean] porte en lui notre propre ambiguïté, notre dualité et toutes les faiblesses humaines.*" François Truffaut, "James Dean est mort," *Cahiers du Cinéma*, 1956; reprinted in his anthology *Les Filmes de Ma Vie* (Paris: Flammarion, 1975), pp. 313–317. English translation in the text by DS.

255 **James Dean gives:** Herbert Kupferberg, *New York Herald-Tribune*, Oct. 11, 1956.

255 **The film only proves:** *Variety*, Oct. 10, 1956.

255 **It's Dean, Dean, Dean:** Hollis Alpert, *Saturday Review*, October 1956.

255 **James Dean's talent:** George Christian, *Houston Post*, October 1956.

255 **This is the finest:** *Time*, Oct. 22, 1956.

255 **The picture belongs:** *Newsweek*, Oct. 22, 1956.

256 **This is a haunting capstone:** Bosley Crowther, in *New York Times*, Oct. 11, 1956.

256 **Dean died at:** Goodman, p. 292.

257 **Dear James:** This and the following letter were quoted in Lee Belser, "James Dean's Fans Still Write to Him," *Los Angeles Mirror*, Sept. 30, 1960.

257 **I identify with him:** Iver Peterson, "Young Drawn to James Dean 25 Years After," *New York Times*, Oct. 1, 1980.

257 **Jimmy's my hero:** Mark A. Stein, "It Was a Caravan With a Cause," *Los Angeles Times*, Sept. 27, 1981.

257 **He was a lot like me:** Ibid.

258 **He had his own ways:** Ibid.

258 For the details of the British bank advertisements, see Catherine Bennett, "The Selling of an Iconoclast," *London Times*, July 31, 1987.

259 **I don't think:** Michael Reidel, "James Dean's Walk on the West Side," *New York Daily News*, Sept. 24, 1995.

259 **although mostly he comes to me:** Goodman, p. 291.

259 **It was Jimmy in his boots:** Laura L. Castro, "Larger Than Life: James Dean's Death Did a Lot for Indiana," *Wall Street Journal*, Oct. 9, 1991.

265 **He didn't have to:** Dick Clayton to DS, Feb. 23, 1995.

265 **To us teenagers:** *Life*, Oct. 15, 1956.

265 **You have a sort of:** Bill Whitworth, "Ageless Memories of the Late James Dean," *New York Herald Tribune*, Jan. 3, 1965.

265 **But I am happier now:** Ibid.

266 For a provocative précis on 1956 as the Year of the Teenager, and the subsequent developments of pop culture, see Stephen Holden, "After the War, the Time of the Teen-Ager," *New York Times*, May 7, 1995.

272 **light, active:** Pat F. Garrett, *The Authentic Life of Billy the Kid, The Noted Desperado*, ed. Maurice G. Fulton (New York: Indian Head/Barnes & Noble, 1994), p. 22.

272 **he expected his business:** Ibid., p. 183.

272 **The Kid's career:** Ibid., pp. xxvii-xxviii.

bibliography

Adams, Cindy. *Lee Strasberg: The Imperfect Genius of the Actors Studio*. New York: Doubleday, 1980.

Adams, Leith and Keith Burns, eds., *James Dean Behind the Scene*. London: Smith Gryphon, 1990.

Backus, Jim. *Rocks on the Roof*. New York: Putnam's, 1958.

Baker, Carroll. *Baby Doll: An Autobiography*. New York: Arbor House, 1983.

Barnouw, Erik. *The Golden Web: A History of Broadcasting in the United States, 1933–1953*. New York: Oxford University Press, 1968.

———. *The Image Empire: A History of Broadcasting in the United States from 1953*. New York: Oxford University Press, 1970.

Beath, Warren Newton. *The Death of James Dean*. New York: Grove, 1986.

Blum, Daniel. *Theatre World, Season 1953–1954*. New York: Greenberg, 1954.

Bodenhamer, David J. and Robert G. Barrows, eds., *The Encyclopedia of Indianapolis*. Indianapolis and Bloomington: University of Indiana Press, 1994.

Boller, Paul F., Jr., *Hollywood Anecdotes*. New York: Morrow, 1987.

Bosworth, Patricia. *Montgomery Clift*. New York: Harcourt Brace Jovanovich, 1978.

Brando, Marlon, with Robert Lindsey, *Brando: Songs My Mother Taught Me*. New York: Random House, 1994.

Ciment, Michel. *Kazan on Kazan*. New York: Viking, 1974.

Cronyn, Hume. *A Terrible Liar: A Memoir*. New York: Morrow, 1991.

Cunningham, Terry. *James Dean: The Way It Was*. London: Electric Reader, 1983.

Dalton, David. *James Dean: The Mutant King*. New York: St. Martin's, 1974.

Dalton, David, with Ron Cayen and David Loehr. *James Dean: American Icon*. New York: St. Martin's, 1984.

Devillers, Marceau (trans. Jonathan Marks). *James Dean*. London: Grange, 1993.

Doherty, Thomas. *Teenagers and Teenpics: The Juvenilization of American Movies in the 1950s*. Winchester, Mass.: Unwin Hyman, 1988.

Fuchs, Wolfgang. *James Dean: Footsteps of a Giant*. Berlin: Taco Verlagsgesellschaft, 1989.

Garrett, Pat F. (ed. Maurice G. Fulton). *The Authentic Life of Billy the Kid, The Noted Desperado*. New York: Indian Head/Barnes & Noble, 1994.

Goodman, Ezra. *The Fifty-Year Decline and Fall of Hollywood*. New York: Simon & Schuster, 1961.

Guinness, Alec. *Blessings in Disguise*. New York: Knopf, 1986.

Halberstam, David. *The Fifties*. New York: Villard, 1993.

Headrick, Robert, Jr., *Deanmania*. Las Vegas: Pioneer, 1990.

Herndon, Venable. *James Dean: A Short Life*. New York: Signet/NAL, 1975.

Hopper, Hedda, with James Brough, *The Whole Truth & Nothing But*. New York: Doubleday, 1963.

Horwitz, James. *They Went Thataway*. New York: Dutton, 1976.

Hoskyns, Barney. *James Dean Shooting Star*. London: Bloomsbury, 1989.

Howlett, John. *James Dean*. London: Plexus, 1975.

Humphreys, Joseph, ed. *Jimmy Dean on Jimmy Dean*. London: Plexus, 1990.

Jacobs, Timothy. *James Dean*. London: Arlington, 1991.

Kazan, Elia. *A Life*. New York: Knopf, 1988.

Levene, Bruce. *James Dean in Mendocino: The Filming of "East of Eden."* Mendocino, Cal.: Pacific Transcriptions, 1994.

McCambridge, Mercedes. *Mercedes McCambridge: The Quality of Mercy*. New York: Times Books, 1981.

McCann, Graham. *Rebel Males*. New Brunswick, N.J.: Rutgers University Press, 1993.

Manso, Peter. *Brando*. New York: Hyperion, 1994.

Martinetti, Ronald. *The James Dean Story*. New York: Carol/Birch Lane, 1995.

Massey, Raymond. *A Hundred Different Lives: An Autobiography*. Boston: Little, Brown, 1979.

Ray, Susan, ed., *I Was Interrupted: Nicholas Ray on Making Movies*. Berkeley: University of California Press, 1993.

Rees, Robert R. *James Dean's Trail: One Fan's Journey*. Katy, Texas: Empire, 1995.

Riese, Randall. *The Unabridged James Dean*. New York: Wings Books, 1994.

Rodriguez, Elena. *Dennis Hopper: A Madness to His Method*. New York: St. Martin's, 1988.

Roth, Beulah. *James Dean*. Corte Madera, Calif.: Pomegranate Artbooks, 1983.

Savage, William W., Jr. *The Cowboy Hero: His Image in American History and Culture*. Norman, Okla.: University of Oklahoma Press, 1979.

Schatt, Roy. *James Dean: A Portrait*. New York: Delilah/Putnam, 1981.

Steen, Mike. *Hollywood Speaks!—An Oral History*. New York: Putnam's, 1974.

Stern, Phil. *Phil Stern's Hollywood: Photographs, 1940–1979*. New York: Knopf, 1993.

Stock, Dennis. *James Dean Revisited*. New York: Penguin, 1978.

Strasberg, Susan. *Bittersweet*. New York: Putnam's, 1980.

Truffaut, François. *Les Filmes de Ma Vie*. Paris: Flammarion, 1975.

index